All Desires Known

Georgie Newbery

HEDDON PUBLISHING

www.heddonpublishing.com
www.facebook.com/heddonpublishing
@PublishHeddon

About the Author

Georgie Newbery is a flower farmer and artisan florist based at Common Farm Flowers, a smallholding in Somerset where she lives with her husband, artist Fabrizio Boccha, two very nice but noisy and generally quite feral children, and a relatively well-behaved border terrier. Her day job involves growing 250+ different varieties of cut flower and foliage, supplying 50+ weddings a year, and teaching lots of workshops on how to grow, cut, condition and arrange flowers from your garden.

In the secret hours between five and seven in the morning she tiptoes downstairs to drink tea and write gardening books and novels, relishing the quiet, and giving space on the page to the people who crowd the stories in her mind.

Non-fiction by the author:
The Flower Farmer's Year (Green Books, 2014)
Grow Your Own Wedding Flowers (Green Books, 2015)

www.commonfarmflowers.com

To Shelley Bovey and Janet Laurence, aka The Writing Ladies, with huge thanks

WINTER

Chapter 1

Stephen scowls as he manoeuvres the hired van onto the South Circular and, with a vicious grinding of the unfamiliar gears, turns west.

The knifing hasn't ruined his looks. In the dirty autumn light, the livid purple slice across his cheek serves only to accentuate the good bits. When he and Tessa met he'd still been almost impossibly beautiful, skin smooth as a child's, his hair a thick shank of black silk. Now his head is crowned by a wiry grey bog-brush, and a rougher face has been carved out of those soft cheeks. Putting on lip gloss (without a mirror), Tessa hugs to herself her pleasure at getting out of London, and flinches as a stone ricochets off the windscreen.

Stephen loves stone-throwing youth. They give him purpose. His current fury (and Tessa's excitement) is all to do with his being forced to leave the stone-throwers behind. When she had married a vicar, Tessa hadn't realised that Stephen's dog collar hid an urban warrior adrenalin junkie. He thinks of this trip to Hindle Green as enforced exile. She's sure it's an escape to heaven.

The sun breaks through as they drive west. Turning onto the A303, the road is crowded with cheering ranks of flaming autumn trees. There's no traffic to slow their passing of Stonehenge and as they top the chalk uplands of Salisbury Plain, a gigantic rainbow frames the view, one end of it finishing at the tower she can see now, rearing up out of Bag Enderby woods.

Turning left off the Stockford road, Stephen growls as they're forced to hold back so as not to hurry a herd of teenage calves being ushered past his mother's house. He grew up here and is easily irritated by things that Tessa, as if still fresh from her own mother's litter-scudding, peeling stucco street in Kentish Town, finds enchanting. The cow men get their skittish charges past the village green successfully enough but a shiny black four-by-four suddenly pulls out of the vicarage and, put off their gentle amble, the cattle tumble into the gentrified yard of Home Farm.

Stephen waits while the newly cow-shit-slicked four-by-four's driver roars past.

'I bet he's not local,' laughs Tessa as Stephen finally parks outside his mother's house; a bright blue painted, corrugated iron bungalow, built in the 1930s by a Raj retiree named Pratt. Across the road, outside a flat-faced council house, a man sorts through tools slung about a cage built onto the back of his pick-up truck. Sitting on the flap at the end of the truck, legs dangling, a girl aged about ten stares at Tessa and Stephen, the pages of the book she's been reading fluttering in the freshening autumn wind. Tessa smiles at her. The girl does not smile back.

A sudden crack. Stephen winds down his window, straining to hear. The man in the back of the pick-up stands straight. Cattle burst back out of Home Farm yard and scatter. The man lopes easily off the back of his truck and walks down the lane, arms wide, to stop any of them causing an accident on the main road. 'Help!' comes a cry. Stephen's out of the van and running. A distraught woman falls out of Home Farm's front door and into his unexpecting arms.

Stephen's mother, Dyllis, leaning heavily on a stick, meets Tessa at the gate of the Blue House. A fluttering hand shields watery eyes from the wind as she peers at the commotion down the lane.

'Bullocks,' says Dyllis. She waves at the expressionless girl across the way before working her way back up the short path to the house. Eighty now, Dyllis subsists on baked beans, toast, instant coffee, Famous Grouse, and one Benson and Hedges a day, smoked slowly after breakfast as an 'aid to digestion'.

'If I don't open my curtains two days in a row, Anna Trester's too nosy not to come and check for a corpse.'

Tessa shuts the door to keep in the stuffy heat.

In the kitchen, Dyllis lowers herself to sit at the yellow formica-topped table, a bottle of whisky and three glasses in front of her.

'There's a time and a place for drinking in the middle of the afternoon,' she says, raising one eyebrow and twinkling at Tessa. She thinks Tessa looks as though she's been run over. Still, they're here. And he's functioning well enough to run to Anna Trester's distress. 'Talk me through that nasty slash across his cheek. And why you packed up and left so suddenly.'

Tessa takes a slug. The whisky whirls about her head. 'Stephen got caught in a knife fight.'

Dyllis tops up Tessa's glass. 'Bit close to the action, even for Stephen.'

'Then the mother of the girl who slashed him threatened to sue him for ruining the girl's chances in some reality TV thing about trying to be a super-model.' Tessa starts giggling at the ridiculousness of it all. Oh, the relief of being out of the city. 'The girl can't take part now because she's on remand. And so long as the threat of being sued is over his head, the diocese says it wouldn't be a good idea for Stephen to go back to work.'

Dyllis isn't sure if Tessa's laughing or crying. She passes over a tissue to catch the running mascara. 'The Living here is open, you know ...'

Old Jack Trester's almost-corpse lies where it fell in the fresh green slime slushing the yard. Anna, his wife, and his son Jonti hang back, though what they're afraid of, Stephen is unsure: this man, whose apoplectic face and angry black eyes used to terrify the living daylights out of him as a boy, now lies helpless as Humpty Dumpty.

'And you can fuck off!' The dying man's rotten apple breath gases Stephen when he kneels to see if he can help. 'I know you,' the old man snarls. 'You can take your religion, sonny boy, and shove it.' Trester chokes. Blood-spattered spittle flecks his lips. Stephen remembers the gun shot. He looks about him for a weapon. Thirty-six-year-old Jonti holds the twelve bore out, as if Stephen might want to finish the old man off with a thump from its antique stock.

'He's too urban to take the living here,' says Tessa.

'But you always fantasised about country living,' says Dyllis. 'And this is your marriage as much as his. And you need to get on with it if you're ever to have any children.'

Tessa takes the whisky glasses to wash them up, determined that her mother-in-law shouldn't see how elegantly she'd scored a bullseye.

Stephen bursts into the room, breathless, bringing with him a rush of cold air. 'Old Jack Trester's dead. The ambulance is coming. I'm going with Anna. She wants me. I'll need to explain the gun to the police, or they'll arrest Jonti for murder.'

And he's gone.

'I don't know,' Dyllis sucks her teeth. 'Anna Trester wants him... This might be your big chance to join the WI and learn to make marmalade, Tessa.'

4

Chapter 2

The new vicarage looks like an illustration from a Ladybird book. Rendered, painted white, with a red tiled roof and an upstairs window in the gable end, it has a picket fence, a garden path, an open fire in the sitting room, and scope for artistic improvement. It's a house that makes Tessa want to pore over colour charts and learn how to manipulate a sewing machine. It's a house in which a marriage could flourish. Tessa wonders which will be easier: the marriage or...

'Is it difficult to make curtains?' she asks Dyllis, who hoots.

'Impossible! You have to have various bits of fabric, all not quite the same size, and not quite sew them all together, and then special tape you pull string through to make them pleat. Much easier to get them ready made.'

'Be nice to make them, though, wouldn't it?'

Dyllis frowns. 'Don't push yourself too hard,' she says. 'It's a steep curve learning to be an old-fashioned housewife. And Stephen says you're only here for a year, remember?'

'Do you think the farm shop will have oranges?' asks Tessa, ignoring the threatened time limit. Dyllis looks blank. 'You're the one who suggested marmalade.'

'Do you own a cookery book?' The answer's no. The furniture decanted from the hired van into this house belongs to literary, bookish types who like wood-cut prints. There's plenty of room for a cookery section.

Tessa laughs. Now that the hired van has been emptied and returned, and since she and Stephen own no car, she feels securely planted in this living-the-dream place. 'Just because we've always survived on ready meals doesn't mean I can't learn...'

'Well don't look to me if you want to borrow a jam pan.'

By the time Stephen and Tessa move into this new house provided by the diocese, the Old Rectory of Hindle Green has a red 'Sold' sign hammered to the gate.

'Be grateful,' says Dyllis. 'The old house may have wisteria and a listed greenhouse, but it's also only got one damp bathroom in a lean-to off the kitchen, and you can see the sky through the roof tiles in the attic bedrooms. And to cook you have to shovel coke into a thing that smokes so badly that every time I left there I used to feel sick.'

'Reverend Jones taught me the trusty basic stew on that stove,' says Stephen.

'I always wondered if his intentions were entirely honourable,' says Dyllis.

'Mum!'

'Well, you were such a beauteous youth.' Dyllis smiles at the memory.

Stephen edges towards the door, round the half-unpacked boxes of their belongings. Grabbing a crisp, white surplice from where it hangs over the back of a chair, he says, 'Well, it doesn't matter where they put us. We're only here for the short term. See you in...'

'Oy! I've just ironed that beautifully!' Tessa protests.

Stephen's not used to her taking such an interest in his work uniform. From up the hill comes a muffled toll. 'Poor Jonti and Anna. Tough to have to play loving when old Jack was such a monster. See you later!' And Stephen's already gone.

Tessa arranges a pair of candlesticks on the dresser, then tries them on the windowsill above the sink. 'Stephen says I don't have to come along to this service, but I think I should, don't you?'

'God, yes! The whole county will be dying for a look at you.'

6

'I want to 'do' the country thing properly. I know Stephen's insisting we won't stay, but I reckon if I play my part properly then maybe he'll settle in and eventually he'll forget he wants to leave.'

'Don't be too subtle about it or he won't notice.' Dyllis hauls herself to her feet and arranges her sticks. 'Come on, then. You ready for your close-up?'

Tessa shrugs on her green corduroy coat. She has a black feather-stuffed jacket, but the material it's made from is too noisy for a funeral. She pulls her lip gloss from her pocket, applies it and turns to Dyllis. 'I don't look too middle-aged or mumsy, do I?'

'You're much too glam for a vicar's wife, thirty-eight-and-a-half years old, dressed like a Londoner, and you have no children. So neither of the above are possible.'

Dyllis sets her jaw at the gentle slope up to St George's as if facing the north face of the Eiger.

'I wish you'd get one of those electric buggy things,' says Tessa.

'Then I'd seize up entirely.' Dyllis is wrapped against February in a felted black cloak and a collection of scarves and shawls, with a dark brown crocheted beret to top it all. 'Jack Trester died of a heart attack in his own yard in the prime of his old age. He may have been a shit, but he must have done something right to have deserved that. I dread a mouldering old age. Doctor tells me if I keep walking, I'll die in my own bed instead of festering in a nursing home. Quite an incentive, don't you think?'

The church is dustier than Stephen remembers, the embroidered altar cloth a little tattier. The cobwebs festooning the timbers in the roof obscure the faded angel faces which somebody forgot to scrub out during the Reformation. There's been no priest in charge of Hindle Green for two years.

In the vestry cupboard, the vestments are faintly spotted with mould. The body of the church hums with people. Afterwards there will be a keg of beer and a quantity of cold red wine, cups of tea and already-curling white bread ham sandwiches at the village hall.

There's a knock on the vestry door and a gust of gossiping voices as Len Fox, the local rector, steps in. Stephen pulls his own black funeral stole around his neck.

'Grateful to you for filling in,' says Len, shaking Stephen's hand.

'So long as you know I'm only a stopgap,' replies Stephen, smiling to show he means no offence. 'When I find the right job, Tessa and I will move on.'

'Course you will.' Len Fox leans against the church safe, empty but for the sixteenth century silver chalice which only comes out for Christmas and Easter. On top of the safe there's a tray on which sit the everyday earthenware cup and plate used for celebrating communion. He picks up the cup and looks at it. 'The diocese hasn't been rushing to fill this job. I expect St George's will just be closed up when you leave. Eight hundred years of christenings, weddings and funerals - finished.'

'Surely the diocese wouldn't have bought the house Tessa and I are living in if they weren't investing in the benefice?'

'They didn't buy it. It's been taken on a short lease. Right.' Len Fox opens the door to the body of the church again. The noise out there is booming.

Stephen knows he's supposed to feel chastened by Len Fox's pointed mention that the Church haven't bought a vicarage because they might not need one for long. Tiny country churches only survive year on year if their parishes can find enough money to pay the parish share, and with a regular congregation of only a handful, how can that be sustainable if the parish share is thousands of pounds? But Stephen needs the challenge of an inner city parish. He's spent twenty years working with the concrete roots, avoiding promotion, keeping himself doing the job he first felt called to do in the favelas of Brazil. And now it seems the stabbing was an excuse to sideline him. It's as though God himself has slapped Stephen in the face and is laughing at him for trying so hard. As a result, this church, his sanctuary when he was a child, has lost its welcoming feel.

He throws a sharp look at the crucifix hanging above the door before arranging himself to look amenable and heading out to face this crowd as their vicar for the first time.

Standing on the chancel step, Stephen waits for the chatter to subside. And then he waits longer as his wife and his mother, smiling and apologising, come in late. In the kerfuffle of their being found seats and settled, the congregation gives Tessa a really good looking over; her fey, pagan beauty, her wild, strawberry-blonde hair and pointed face, her pale, freckled skin and mesmerising grey-green eyes outlined in black. She's more feral cat than church mouse, he thinks.

It's unsettling, Tessa pretending to be the kind of woman who irons his surplices, let alone comes along to services. She keeps protesting that village life will suit them. But how will she survive in the country? She's never even passed her driving test.

The address is given by a dignitary who waxes lyrical from the pulpit about generations of Trester generosity culminating in Old Jack giving the Black Barn in Stockford to the community - 'In exchange for planning permission to build fifty houses on ancient common land the town side of Sink Wood,' hisses Dyllis to Tessa in a stage whisper.

At the top of the lane a school minibus drops off a lone figure. Abbie Stoke runs down through the wintry gloom, squeezes through cars parked nose to tail all along the lane for the funeral, and lets herself in the front door of No. 3 Pratt Cottages. The lights are on. Abbie pulls up short in the kitchen. It's gleaming. Lauren won't have done this. And Carter's been out at work all day.

'Mum!' Abbie throws herself upstairs. But her mum's room's empty, clean, tidy, abandoned.

Abbie leans against the doorjamb and digests her disappointment. She never cries. Eventually, she pads downstairs. If her mum was here, then where's she gone already? She begins a patient, methodical search for clues.

Not brave enough yet to face the village women and offer to help – there's a limit to how keen she needs to be on day one – Tessa pays her respects to the Trester widow and then slips out of the wake at the village hall and cycles down to the farm shop to buy supper.

'I was just getting ready to close,' says the lady behind the counter. 'I'm Amy, by the way. Welcome to the village. Big crowd up at the hall, is there?'

Tessa smiles. 'It's heaving.' Uncertain, she picks over a selection of muddy vegetables – how do you whiz up soup? No ready meals to microwave here. Lamb and leek sausages: she knows how to use a grill. A pamphlet entitled *What's Cooking in Hindle Green* catches her eye. Tessa takes one, along with a bottle of wine from the Bag Enderby estate. Too late she sees its price. Ringing up the contents of Tessa's basket, Amy raises an eyebrow at the eight pound bottle of wine. In future, Tessa will have to buy her alcohol elsewhere.

'And how much milk will you need?' A little cashbook is reached for and a pen poised to take Tessa's order. 'We deliver

Tuesdays, Thursdays and Saturdays. Shall I say a pint a day to start with? Or are you cereal people?' This is not a question Tessa's ever considered. 'In which case you'll need two. You don't have any children, do you?' Ouch! 'And shall we say half a dozen eggs on Saturdays?'

Anna Trester plays the brave widow with aplomb. Wearing a rusty-black knitted ensemble and pearls, she receives her guests from where she perches girlishly, her ankles crossed, on the edge of the village hall stage. Luke-warm tomato soup from a teacup edges her lipstick with extra orange. At her side her son, Jonti, obediently shakes hands with strangers while forcing himself to look them in the eye, as if his dead father might appear at any time and clout him for bad manners otherwise. A vicious draught whips the ankles of the mourners while their hair is singed by antique overhead heating.

A youngish, energetic-looking woman in a sheepskin jerkin and rubber clogs appears at Stephen's elbow with a tray of cheese straws. 'Your wife's escaped already?' Stephen knows Tessa should have stayed. 'Don't blame her,' continues the woman. 'Have a cheese straw. I tried paprika to see if it would give them a smoky bacon taste.' Stephen feels obliged to take one. 'We could have them at the party after your installation as priest-in-charge. Will you want to invite members of the congregation from your previous parish?' Not-so-guileless Ellen Wiseman, churchwarden from Pendle, asks this with a wicked gleam in her eye.

Unconsciously, Stephen touches the healed slash across his face. His nose still feels bruised when he blows it. 'Seems to me that if the benefice is to be kept going, the last thing we need do is waste money on parties,' he says.

'You don't remember me, do you?' asks Ellen.

Stephen shakes his head. 'Should I?'

'Stockford Primary. I was younger than you. You remember the people who were older, don't you? But not those coming along behind.'

Stephen can barely remember his primary school: his childhood memories nearly all revolve around the mesmerising whirl that was Kat.

'The lady in the farm shop said I'd get a chimney sweep out of the *Advertiser*. She said she'd keep a copy for me on Friday.' With some ceremony, Tessa serves up sausages on a bed of roasted parsnips with a garnish of wilted kale. She's laid their skip-rescued kitchen table with candlesticks, and napkins she thinks they've never once used since they were married. She's decanted salt into an egg cup. The oil-fired Rayburn makes the room snug. Tessa gives Stephen his plate and hugs him.

'It's hardly Cordon Bleu,' she says keenly. 'The Rayburn doesn't have a grill, so I fried the sausages.' They both look at the burnt offerings for a moment. 'Not bad for a beginner, don't you think?'

Stephen picks up his knife and fork and moves things around on his plate. He changes the subject. 'I hadn't considered the necessity of a grand installation as priest-in-charge of these three little parishes. Especially as we don't intend to stay.'

Tessa knows her desire to settle permanently in the country won't be satisfied by arguing now. She must be slow and subtle. So she says, 'I cooked it all myself. Please eat something.'

Stephen cuts off the end of one sausage and looks at its pink interior. He puts the fork down. 'Can't I just be interim vicar and get on with it?'

Tessa pours them both a glass of the eight pound Bag Enderby white: it's a little sour, but supporting a local producer makes the experience of drinking it sweeter. She's taken the price label off and burnt it. 'Cheers,' she says.

'I just want to do my job. There's to be a party afterwards. In the church. With wine and Ellen Wiseman's cheese straws.'

'What's wrong with cheese straws?'

Tessa hasn't quite drained the kale enough: on her plate, water is cooling round the rock-hard parsnips. She picks up a carbonised sausage and bites the end off. Most of the recipes in the booklet she bought are credited to Anna Trester, who says things like 'pour gravy over and serve'. She doesn't tell how to make the gravy. What Tessa's made looks disgusting. She grabs both plates and scrapes the contents into the food recycling bin.

'What are you doing?'

'You make us baked beans.'

'Is there any bread?'

Shoulders shuddering over a pouring hot tap at the sink, Tessa tells herself not to be so stupid. She may not yet be forty but she is too old to cry over spoiled sausages.

Chapter 3

It's so cold upstairs, they sleep clinging together like newlyweds, spooning in the dark. In the morning, as the night is pushed away by a grey February dawn, Stephen buries his nose in his wife's hair. She smells warm to him, sweet as hay. He might have tried making love to her if fear of failure hadn't made him shy. The knifing and subsequent exile to the country has given his confidence so great a blow he can't even be sure he'd be able to make love to his wife if he wanted to. Besides, she's so deeply asleep. He hugs her tight. He loves her. She doesn't stir. He feels as sexy as a stale crust of bread.

Her hair tickles. He sneezes. Gets out of bed and stomps downstairs, puts the kettle on and opens the kitchen door to a blackbird concerto being conducted amongst the last of the rotten windfalls up the lawn. His feet freeze on the bare linoleum. He takes Tessa a cup of tea and now finds her sitting up in bed with the duvet wrapped tight under her armpits and some work already laid out on her lap, her newly acquired reading glasses perched on the end of her nose, her hair a bird's nest. He gives her the tea. He loves the bossy glasses. She says they make her look old. He kicks off his pyjama bottoms and, shivering, reaches for clean underpants.

'I'm off to look at this youth club the rector's putting together,' he tells her.

'Wouldn't you rather drink tea in bed with me?'

'I promised I'd meet him there at eight thirty.'

And he's off, roaring up the hill in his mother's vintage Mini.

Listening to the fading, old-fashioned *broom broom* of Dyllis' vintage Mini Clubman, in which Stephen has bustled off importantly, Tessa looks out at the meadow. It's the second

Tuesday in February, supposedly the most depressing day of the year, but through the window she can see a bank thick with snowdrops under the back wall in her new garden. Daffodils are pushing up in great clumps under the apple trees. She sips her steaming tea. This could be heaven, she thinks.

If only Stephen weren't so edgy all the time. And if they had sex once in a while. And she got pregnant. She should have grabbed him when she had the chance this morning. She should never have let him get out of bed to go and put the kettle on.

Once upon a time, not that long ago, she was a blushing bride in a vintage 1920s wedding dress, holding tight to Stephen's hand while being showered with real rose petal confetti under the thatched roof of the lychgate at St George's.

They'd met at a publisher's do. Stephen had helped with a memoir a colleague of his had written about being a sexy young man finding his vocation with Stephen in the Sao Paolo favelas during their gap year. Tessa had edited the work and fallen for Stephen on paper before meeting him. He'd written an introduction in which he'd lovingly described his English country childhood in contrast with Brazil with a light and amused touch. And at the party he'd laughed at himself and she'd admired his confidence. She'd even fallen for the peculiar (she thought) nature of his work. Not that she was about to get religion herself. But she found his faith only added to his appeal. They'd married fast because he'd refused to sleep with her otherwise. They had love, and all their lives to make a necklace of memories with the grit of one another.

She'd never anticipated that he'd just add her to what he did, instead of cut back to make room for her. Which at first impressed her. They'd been almost competitively busy with their different careers. She'd been comfortable with the loose knit of their marriage, because when they slept together he

15

focused on nothing but her, and their love-making was intense and precious as a result.

Hindle Green vicarage would be the place to be a mother. Tessa imagines the garden with a swing and a slide in it. A child would benefit from all her soon to be new-found country lady cooking skills. She can almost smell the cupcakes rising.

But she and Stephen have been together ten years, and even when they were freshly married and could barely keep their hands off each other, she didn't get pregnant. She's hardly going to find herself magically up the duff now.

Besides, in one year and four months she's going to be forty, the age at which country ladies stop being cool, pregnant, hippie chicks and overnight morph into heavy-footed types who chop their fingers off to feed their dogs.

Try, insists that voice in the back of her head.

'Oh, shut up,' she says out loud.

She leans back into the pillows and thinks about how she'd like to be seduced. She smiles to herself. Ravished is such a ridiculous word. But a bit of unexpected ravishing... *I'm a spoilt brat,* she thinks, resolving to be more receptive next time Stephen shows himself even tentatively willing. However remote they might have become from one another, Stephen's her only bet if she's looking to conceive. And a baby would bring them together again, bring a bit of jam to the staling bread of their marriage...

The blackened remains of what had been going to be Stockford's youth club still smoke in places. A charred beam has crashed laterally across the space; once a tractor barn, then derelict, now destroyed.

Stephen eyes the disaster with amazement.

The rector gives an exhausted smile. 'And you thought it was going to be all fêtes and flower shows, did you? They're not bad kids... They're bored. And they egg each other on.'

'Will you prosecute?'

'If we can single out a culprit. It's not so bad. We hadn't got going on the building yet: our grants are still intact. Now we can brush away all this debris and start again from scratch. No VAT on a new build.' The rector grins: he's obviously a cheerful type, even when faced with this kind of disaster. 'We've had a terrible time getting permission to turn it into anything useful. Trester wouldn't have been so generous if anybody else had wanted it. But a Grade Two listed barn in the middle of a council estate is hardly the potential des-res an old cowshed in Bag Enderby might be. Doesn't stop the planners protecting it though, does it?'

'What do the police say?'

'Not much evidence when the weapon is petrol. It's the committee meetings I dread.' The rector's abrupt change of subject leaves Stephen nonplussed. 'Took us two years to decide what to do with a barn with planning restrictions. Imagine how long it'll take the town's do-gooders to come up with a design with no limitations at all.' The rector almost trips climbing out of the space. He's older than he looks.

Beyond the singed bramble edging the plot, a girl appears. Yellow hair is scraped back off a face which is all eyes. She looks about nine or ten years old. She pulls a pack of ten out of her school uniform sweatshirt pocket and puts a cigarette between her lips. Out of the other pocket comes an old-fashioned wind-proof lighter. She throws Stephen a mutinous glare, lights up, takes a deep drag and exhales so that her face disappears behind the smoke.

'What's Abbie Stoke doing here so early?' asks Stephen, pointing. The rector turns to look, but the girl is already gone.

'Practice, that's what we need,' Tessa says to herself, as water chokes out of the green-striped, calcified bath tap. *Practise being happy, country people, and that's what we'll become.* The cold cast iron of the bath cools the water in minutes. She's out and dressed in no time: thick grey socks, brown corduroys, an aubergine roll-necked sweater she bought last year in a boutique near her publisher's office. She wears Stephen's red spotted handkerchief tied jauntily as a note of colour round her neck. She loves the change from dressing as a serious London editor. Looking at herself in the mirror, she decides that black was never really her colour. She'll wrap up all the black stuff, she thinks, and take it to the charity shop.

Downstairs she laughs out loud when she finds full milk bottles on the front doorstep. A woman passing with a child in a buggy wishes her a cheery 'Good morning' and Tessa smiles and waves, allowing herself a split second to determine, *New house, new baby.* She bends to pick up the milk.

Behind her, a diesel engine growls to a halt. It's Dyllis' neighbour's pick-up truck loaded with pungent, green-smelling logs.

'Beech,' says the man, dropping out of the cab. He pulls off a beanie to reveal stand-up straw hair. His face is wide, his smile warm, his blue eyes look straight at her through brushes of pale lashes. He's wearing overalls covered in sawdust. Steel caps gleam through the toes of his worn leather boots. Behind his ear nestles a roll-up. Tessa blushes.

'House warming from the Bag Enderby estate,' explains the deliverer.

'Oh.' Tessa's lost for words. There are such a lot. Where to put them?

'Mind.' The man presses a button at the side of the truck and the back lifts up, the logs flumping heavily into a tumbled heap beside the house.

'They'll need chopping,' the man says, thoughtfully, pulling the cigarette from behind his ear and cupping an oil-rimed hand to light it.

'Oh, yes, I suppose they will.' There's nothing like a country drawl to make a middle class freelance editor's voice sound like Celia Johnson's in *Brief Encounter*.

'Vicar do it, will he?'

Tessa opens her mouth. Stephen's hands are soft. He doesn't have the shoulders for wielding an axe. He's a forty-year-old priest, Tessa chides herself. What does he need shoulders for?

The log man is in no rush to interrupt Tessa's interior monologue. After a few draws he flicks the smouldering stub of tobacco onto the road before tucking the rest of the cigarette back behind his ear. 'I'll do 'em for you,' he tells her, eventually, as if he's only just had this genius idea. 'Best while they still green.' He doesn't quite suck his teeth as he considers his price. 'Forty quid the lot.'

'Deal,' says Tessa, sounding horribly keen. 'Will you cut the grass for me too?' she asks as he brushes past her, light sharping off the blade of his axe. He smells of bonfires and unwashed hair.

'Not till the spring now,' he tells her with a gleaming grin. She flushes again, hating her pale, revealing skin: of course grass won't grow in the winter.

'Cup of tea?' she asks in that proper voice that suddenly sounds so grating.

'White, three sugars.' He positions a fat log upright, puts another on top of it and *chock* - the first chunk is split three ways. By the time Tessa brings the tea out, he's half-way through the pile.

She leaves him to chop: she can't very well stand there all day and watch, can she? Upstairs, she switches on her computer in the spare room. She needs to change the contact details for her entry in the Society for Freelance Editors and Proofreaders' listings. Instead, she starts searching the internet for the best reviewed learn-to-cook-from-scratch book.

The office had been a child's bedroom. It has a Peter Rabbit frieze glued hip-height around it. Tessa should have taken a steamer to the paper and painted the room inspirational green before even installing her desk. She smooths a curling corner of the frieze back onto the wall. She ought to take it down if the room's going to be an office.

Tock. The axe slices through the logs as rhythmically as clockwork.

Unable to settle, Tessa switches off the computer. Stephen says she'll feel isolated in the country because she's never learned to drive. Well, she can easily prove him wrong on that count. Four miles to Stockford is no distance. She'll cycle in and buy the book that will transform her into a domestic goddess. She's heard about country facilities, that she must 'use them or lose them'. Why pay over the Internet to have books sent when she can save on the postage and buy them locally?

Outside, Dyllis' neighbour is slicing two-inch wedges off the split logs to make kindling. Now he's just showing off.

Tessa's purse is empty.

'Can I give you a cheque?' she asks. He looks as if he might spit. 'Or I can get cash in town and have it for you later?' That's more like it. He slings his axe over his shoulder and slopes off to his truck. She realises she doesn't even know his name.

Tessa buys a basket to hook onto the handlebars of her bicycle at the car parts shop on the trading estate: in Stockford, nobody's going to snatch her shopping. She's given a sack-cloth bag featuring the slogan 'I'm already recycled' by a woman with a stall at the crossroads outside the deli, where Tessa signs a petition to make Stockford plastic bag-free. At the stationers-cum-bookshop she buys twenty-five pounds' worth of cook book - extravagance! She spies a tray of knobbly Seville oranges in the window of the health food shop. The owner gauges her nervousness as she handles one.

'They're the last,' he says. 'Marmalade has such a short season. No more till next year after this lot. You'll need three pounds of sugar to go with three pounds of oranges. Organic would be best, then you can say it's organic marmalade.' Tessa holds out the recycled hessian bag and hopes it'll be up to this challenge.

'She's had those bags made especially badly. You'll have to pay for your next one,' the woman in the deli warns Tessa, laughing when she sees the sisal bulging at the seams with oranges and sugar. 'I'm April. And I'll bet you're the new Hindle Green vicar's wife? I'm a blow-in from London too. You'll settle in soon enough. Here...' and she gives Tessa flyers about yoga classes and a film club. 'You heard about the burning last night?'

By the time she slings her oranges into her new, front-mounted basket, Tessa feels as though she's found a friend. Thanks to April she knows that the log-chopper's name is Carter Stoke, that Jack Trester was a renowned local lech. Over her sweater she's now wearing a green corduroy waistcoat, found for 50p at the charity shop. She's formally registered with the library, and taken the phone number so she can make an appointment for a new patient check-up at the surgery. Tucked in with the rest of her loot are two pasties, a cabbage and some onions she thinks she'll fry up with butter. At the hardware shop she decided against a jam pan; it wouldn't fit in her bicycle basket. Surely an ordinary saucepan will do?

Tessa flings herself into the four-mile ride back up to Hindle Green. Her legs shake as she leans her bicycle against Dyllis' front fence, walks round the back and lets herself in through the kitchen door. She banishes all thoughts of sex or children - Dyllis has a sort of sixth sense on that subject, and whenever it appears in Tessa's head it'll soon be brought up – and calls through to the sitting room as she puts on the kettle, 'It's only me...' Silence. 'Dyllis?' A heartbeat of fear at the silence: now they live close enough to see her every day, Tessa is much more conscious of the old woman's frailty.

Dyllis is ensconced in her armchair, feet up, an electric fire cooking the soles of her especially comfortable shoes.

Hiding her fright, Tessa babbles, 'The gardener man who lives across the road from you delivered us a great heap of logs this morning.'

'Did he just?' Dyllis' voice is amused. She yawns, wide as a cat.

'Forty pounds! The whole load of logs wasn't worth that much.' Tessa sits at the kitchen table, pretending she doesn't have cramp from cutting up orange peel with scissors – how else is she going to get the pieces small enough for marmalade? She has a system going: the biggest of her saucepans is filling with orange juice, she's planning to tie the pith and pips in a clean tea towel for lack of the muslin the recipe tells her she needs. Four large Kilner jars she found mouldering under Dyllis' sink have been scrubbed out with boiling water and are sterilising in the top oven of the Rayburn. She doesn't have a lemon but can't see that it'll be the end of the world without it. The pleasure she's taking in her industry is not quite destroyed by Stephen's telling her off like this.

'How long would it have been before you got round to chopping them?' she asks.

'You'll upset the local economy if you start paying that kind of money. You've been had.'

'I thought it was a fair amount for the job. I haven't paid him yet. I had to go and get him cash. It was that man who lives across from your mum.' Stephen's head shoots up. 'April in the deli said his name is Carter Stoke.'

'Well, here then,' Stephen holds his hand out. 'Give it me and I'll drop the money round while you're cooking.'

'I'll pay him when he comes.'

'You don't want to encourage they Stokes to snoop about the house, Tessa.'

'What? Usually you're desperate to give our every last belonging away.'

Stephen recovers himself. 'I was joking. Ha ha! They Stokes? Joke?'

'Not funny.' Concentrating on the marmalade, Tessa pulls an elastic band round the neck of her bundled tea towel full of pith and pips and dunks it into her saucepan. It's very full. She carries it carefully and puts it on the Rayburn hotplate. The book says simmer for two hours. She'll be up all night at this rate. How should she warm sugar? She pours it into the next sized saucepan and puts that on the hotplate too.

'I'm sorry,' Stephen tries to waylay her. 'Do you want some help?'

She pushes past with her chopping board, scissors and orange squeezer and turns her back to him at the sink.

He stirs the sugar: it's beginning to stick. 'Are you sure you're supposed to..?'

'I'm doing what it says in the book!'

Stephen sits down at the far end of the kitchen table to show he's really not fussing. 'The Stoke children used to come to primary school barefoot in the summer. They lived in some old cottages on the Stockford Road. They kept pigs inside the house.   Eventually, old Jack Trester had the cottages condemned, knocked them down, and built an executive eyesore instead. They were all clever. Passed their eleven-plus but didn't go to the grammar school because, Ma Stoke used to say, 'Don't do nothing, do it?' The brothers moved away. I don't know what happened to...'

And there's that sudden flash of Kat again, as he'd last seen her when he was still not much more than a boy; two years older than him, with her waist-length gypsy red hair, crooking her finger, dancing away towards the Black Barn, laughing at him. He hasn't thought about her for years. But now it's as if she's haunting him, appearing un-bidden all the time now they've moved back to Hindle Green.

There's a vicious hissing. The marmalade boils over and slithers of rind burn all over the Rayburn top. 'Shit!' Tessa pulls the pan away and the mix sloshes onto the floor and cooks the lino. 'Bugger!' a spoon in the sugar tells her what she already knows: it's burned. 'Why didn't you take it off? Shit! Stephen!'

Chapter 4

It still astonishes Stephen that his faith is stronger than reason. He can't bear the thought that anyone might be denied the opportunity to experience the reassurance he finds in the knowledge that God is good, and so are we when we give ourselves the chance - knowledge he still has, even now he's been stabbed by a frustrated teenager, kicked out of his job and banished to the depths of the country as if he's incapable.

And now he's got over that horrible moment of facing a new congregation for the first time, St George's is still a sanctuary to him. It has been since the morning Stephen guiltily ventured home after his first ever sexual encounter to find his father dead from an unexpected heart attack, the body removed by efficient undertakers. The information that his father was dead had barely penetrated his brain when Dyllis, turning vicious in an effort to hide her shock and grief, shouted at him to go away, physically shoving him out of the front door.

Until the night before, Kat had always been his touchstone. Even now, aged forty, he still cannot understand how he could have been so careless as to fall asleep beside her after that unexpected, terrifying, thrilling moment of intimacy. But fall asleep he did, and when he woke to a perfect, hay-scented, misty summer's dawn he found that she was gone. So, thrown out by his mother, habit drove him to her house, where he was told Kat had packed up that very morning and left.

Reeling, Stephen had sought refuge in the muffled silence of the village church. There, while summer rain stormed against the ancient stone, he wept snotty, childish tears. Exhausted, exhilarated, grieving, he sat on a three-hundred-year-old, bottom-polished elm pew and breathed in the damp, mouldy air. He wiped his nose on his sleeve and when he looked up at the stained glass dove above the altar the sun broke through the clouds so that the bird hovered in a blaze of light. It was his sixteenth birthday.

It might have been hours later that Reverend Jones found him, curled up asleep on the chancel step. Stephen knew he'd never be able to describe how God led him there and gave him space to rest, completely reassured that all would be well. But from that day forward his Christian faith was the cornerstone upon which he built his life.

'Might as well make yourself useful.' Reverend Jones had appeared at his elbow with a tin of Brasso and polishing cloths. Stephen has never forgotten the clever kindness of the village priest who neither pried nor lectured but simply gave the overwhelmed boy something to do before taking him back to the Old Rectory and teaching him how to make stew.

So it is gratitude (as well as a certain finger-jabbing 'up yours' to the Church authorities for thinking him so useless) that has driven the grown-up Stephen to decide that by the time he leaves Hindle Green this time, St George's will be so flourishing it will be counter-intuitive for the diocese to close it. He may be certain his talents would be better deployed elsewhere, but Stephen still thinks it grossly unfair that his country congregation should be threatened with the loss of a functioning church.

'Hello?' a voice calls down the aisle from the West door.

The woman coming towards Stephen is all come-to-bed hair and three shades of eye shadow, her hand held out as if she wants to sell him insurance.

'Amanda Davis,' she says. 'Great to get your call. The previous incumbent always used to consult my competitors. This is the first Quinquennial I've been commissioned to do under my own name. I've only just gone solo, and the practice needs all the work it can get. You know, if necessary English Heritage can help protect St George's as much as prayer... with respect,' she says.

Stephen laughs. It's a relief to be talking to someone who doesn't know anything about him. He can switch on the Stephen Wilkinson glitter and her being charmed by him will soothe his battered self-esteem.

'I'll accept that on behalf of anyone who might be listening,' he says.

'Shall we start up here?' Amanda Davis turns to the door of the tower. 'You could make a tourist attraction of this,' she shouts over her shoulder. 'It must have the most incredible view from the top.'

She's right. From the heights of St George's crenellations they can see all the way to its mirror image, the folly on the Bag Enderby estate. In the opposite direction there's Ellen Wiseman's smallholding, where the road ribboning out of Stockford turns round the hill to Pendle. Nearer to home, muck-spreaders stream out from Green Farm to spatter the meadows. Carter Stoke's pick-up pulls up at No. 3 Pratt Cottages.

How would it be if Stephen just knocked on the door there and asked after Kat? He should have done it before. If he asks now it'll look odd that he's left it so long. And he's frightened that the weight of the question will show on his face. Married vicars aren't supposed to be lumbered with emotional baggage from their extremely distant past.

'Master of all you survey?' asks Amanda. Stephen leans against the parapet and crosses his arms. Amanda kicks at the cold grey curves of the ancient roof as if to test it. 'You're lucky to still have your lead. Look, a footprint.' She points out the stamp of a square-toed boot, a line drawn round it, the date, 1707, cut into the lead beside the heel.

'Churchwardens used to do it,' says Amanda. 'He hasn't written his name. Or... here... Tr... No, it's worn away. You could go back through the records and find out who it was. We'll have to check underneath. Where he made the print he might have thinned the lead enough to let the water in. And here.' She squats down to take a closer look. 'Where the joist ends are built into the wall, there might be rotten roof and stonework problems. Double whammy!'

'I've only ever worked with younger churches than this,' says Stephen. 'There was nothing particularly important or interesting to protect in shoring them up. If we did need money for St George's, would a grant be dependent upon turning this building into a tourist attraction?'

'How much do you think you could generate from the village?' asks Amanda. 'Ballpark for a tower like this – if we do find major problems - would be about £100k. Is your fabric fund up to that? You could apply to English Heritage to make up the shortfall on what the parish can contribute, but they would never fund the whole works. They tend to go for meeting what the locals can raise, like for like.'

'What little money there is I've been hoping to use to put in a hearing loop and sensible heating. And we have no loo. And the organ had mice nesting in it last year. This place needs updating if we're to be able to use it for money-raising activities to keep the church standing. The parish share alone is £14,000 a year, which the congregation really struggle to find. There is a heating system, but it was installed by a rich nineteenth century incumbent who based it on the way he kept his greenhouses warm for his peach trees. Works fine if you're prepared to feed a coal-fired boiler all day long.'

Twenty-year-old Lauren Stoke sits at the kitchen table, smoking. In front of her she's laid the forms she must fill in to begin the process of reclaiming her six-year-old twins, Trixie and Belle. Her hands no longer shake. Her thoughts no longer wander. She's daring to think she might be clean. Kat always said she wouldn't be able to do it. Well, she's going to prove Kat wrong. Lauren lights one of four remaining cigarettes. Kat can go fuck herself for all Lauren cares. Kyle fucked off. Kat fucked off. Well, Lauren will just do it all on her own. There's nobody out there she trusts, anyway.

According to her probation officer, she and her friend had been 'Recreational users of crack cocaine and heroin'. The friend is dead from all that recreation. Lauren takes a final suck from the cigarette and stubs it out. Social services don't like giving kids back to smokers. She folds the top over to hide the three she has left and tries to focus on the densely questioning forms. Her probation officer asked if she needed help filling them in. She should have said yes.

'All right?' Carter shoulders his way into the room with a strimmer that needs stripping back before the season starts. Lauren puts the forms into a neat pile and opens the *Advertiser* at the jobs pages. Cleaning in a school: that would be regular and she'd get time off in the holidays. But she'll never get school work now; they'd worry she'd try dealing, however clean she said she was. She lights the third-last cigarette.

'You got anything in for dinner?' asks Carter, strimmer string between his teeth.

'Sandwiches.' Fighting frustrated tears, Lauren slams a loaf of bread onto the table and a half-empty pot of peanut butter. Her forms scatter across the floor. She shoves the pack with its two remaining cigarettes into the pocket of her body warmer and storms upstairs.

Carter stops fiddling with the strimmer. He wishes he could magic Lauren happy. He thought it would be better without his mum here to scratch at her. His feelings for both his sisters are animal-protective. But it's easier to defend ten-year-old Abbie from the world with his twenty-two-year-old authority. Lauren's more difficult. He can't very well send a woman only thirteen months younger than he is early to bed for screwing her life up. Prison's already tried that.

At the railway station in London, people bear down on Tessa in solid ranks until at the very last moment they break round her. Country habit already has her looking people straight in the eye and smiling, until a man takes her openness as a challenge and snarls. The second-hand, leaf-coloured ensemble that had appeared clever and zeitgeist this morning seems dowdy now among the Londoners' matt black winter wardrobes. Unless they're going to a funeral, nobody wears black in Stockford.

The publisher wants to take her to lunch. Generous of him since she hasn't finished half the work she promised him by Christmas.

The truth is, Tessa's lost her drive. She used to go to the British Library every day and the atmosphere of mildly competitive intellectual activity was enough to make her concentrate. In Hindle Green she spends her time making tea, thinking she might paint the sitting room in buttercup, wondering how she can persuade Stephen to build her some raised beds to plant vegetables in, practising successful flapjacks and taking them up to Dyllis who says they're so good Tessa should sell them at the WI market in Stockford on Fridays – and trying to think of ways to inject rising sap into her marriage.

Tessa's been to the WI market: she was overawed by the apparently easy achievements of the busy ladies presiding over cakes, eggs, spicy winter salads, bunches of early daffodils... Easter's not far off: somewhere, Tessa read she should plant potatoes on Good Friday. And Stephen's busy: his part-time, gap-filling job occupies him seven days a week. At night he's asleep before his head hits the pillow: in the morning he's always already downstairs, no matter how early Tessa stirs.

Talking into his mobile, the publisher's waiting for her on the pavement outside the pizza house he uses as his canteen.

He ushers her inside. 'No wine for you,' he says, putting down his phone at last. 'You haven't earned it. Tessa, what are we going to do with you?'

A flush burns up her neck. She hates being told off. But she and Stephen will practically starve if they have to live on his stipend. There are other jobs he could go for in the rural deanery, but he says there's no point applying for them since he and Tessa aren't staying. Tessa doesn't earn much as a freelance editor, but it's enough to cover running the car, for instance; it's all very well Dyllis letting them use her car for free but it has already cost them three hundred pounds plus buying and fitting new tyres, and the garage man in Hindle says there'll be more needs doing if the old car is to pass her next MOT. However, in the country a car is a necessary indulgence which has had to replace the ready meal habit.

'Gavin,' she says to the publisher, 'be gentle with me.' She can't tell if her voice sounds desperate. 'My husband nearly died of a stabbing in October, since when he's changed his job, we've moved house and exchanged our lives for something completely alien. I promise I won't let you down any more than I have already. Give me till June,' she says, her fingers tightly crossed under her thighs so he can't see.

A waiter hovers.

'Salad Niçoise for me,' says the publisher, 'And she'll have a pizza with everything on it.'

The waiter scribbles. 'And to drink?'

'Jug of tap water,' says Tessa quickly. 'Please.'

'For God's sake! Red wine. House red. You look so wan, Tessa, you clearly need the iron.'

31

'And I'll have the pizza with spinach and egg,' says Tessa to the waiter. She turns back to Gavin. 'So will you give me till June?' Tessa can't bear the suspense.

The publisher's playing with his BlackBerry again. 'Can't, sorry.'

Is he serious?

'Listen.' Now he manages to meet her eye. 'We've already missed three publication dates because the author was late. And now he says you don't answer his emails fast enough.'

'It's our crap broadband,' Tessa protests. 'The phone company says we have an old wire serving nearly all the village. Every time a bird lands on it or the wind blows, the connection goes on the blink, so it's hardly worth paying for. I'm arguing with them. But we're second class citizens in the country: we don't make enough business for the phone company to bother dealing with us. I need the work, Gavin.'

'I'll get you other work.'

'What other work?'

'Hey, you know who bought the Old Rectory in Hindle Green?' he asks, changing the subject as if they're making conversation at a cocktail party.

'What?'

'Well, we had an alright year last year so, oddly enough, I looked at the place for us. We'd have been neighbours.' He stops for Tessa to say something. She's still biting her tongue about the work being taken from her. 'But now you say the broadband connection's so bad, I'm glad we left it. God, the house was a mess! And the Listed Buildings' Consent you'd need to make that place habitable... Anyway, I saw in the paper something about Rufus Stone's brand new country pile. How's that for a small world? Didn't you and he have a fling once, years ago?'

Tessa's tongue finally escapes her control. 'Well if he's bought it, I expect the broadband connection to the village will be sorted out in no time. Then when you need me I'll be working for someone else.' Absorbing the shock of her summary dismissal, she struggles to her feet and slings her bag over her shoulder. How could he be so unsympathetic? They've worked together for fifteen years. Once she'd have kissed this man. Now she doesn't even offer him her hand.

'What about your pizza? Tessa! Don't be like that...'

Stephen knocks on the open cottage door. A black cat purrs welcoming figures of eight around his legs. A goat peers at him from its tether in an orchard. Chickens peck about the place, kept in order by a bright yellow cockerel standing proud on a pile of stable sweepings heaped against the stone wall of a vegetable garden. Stephen escapes the cockerel's malicious glare by stepping into Ellen Wiseman's kitchen.

'Hello?' he calls.

'Sorry,' a breathless Ellen appears from the next room. 'If I stop hanging the washing I never remember to go back and it rots in the basket. Here.' She pulls a chair out and shoves old copies of the *Advertiser*, a tool kit, and a half-empty sack of seed compost down the table to make some space. 'Tea?' she asks, putting a kettle onto a stove all heaped about with logs and faggots. 'There.' A plate of little buns appears, the tea's made in a chipped brown pot, mugs and a jug of milk are put on the table. 'It's Pearl's,' she explains. 'You don't mind goat? Right. Here's the list.' She pulls a file from the detritus at the other end of the table. 'I know we would normally wait and go through all this at the next meeting but Lent starts next week... Did they do Lent Lunches where you were before?'

Stephen shakes his head. 'Things weren't so genteel.'

'Of course. I didn't think.'

She can't help herself, thinks Stephen. 'Does the scar still...?' Ellen gulps at her tea, puts it down. 'Sorry. Natural nosiness. Gentility aside, the Lent lunches and things do bring different people together.'

Stephen wishes he'd thought of another word. Now Ellen thinks him an inverted snob. Which he is.

'We start with the pancake party, that's Hindle Green...'

She's interrupted by a terrible squawking and squabbling outside.

Running after Ellen into the yard, Stephen sees that the goat is being ridden like a race-horse by the territorial cockerel. The terrified goat has pulled her chain out of the wall, smashed through the gate, and is rampaging through the vegetable garden. She's already reached the fruit cage where she's caught in the sagging green netting which protects the raspberries in summer.

Adrenalin pumping, 'I'll get the cockerel,' shouts Stephen, 'You see if you can catch the goat.'

He strips off his jacket, rolls up his sleeves, and goes for it. The cockerel abandons the goat and challenges Stephen. Fluffing his neck feathers into a great yellow ruff, the cockerel puts his head down and charges, flying feet-first to attack Stephen's legs. Stephen, blood pouring, tries to get hold of the bird.

'Get him round the neck and put his head down,' shouts Ellen from the orchard where she's already tying up the rescued goat. Instead, Stephen slips, and lands face-down in a heap of old cabbage leaves. The cockerel's on him instantly, standing on his shoulders and crowing in triumph. Stephen lies there, spurs digging into his back, and considers his next move.

'Here, silly thing.' Is Ellen talking to Stephen? The cockerel's lifted off and Stephen sits up. Ellen grins; the cockerel, meek as a newborn lamb, is tucked cosily under her arm. 'I'm sorry,' she says, fighting laughter. 'Oh, Vicar. If you could see yourself.' Stephen struggles to his feet. He brushes off a mixture of cabbage leaves, teabags and carrot scrapings.

'Next time,' says Ellen, 'you just get him like this.' She puts the cockerel gently on the ground, takes him by the neck, covers his eyes. The cockerel slumps. 'You see? He thinks it's night time now and he's gone straight to sleep.' Stephen forces a smile. He wishes he could ask her to hold on to the bird while he legs it to the car. Can he not even face down a cockerel?

'Would you like a bath?'

'I'm sorry. I'd better...' He needs to get out of here.

'Oh. What about the list?'

But Stephen's already getting into his car, revving. 'Email me,' he shouts.

The hens calmly take advantage of the smashed gate and tuck in to a row of spinach. Shooing them gently back towards the yard, Ellen goes to answer her phone. It's April at the deli, wanting to ask about herbs and what the new vicar's like. 'Bet that nice wife has to fight off lonely lady parishioners who fancy getting lost in those big black eyes of his.'

'If they don't mind his being squeamish about mud. He's a bit pathetic, I think. Mrs Trester might have him for a Lent lunch. He was a couple of years older than me at primary school. Used to hang out with those Stokeses all the time. He seemed much tougher then.'

Fighting a wasting, drowning feeling, hating himself for being completely unmanned by the cockerel incident, Stephen slams about the kitchen making the stew Reverend Jones taught him. *Bang* goes the cleaver chopping up the lamb neck, *thudthudthudthud* as it slices onion, carrots and celery.

Caramelising sugar is chucked into the casserole from too aggressive a height and goes everywhere. Stephen shoves the mix into the bottom oven and the Rayburn shudders as he kicks the door shut.

Still burning with pent-up energy, he spends an hour ferrying the logs from their roadside heap into a rough arrangement around the kitchen door using a squeaky-wheeled barrow he finds in the garden shed. He lights the fire in the sitting room.

He feels thwarted, caged, yet in desperate need of a shoulder – not to cry on, just for warmth. He calls Tessa's mobile to see if she wants fetching from the station. A recorded message tells him she's unavailable. He goes upstairs to have a bath. He's going to prove to himself that he's not sexually defunct. If he can do it now, then seducing Tessa later, tomorrow, whenever, won't be fraught with the fear he's got from nowhere that he won't be able to perform. Luke-warm water spurts down green-striped calcium deposits into the bath. OK, so maybe the bathroom's not the place. He washes perfunctorily. Scrubs himself dry. Puts on pyjamas. Gets into bed. And picks up the book of Season Songs he found in his bedroom at his mother's. His father gave it to him one Christmas. Snuggling under the duvet, what he wants is a cup of Horlicks, not sex. He settles for poetry.

Tessa doesn't ring Stephen to say what time her train gets in. Her anger at herself for storming out of her meeting is not something she wants to share yet. She needs some anonymous time. Stockford High Street is deserted. The place looks dead and it's only five thirty. Wandering down Watery Lane, she comes across the Kingsmead Arms, claiming to have been built where somebody supplied beer to the gathered fighting men at a rallying point for King Alfred. She buys a glass of red wine from a girl who tries to begin a chat with, 'Half the time it's as if the weather has a mind of its own.'

Tessa escapes to a table beside the fire where she huddles, her enthusiasm for life dribbling down the gutter with the rain.

I should be ashamed of myself, she thinks, feeling instead like a rebellious teenager.

There's Carter Stoke, the log deliverer. He's drinking beer from a pewter mug with a glass bottom which the simpering barmaid had taken from a special hook

'All right?' he asks.

'Not really,' she's too tired to be discreet. 'What about you?'

'My sister's out of prison and come to live with us.' He stands with his back to the fire, his hair glistening with fine rain. 'So it's pretty shit at our house an'all. Parade gets going in half an hour. And then the Fair starts.' Tessa looks lost. 'It's the Carnival. Come on, I'll show you the best place to see from.' Tessa can understand the barmaid's blushes. It's warm in the beam of Carter's eyes. She smiles. Why resist this excuse to avoid reality? Tessa finishes her glass in one gulp and stands up too quickly.

'Whoa,' Carter steadies her. She knows she should eat something but this evening she sees no reason to be sensible.

Carter leads Tessa down the high street through crowds that have materialised from nowhere. At the deli, April's put up a makeshift bar on which a cauldron of spiced wine steams beside a gorgeous array of mismatched vintage teacups on a wipe-down, red and white gingham-patterned cloth.

'Carter!' April runs out and grabs him, drags him inside the shop and hugs him keenly. Tessa follows and finds herself in a crowd of educated voices dressed in faded cotton, corduroy and moth-eaten wool. She's introduced to Hugo, a blacksmith;

Orlando, a plumber; Sarah, who makes cakes; and Daisy: 'She grows the biggest selection of chillies in the county, don't you darling?' says April, diving off to ladle more wine.

'Welcome to Stockford,' says Daisy, the chilli-grower. 'Is it being nice to you so far? Where are your children going to school?'

Tessa keeps the smile going. 'We don't have any children.'

The chilli-grower slaps her hand over her mouth. 'Oh, I hope I haven't put my foot in it. Are you a major career woman then?'

Tessa finishes the wine in her glass. 'I'm a freelance editor,' she says. Daisy claps her hands with glee.

'Thank God for that! I've got to write a book about growing bloody chillies. Will you advise me?'

Tessa reaches for a jug of wine and fills both their cups. 'Absolutely, I'll advise you.'

And suddenly, 'They're coming!' shouts the cake-maker.

First there are tractors pulling themed floats on which chained children dance and lip-sync songs from musicals. The tractor and trailer ensembles are interspersed by bands of pre-teen cheerleaders, dressed mostly in pink lycra, dancing their routines behind smaller tractors pulling carefully arranged stands of the troupes' trophies. Then come the souped-up cars, more sound system than wheelbase, and from time to time a solitary child, almost asphyxiated by diesel fumes, shivering in the March evening wind, carrying a sign to say that their fancy dress is 'Snowflake', or 'Chimney sweep'. Tessa's mesmerised.

Carter re-fills her teacup and puts a few cheesy whorls cut through with the salty tang of anchovy into her saucer. Tessa lets them melt, one at a time, in her mouth.

Now there are twin girls parading. They can't be more

than five or six. Blue-lipped with cold, they're dressed as a miniature Dannii and Cheryl. Across the road a couple in their forties are cheering them on fit to burst.

Then from the alley next to the deli a figure flits and grabs them.

There's a collective intake of breath. Even the music seems to stop. And with barely a look back, the children take the hands of their assailant and abandon the parade, running off down the alley and into the yard behind the shop.

'Shit!' Carter drops his pastry whorls, ducks under the counter and through the door to the back. Tessa follows.

'Lauren!'

In the yard, Tessa stops beside him and they watch together as his pick-up disappears down Watery Lane and towards the A-road which runs beside the river at the bottom. Carter looks as though he might cry.

'What was that all about?' she asks. He runs his hands through his hair and doesn't seem to notice her.

'Fuckin' stupid bitch,' he says.

Chapter 5

'Surely batter's supposed to be runnier than this?' Tessa asks the air.

Anna Trester caught her defenceless when she rang at seven fifty-eight this morning and told Tessa to make twenty stuffed pancakes for the party tonight. Game, Tessa's tied her new blue and white striped butcher's apron over her jeans with a tight bow in front: it's a good look, she thinks, admiring herself in the long mirror in the bathroom. Normally she considers herself scrawny, but the tubular wrapping of the apron makes her appear elegantly svelte.

Only mildly irritated by it (on account of having Project Pancake to get her teeth into), Tessa's cleared up the mess made by Stephen's last-night stewing – bachelor Reverend Jones never taught Stephen that a good cook cleans up as they go - and puts a chicken in the top oven of the Rayburn. She and Stephen are going to have some of it for lunch, and the rest she's going to pick apart and put with mushrooms in a white wine sauce as a pancake filling - very country lady, making-two-meals-out-of-one. And never mind Stephen's leftover lamb stew in the larder – they can eat that tomorrow. Tessa's not quite feeling out of her depth, though this whole project is much more complicated than flapjacks. And she forgot to buy the mushrooms when she went to the shop.

'Hello?'

'Dyllis – help!' Dyllis leans, breathless, against Tessa's kitchen doorjamb. 'You haven't run down the hill, have you?'

'It's the wind,' says the old lady. 'Takes my breath away.' And she eases herself onto a kitchen chair and nods at the kettle. 'I've come for elevenses. How was yesterday?'

'Terrible. Carter's sister, Lauren, the one just out of prison, abducted her daughters and drove off into the night with them. Nobody knows where they've gone.'

'I meant London. What are you doing?'

Tessa is adding beer to her pancake batter from a bottle which cost her nearly two pounds. 'It's an expensive business making charitable suppers, isn't it?' she says. 'In London, Stephen used to buy frozen party snacks from the cash and carry. This recipe says use chicken pieces. But a whole chicken was cheaper so I'm roasting it and I'll pull it apart later. What do you think?'

'Darling, the best pancakes I've ever had are those frozen ones. Besides, aren't you supposed to be working?'

Tessa puts a frying pan on the hot, left-hand end of the Rayburn hob, and cuts a knob of butter into it. 'This mixture seems horribly gloopy to me,' she says, 'even with the beer. Can I try one on you?'

'Couldn't we have tea?'

The butter's fizzing round the pan, the edges of its froth browning already. Tessa can't let it burn. She hurriedly sloshes a ladle of batter into the butter. 'Whoops!' She stands back, hands on hips, peering forward, hopeful. A knife to smooth the mixture, she thinks.

'Careful,' says Dyllis. 'You don't want it to look like an omelette.' Tessa takes the egg flip from the drawer and wields it in the direction of the pancake. The edges look worryingly stuck to the pan.

'Here we go.' To her astonishment, Tessa manages to flip the circle of mixture, which has solidified quite nicely. 'One minute on this side...' she looks blindly at the kitchen clock, back at the pan. 'Must be done now, don't you think? What would you like on it? Butter? Jam?'

Dyllis eyes the object she's offered and says, 'Or whipped cream and strawberries since it's almost thick enough to be called cake.'

'Please, taste it. Tell me it's not horrible.'

Dyllis dutifully tucks in, makes a moue, puts down her fork. 'I seem to have a very distant memory of my mother leaving her batter to rest overnight. This might be much improved tomorrow morning.' Tessa slumps at the table and puts her head in her hands.

'The party's tonight. It's so time-consuming, all this cooking business,' she says, pulling at the edge of Dyllis' abandoned pancake and testing it. She grimaces. 'It tastes like half-set concrete.'

'Better ring Anna Trester back and tell her you've too much work to do.'

Tessa groans. 'If that weren't a horrible lie.'

And so it all comes out: the being late with the editing, the row with the publisher, the childish storming out. 'I can't believe I'm arsing about making pancakes when we won't be able to afford to fill the oil tank when it's empty.'

'Oh, bollocks to that,' says Dillys. 'You are the most thrifty couple I've ever come across. Your wedding dress was second-hand.'

'Vintage.'

'You bought it in a charity shop. You'll be fine for money.'

'Stephen's only part-time.'

'They'll dragoon him into some diocesan position soon enough. You don't think they're going to let an able priest like Stephen go as easily as he says they will, do you? Perhaps it's time for you to change direction? People round here do it all the time. I think they call it 'Downshifting'.

'I thought you'd say I should have a baby.' The words are out before Tessa can stop them. She flushes puce.

'Good Lord! It's a bit late for that. You're nearly forty, for God's sake! What did Stephen say when you told him you'd lost the job?'

Reeling at Dyllis' brusque dismissal of her fertility, Tessa says, 'I haven't yet. I got caught up in Stockford carnival when I got off the train.' In the middle of the night she and Carter had walked back to Hindle Green together. He lent her his coat when she shivered, and left her at the gate. He hadn't been able to find his sister, or her twins, and there'd been no sign of his pick-up.

'Stephen was asleep when I got in last night and gone already when I woke up this morning. All the Stockford area priests get together once a month for a working breakfast. They're having it today because Lent starts tomorrow.'

'Excuse for a fry-up, more like. Right,' Dyllis pulls herself upright. 'Never mind the tea. I'd better scarper so you can lay a pretty table for your husband's lunch and then seduce him quick afterwards in case he says he won't have intimate relations -' (this in a leery voice) '- during Lent.'

Tessa flushes purple, but gets out napkins all the same. She puts a damp cloth over the bowl of batter and tucks it onto the shelf in the larder. The chicken smells delicious. Forgetting to remove her apron, she cycles down to the farm shop where she buys a handful of only slightly over-the-top mushrooms. She's already got a bottle of cheaper white from April.

It occurs to her that to be a happy countrywoman it helps if you delight in the creative challenge of daily chores. She hangs out the washing with artistic flair and laughs at herself for being ridiculous. She picks daffodils in bud and blue and purple flowers with a spotted leaf and arranges them on the table in a milk bottle vase. She peels potatoes and puts them to boil. They'll take forever. The Rayburn may be romantic, but it certainly isn't speedy: the more she uses it, the cooler it gets. She wishes she hadn't given their electric kettle to the hoarder responsible for the white elephant stall at the fête. They should get some chickens to eat all these peelings, she thinks, as she chops the sweet hearts out of some muddy, farm shop leeks. Chickens would look pretty pecking about under sheets snapping in the breezy spring sunshine – except now it's suddenly pouring.

She wipes her hands on her batter-spattered apron and pushes her hair out of her eyes, leaving a smear of mud across her cheek. Then, wet washing heaped once again in a basket inside the back door, and still waiting for the potatoes to boil, the table laid prettily and the bed clean-sheeted and turned down expectantly, she arranges herself against the warmth of the Rayburn and picks up last week's *Advertiser*. There's a photograph on the front of a forty-eight year old woman who's just given birth to triplets.

'All right?' Without knocking, Carter Stoke's opened the kitchen door. He shakes himself and water sprays all over the lino. 'Just saw old Dyllis in,' he says. 'She got caught in it and all.'

Uninvited, he eases off his muddy boots and arranges them carefully on the doormat. Then, beanie in hand, he steps into Tessa's love nest and asks, 'Where's the vicar to?'

'He'll be home soon. Would you like to wait?' So much for romance with Stephen. That's the thing about being a vicar: you work from home and your congregation has the right to drop in on you at any time of the day or night. Tessa crowds the kettle onto the Rayburn hob.

'You looking for anything in particular?' Carter swings the *Advertiser* round to face him on the table. 'Most things, I'll know someone. Don't have to pay *Advertiser* prices.' What's most attractive about Carter, realises Tessa, is that he looks straight at you. He talks to you directly: he's not thinking about anything else, or making a list, or reading a document. He's speaking, then listening, and concentrating on you all the time.

Remembering the forty quid he charged her for the log chopping, Tessa says, 'I was going to look for some chickens.'

'Nice bit of ground you've got back here. I could set you up with two runs: dozen to fatten and a dozen layers. Sell your surplus, you could.'

'I don't know I'd be any good at it.'

'Nothing to it. Just remember it's always worth feeding the layer a bit of corn. Bit dearer, but it keeps the eggs coming regular and stops him going broody if you spoil him a bit.' Tessa loves the idiom: why's a hen a he?

'What's all this?' Tessa hasn't heard the front door open. Stephen's entry from the hall makes her jump, look down, fuss with the *Advertiser*, closing it and turning it over so that the woman with triplets is hidden. Stephen dumps his dripping coat on the back of a chair and holds his hand out to Carter. 'I'm Stephen. Are you Kat's son?'

'Yeah. Your wife's been telling me how she fancies keeping chickens.' Stephen shoots a look at Tessa, who still doesn't know about the cockerel incident. She blithely pours Stephen tea. Who's Kat?

Stephen offers Carter a seat beside the wood-burner in the office and, to stop himself staring, starts lighting a fire. Carter's a hearty spitting image of Kat, his young man's face still rounded, skin smooth beneath the stubble he forgets to shave, his eyelashes thick as hers had been as a girl... Stephen shakes himself: sounds as though he fancies the boy – he wonders what the years have done to her. 'Won't take a minute.' He breaks the first match. Breaks another. Finally lights the third. 'You did a fine job on these logs for us.'

'Thanks.'

Stephen fiddles about, pushing newspaper and kindling into the flames. He won't reach for the firelighters. 'So,' he stands up, his knees creaking, abandoning the reluctant smoulder he's made instead of a fire. 'How can I help?'

'Well I got to ask somebody and the social services just tell you how the system works. My sister saw you at the youth club when it burnt down. Said you winked at her.'

'You want to talk about little Abbie?'

Carter twists his yellow jacket in his hands. A reflective band gleams through the grime.

'No. My other sister, Lauren. What's been in prison.' Carter throws Stephen a challenging glare. Stephen doesn't react. This is what he's good at. He's absorbent as a padded wall.

Carter continues, 'But now she's out she wants to get her girls back. They're six and they live with they Nanna. Lauren moved in with me and tried to get it together, but she thinks everyone's against her. She didn't have the patience to let the system work itself out. Last night she grabbed the kids at Carnival and drove off with them.'

'Do you know where she's likely to have gone?'

'Fair packed up this morning. Been around the area for carnival season but I don't know where it's to now. I expect she's with that one who does the waltzer. She's been going to all the carnivals so she can see him. She took my pick-up.' Carter doesn't mention that, though she can drive perfectly well, Lauren's never passed her test and therefore has no licence, and couldn't get insurance if she asked for some.

'Well, we should at least go and see where they were,' says Stephen.

It's not just the way the boy looks like her physically, but the energetic way he's sitting, pushing the hair off his face, restlessly leaning forward to try resting his elbows on his knees for a second, the way he flicks a look at the ceiling when looking for the right answer to a question: it's all pure Kat.

'There might be somebody left behind at the fairground,' suggests Stephen. 'What did the police say?'

'Wass the police to do with it? They her kids.'

Stephen's sympathetic but the police must be told what's happened. 'What about the insurance on the pick-up?'

Carter frowns.

'You won't be able to claim for it unless you've reported it stolen... And without it I assume you won't be able to take your tools to work?'

So much for Tessa's dream lunch. Stephen apparently doesn't see the roast chicken proudly set in the middle of the table, or the bowl of steaming potatoes running with butter, or the melt-in-the-mouth leeks - already served onto hot plates - let alone the napkins. He simply pulls on his wet coat.

'We're off to do something about this man's sister.' He's already half-way out of the door. No wonder Tessa didn't bother learning to cook. What was the point when Stephen would never stay still for long enough to eat? Carter shrugs his apology. Then, grinning, he swivels the plate of chicken, expertly pulls off both legs, waves them at Tessa, and hurries after Stephen. Tessa shoves her lip gloss back into her pocket and jabs a V sign at the sound of the explosive farting the Mini makes when roaring off. She cuts herself a bit of breast. The chicken seems to have made a little sauce all on its own and she dips slices into it as she eats, standing, leaning against the Rayburn.

Stuff Stephen. Stuff Dyllis for inspiring Tessa to change the sheets especially.

It occurs to her she ought to be proud of herself: she's just successfully roasted her first chicken. At least Carter noticed the effort she made. Tessa clears the lunch away and goes upstairs to Google-search 'keeping chickens.' Instead, she types in: '1st time mother age 39'. She's amazed, though not very amused, to discover that if she and Stephen ever actually had sex and she magically managed to produce a baby she'd be referred to as a 'geriatric mother'.

Inside Hindle Green's silvered-oak-clad village hall, tables are arranged for supper with cotton cloths and jam jars of snowdrops, and a few early daffodils. This year, on account of the keg of beer Mrs Trester's persuaded the new owner of the Old Rectory to donate, tickets for the pancake party have sold like hot crêpes. Tonight there are not more than five left for any Johnny-come-latelies.

The place is buzzing. Everyone's here early because, they say, the new owner of the Old Rectory might be coming, and nobody wants to miss their chance to cosy up with the village's new star resident.

There's no sign of the celebrity as yet, but his beer's going down a treat. No sign of the vicar, either, or his wife, or the twenty chicken and mushroom pancakes she promised for the main course.

'Stephen says she works for herself,' says Anna Trester, shuffling trays of pancakes in and out of the oven in the hall's tiny kitchen, her upper lip beaded with the sweat of responsibility. 'She should have said no if she didn't have time to make them.'

'Is *he* coming, then?' asks Amy from the farm shop. She's not interested in the vicar's wife when there's the possibility that tonight she might meet Rufus Stone.

'Well, you know, he's filming in Scotland at the moment.' Mrs Trester's intimate knowledge of Rufus Stone's movements is, in fact, second-hand: what little she knows is gleaned from the secretary she spoke to on a London telephone number. Her voice pierces a sudden silence. She grapples with her apron's strings and yanks it over her head. 'It's him,' she hisses to her acolytes. And she dives out into the hall, patting her hair, and rubbing what's left of her lipstick out of the creases around her lips.

But the hall hasn't fallen silent for the entry of Rufus Stone. The silence is in honour of the vicar and his wife, who stand at the door flanking the blinking figures of Carter Stoke and...

'That Abbie!' Mrs Trester is indignant. 'This is hardly...' She bustles forward. She'll remind them that this is a ticket-only affair, that you have to have bought the tickets at the farm shop before the evening, and that they cost five pounds each plus contributions for the raffle and payments for the beer.

'Mrs Trester,' Stephen reaches forward to kiss and disarm her in one easy move. 'I hope you don't mind, but we brought some friends. You did say there would be a few spare places.' He pulls a rumpled tenner from his pocket and hands it over to the flushing Jonti, who shuffles, waiting for instructions from his mother.

But Stephen's already marched straight into the hall. 'Hi Ellen,' he says. 'How's the goat? Can we sit with you? Are we late? Where do we put Tessa's lovely Chicken Surprise Pancake Bake?' Tessa winces. She'd wanted to throw her effort away.

Ellen smiles at Tessa and says, 'Vicar, I think they're waiting for you to say grace.'

'They were feculent!' Tessa shivers as she pulls on pyjamas and bed socks.

'Doesn't matter!' insists Stephen from the bathroom where he's cleaning his teeth. 'Anna Trester shouldn't assume that just because you're a vicar's wife you're also a Cordon Bleu cook.'

'And she was horrible to Carter.' The sheets are icy. Tessa hugs a hot water bottle and tucks the duvet around her ears.

'Miserable business, having to report his pick-up stolen to the police. But it was the only way I could get him to witness the report of Lauren taking her daughters.' Stephen climbs into bed and sets his alarm. He turns off his bedside light.

'You didn't make him?' She sits up. Stephen opens his just-closed eyes.

'Trixie and Belle are only six. Lauren's a recovering heroin addict. Of course I made him.'

'Last night he seemed to think they'd be perfectly safe.'

'What do you mean 'last night'?' Stephen turns his light back on.

'I was there. When she took them.' Tessa flushes with a guilt she has no reason to feel.

'Now you tell me! And you didn't report it?' Stephen doesn't ask what Tessa was doing with Carter.

'The grandparents will have reported it. Anyway, he said they'd be fine. I talked to him.' She doesn't say she talked at midnight as they walked back through the lanes under a magnificent reach of stars.

'Tessa! You're a witness. The police will want to know why you didn't come forward last night. Now they could be out of the country for all we know. It's basic stuff, Tess.'

'Don't patronise me, Stephen.' He got away with there-thereing about the pancakes: she won't have him question this judgement call.

He doesn't let it lie. He never lets it lie. Every time they have a row he ruthlessly claims the moral high ground.

'It's my job to watch out for people,' he tells her, as if she doesn't already know. 'I know you're not the classic Busy Lizzie-type vicar's wife but people here see us as a team. You behave irresponsibly and it reflects right back on me.'

'Oh fuck off, Stephen!'

Clean sheets forgotten, tonight they lie back to back, he spitting tacks because her instinct about those disappeared children was so wrong, she furious because he still hasn't shown any interest in how her meeting went with Gavin. She's boiling with the loss of her work and she punishes Stephen by not telling him about it. How can he bang on about how important his job is when they rely on hers to pay for the car, the insurance, the heating oil... *And the rest!* she shouts in her mind. And she has been being the perfect country vicar's wife. She ironed his surplice. She went to Jack Trester's memorial service. She invited Carter in despite her plans for a seductive lunch. Stephen's the one always telling her she shouldn't feel obliged to get involved: in fact, he practically shuts her out of his work...

Stephen wakes at three in the morning. Tessa's face in the moonlight is smooth as alabaster. While he was passed from one parishioner to another during supper, Ellen and Tessa hooted with laughter about something. Stephen envies Tessa her easy ability to make new friends. He expects the laughter was caused by the story of Stephen's grappling with the compost heap while the cock crowed triumphant on his shoulders.

And what's this Anna Trester says about Rufus Stone buying the Old Rectory?

Too unsettled to sleep, he goes downstairs and switches on his computer, determined to write a sermon about welcoming the strangers already in our midst. He starts by Google-searching Rufus Stone. And then he tells himself not to be so stupid. Doing something useful (but still not writing the sermon), he adds the Church of England vacancies list to his 'Favourites'. There's a job in Blackburn that might be interesting. If only he spoke Farsi.

Stephen's slipping out of bed wakes Tessa from dreaming of a woodland encounter with a fellow whose hair glistens in the starlight with a million droplets of mist. This is mad. Carter is twenty-two-years-old, and she's married to a vicar. But Stephen's not there when she reaches gingerly towards his side of the bed. This might have been an opportunity for a bit of reconciliation but finding herself alone, Tessa flings herself onto her back and stares angrily into the dark. Her hands cup her hip bones. She's slim. She keeps her legs waxed no matter how tight money gets. She makes an effort. They need some intimacy to remind themselves that they're not just flatmates. Will she and Stephen never have sex again?

Next day, she comes downstairs resolved to be friendly, but Stephen's already on his way out.

'I told Carter he could use the Mini.' Stephen grabs a mouthful of toast, slides notes into a folder, pats his jacket for his house keys.

'And what are you going to get around in?' Tessa keeps her voice sweet.

'I'll take your bike,' says Stephen, blithely imprisoning Tessa within walking distance of the house. 'You're working.' She still hasn't told him about her trip to London. 'And what have we got that we need so much we can't lend it to a Stoke?' Stephen's rung the rector who said Stephen wouldn't be treading on his toes if he went today to see the grandparents who normally look after Lauren's twins.

They might tell him what happened to Kat. He's still been too pathetic to ask, but this grandmother might be Kat.

For lack of clips, he tucks his jeans into his socks, slings his leg over Tessa's bicycle and wobbles off up the lane towards the T-junction at the top.

He's never told Tessa about Kat. Since his father's death,

52

Kat's been bound up in a package of guilt and grief that Stephen has always ignored. But moving back to Hindle Green has sliced the ties on that package, thrown it open at the front of his mind. Every inch of this village and the fields around was their playground as children.

There's the deafening blast of an indignant horn as, without looking, Stephen blindly pulls out and turns right towards Stockford. A black Lexus is forced to over-shoot the turning to Hindle Green, and then back up, the driver shaking his fist at Stephen's back as Stephen, recovering his balance, disappears, freewheeling down towards the town.

Should Stephen have worn a more uniform priest's garb instead of jeans and a denim shirt to visit Carter's nieces' bereft grandmother? Not if it's Kat. Though this immaculate bungalow with its striped mown lawn and winter bedding pansies doesn't seem a likely home for the wild girl he once knew. His heart's beating hard in his ears as he rings the doorbell and hastily yanks his trousers out of his socks: at least he remembered his dog collar. Does she know he's become a priest?

The brassy blonde-haired woman who opens the door has a face purple and blotched with grief. She accepts Stephen's arrival as nothing unexpected and leads him back into the kitchen where she's kept company by a neighbour who leans against the sink, cup of tea in hand, head sympathetically cocked to one side. The woman slumps down at the table, puts her head between her hands, and wails.

The woman is not Kat.

The neighbour squats down and rubs her back. 'Look, vicar's here to help now, isn't he? They won't be lost forever.'

The neighbour picks up the kettle and raises a questioning eyebrow at Stephen. He's got to be at Pendle for the service of reflection and penitence in half an hour. He shakes his head.

The grandmother blows her nose. 'I can't. I can't... Ohhhh...' And she stumbles out of the room, followed closely by the neighbour. Stephen can hear a whispered consultation before the neighbour returns.

'I've put her to bed. If I could get something from the doctor to calm her down it wouldn't do no harm. You the new vicar at Hindle Green, are you?'

'I'll ask the rector to give the doctor a call,' he offers. 'Given the circumstances he might be able to arrange a home visit.'

'That Lauren... She was a lovely child. In and out of everybody's houses, big smile.' Stephen doesn't have to look at his watch to know he's going to be late at Pendle unless he gets going.

'Shall I come back later?' he asks

'Oh, it's nice of you to offer, but they're not church people. And they don't know you, do they? And you're Hindle Green and that's where that Carter Stoke lives, isn't it? Lauren too, until she left. How's that Abbie doing?'

'Fine,' he lies.

'Course, if their mother was still around...'

'Kat?'

'Oh, I could go on all day about that family.' The neighbour's ushering him to the door, looking at her own watch. 'Still, nice to meet you. Better get on with my rounds, though, eh? Avon calling,' she sing-songs. 'I can tell everyone about Hindle Green's good looking new vicar, can't I?' Stephen hooks his leg over Tessa's bicycle. The neighbour seems genuinely shocked. 'You're not getting about on that!' He doesn't like to say who's using his car.

'Bye then,' he says, before pedalling off down the close, turning left at the bottom towards Pendle, but screeching to a halt to stop himself freewheeling through a herd of cows ambling across the road, back to their indoor winter quarters after milking.

Luckily, Pendle has a vestry door through which Stephen sneaks so that he can robe up quietly before entering the body of the church, looking as if he's simply been collecting his thoughts in private all this time.

Tessa does not follow Stephen to church today. She comes from a long line of socialist realists, gently poor intellectual snobs who hold religion to be the opiate of the masses and are above being treated like children needing fairy stories to entertain them. Although Tessa loves a fairy story, she's never gone so far as to allow herself to believe in Stephen's God. It seems to her that all the gods in the world are teaching the same thing: be nice to one another. You don't have to believe to agree that's a good idea, thinks Tessa.

Tessa's mother still lives in Kentish Town in the house where Tessa was born. It is the only house in the street not to have been done up and painted pistachio or sugar-mouse pink. Tessa's mother keeps lodgers and has voted Green ever since there's been a candidate to canvass for. Tessa avoided learning to cook at her mother's knee because she didn't like the smell that came off pulses left to soak and then forgotten about.

Though she's married a vicar, it was him she fell in love with, not his faith. Being a vicar, to Tessa, seemed brave, aggressive; rebellious, even. Standing up for what he believed in made Stephen manly.

And when they were courting (she loves that old-fashioned word), she made him bring her down here to Hindle Green because she needed to know where he came from. Dyllis welcomed her with, 'At last! I knew he'd find you eventually.' Tessa persuaded Stephen to take her for a walk through the woods where she discovered he could identify every tree – even when they were leafless after a wild autumn gale. Walking along a path cut deep between shooting boles of ash and hazel, his cheeks flushed in the winter gloaming, he held her hand and she felt the blood pulse between them. He pointed out bracket fungus you can eat in the summer and good places to find morels. The potential for children fluttered low down in her solar plexus. She didn't mention them then, for fear of frightening him off. But she shivered with anticipation, and his coat when he pulled it round her shoulders was warm inside and smelt of him.

It's only now that she's living in Hindle Green that Tessa admits to herself that, children aside, the country was also part of the deal she'd thought she would get in being with him.

'You don't marry a person, you marry a life,' she says, frowning at a recipe for Victoria sponge. Stephen gives up wine for Lent. He's never said anything about cakes. And if those fluttering children are to be made reality, she needs to inspire him with something. With no job, no transport, and no way of getting the number for the chilli lady who said she needed help writing a book, Tessa's decided today's the day to expand her culinary repertoire. A proper country lady can rustle up more than just flapjacks. She's run out of butter; will sunflower oil do?

'Bored yet?' Dyllis stands at the back door, not coming in.

'No!'

'Oh, come on,' insists Dyllis. 'Looks as if Rufus Stone's moving in.' Tessa doesn't want to have anything to do with Rufus Stone. Why should he be allowed to disturb the creation of her Hindle Green idyll? Besides, it's so long since they had anything to do with one another, she's sure he won't remember her. But she is butter-less, and the Old Rectory is on the way to the farm shop.

Tessa pulls on her coat and gives an arm to Dyllis, who fairly drags Tessa down the hill as fast as her twisted joints will let her. 'How much do you bet Mrs Trester's already on to the council?' From the other side of the ivy-clad stone wall they can hear the roar of machinery.

Round the corner, past the wrought iron gates - already taken off their posts and laid flat on pallets in the cider orchard - Tessa and Dyllis march up the drive towards the open-doored, red brick Queen Anne front.

Tessa stops. 'We can't just barge in.'

'We've got to find out what's going on.' Dyllis' face is hot with indignation. 'They haven't got planning permission yet. Hey!' And she lets go of Tessa and stumbles forward, straight into the path of a reversing digger.

Chapter 6

Tessa's taken to the kitchen, given a seat.

'There.' Squatting before her is the famous face of Rufus Stone. 'Poor thing, you're shaking. The old lady will be fine, I promise.' Dyllis is being checked over in another room by a man Rufus claims is a doctor. 'It's the driver you should be worried about. Rolling the digger into the hole left by that bloody great tree.'

Getting her bearings, Tessa casts about. The kitchen is cavernous, furnished with nothing but this table, a jumble of mismatched chairs, and a range set back into a fireplace large enough to be considered a room.

'Rufus Stone. You cut down the magnolia!' Dyllis stands in the doorway, strips of plaster on her nose and forehead, bandages where the fall has scraped the tissue-thin skin off the palms of her hands. In spite of her injuries she's coquettish in accepting the carver at the end of the table, which is solicitously pulled out for her. 'Did you not know that tree had a preservation order on it?'

'It cut out all the light.'

'Bollocks! There'll be a hefty fine for cutting it down.'

'I'll pay it. Have a slug of whisky in your tea, Mrs...?'

'Wilkinson.'

'Wilkinson,' says Rufus, and Dyllis positively shivers with delight as he uses the voice you hear in the advertisement for luxury cat food.

'Anna Trester will be spitting tacks that I got into your kitchen first,' she says, patting at her hair and accepting a cushion for her back.

Tessa's amused by Dyllis' flirting: it must mean she's not too badly hurt. 'Glad to see you haven't touched the inside yet.'

Tessa looks round at the peeling scales of plaster, the cast iron range with a great crack in the pipe going up into the floor above. There's no sink. There must be a scullery somewhere.

'Is Anna Trester the lady from Home Farm?'

'That red house immediately across the road from your gate,' Tessa winces at the breathy keenness in her voice: she doesn't need to curry favour with a boyfriend she never slept with and whom she dumped, however famous he may have become since they last saw each other.

Rufus Stone puts a tray of tea on the table and perches his famous, especially-insured bottom beside it.

'Well, she has been slow on the uptake, letting you get here first.' He pours. 'So, is this one of those calls where you leave a card and I visit you back another tea time?'

'Of course not,' snorts Dyllis. 'I've come to find out how it is you've started ripping out rare original features while your planning application's still pristine on the gate. I know full well nothing can have been passed yet.'

Rufus Stone doesn't bat an eyelid. 'We had to get on. Without a few basics, this place is unsafe. And one can hardly expect workmen to do a thing without proper health-and-safety-box-ticked facilities, can one?'

'They can have a portakabin and a chemical toilet, like every other builder,' says Dyllis.

'Ooh, he's got a nerve!' Dyllis and Tessa huddle together as they hobble down the drive. 'If that man thinks he's got an in with the planning inspectorate to get round restrictions, he's got another think coming.'

'He didn't recognise me,' says Tessa.

She hasn't decided yet whether to be offended or relieved about this.

'I worked on a book his agent wrote. Years ago. Rufus

asked me out to dinner a few times. Nothing happened. But then I met Stephen.' Dyllis squeezes Tessa's hand. They walk on into the wind.

Back at the vicarage there are messages. Two people have died in two different parishes and Stephen must visit to arrange funerals.

'That's the spring for you,' says Dyllis. 'Sap rising. Always a killer.'

A third message is from Daisy, the chilli-grower. 'Will you come and see me? I need your advice re: this bloody book. Don't know how much money'll be in it.'

'Well, that's a start,' says Dyllis. She's blue round the lips and she's clasping at her hands to stop them shivering. Delayed shock, thinks Tessa as she pulls an armchair in from the sitting room and installs Dyllis beside the Rayburn, putting her feet onto a pile of cushions to get them off the chill of the floor.

'Stay here. I'm going to get your buzzing cushion for your back,' she says.

Dyllis smiles bravely. 'I'm lucky not to have broken a bone this afternoon. If it hadn't been for the long grass... Really, a surprisingly soft landing.'

Tessa's frightened of a brave smile on someone so frail. She switches on the radio to keep Dyllis company and nips up the road to her mother-in-law's unlocked house where she stuffs into a bag the orthopaedic cushion, toothbrush, nightdress, and *The Sabres of Paradise* from beside her bed. And then she runs back to the Old Rectory. The JCBs have finished for the day and the place looks deserted but for the front door, still standing open.

'Hello?'

'Hey, come back for more?' Rufus Stone's in the kitchen

with his mate, the doctor. The doctor looks familiar. Tessa can't think why. She's only interested in his thoughts about Dyllis.

'I'm sorry we stormed off like that but she wouldn't have let me talk to you about her. I wanted to ask how was she, did you think, when you examined her?'

'As you saw, cuts and bruises. Lucky Rufus here has such a first class first aid kit to hand.'

'The thing is she has terrible arthritis. She's lucky not to have broken a bone. I think, maybe, I should get her to casualty.'

The doctor flushes. 'I think you'll find she's fine. Tuck her up warm. She'll be right as rain by morning.'

Tessa has never felt less confident in a doctor's opinion. 'You're...' it's coming back to her. 'You're the doctor on the telly!' The doctor smiles and accepts the recognition as a compliment. 'Are you a real doctor?' He flushes. 'I mean, if you're just a telly... you know... I don't mean to be rude, but...'

'Course Benjy's the real thing. Aren't you, mate? I should know. We were at Oxford together.' Rufus is standing a little too close. His eyes glisten. With a shock Tessa realises both men's nostrils are rimed with white.

'Right,' she turns to leave. 'I'm calling an ambulance.'

'Wait!' Rufus Stone bars her way. 'Now you're the one who looks familiar. Telly? Theatre?' He raises one eyebrow. 'Date?'

Tessa shakes her head. This isn't the moment for reminiscence. 'Excuse me,' she tries to duck under his arm, but it closes around her waist and he breathes wetly into her ear. 'Now I remember you. Stay. You always used to like to party.'

'Mum?' Dyllis doesn't wake.

The skin on her hands is black through the gaps in the bandages. There are two separate stars of plaster on her face. Her breathing's shallow. Carefully, Stephen lifts a foot back onto the makeshift stool of cushions and tiptoes out of the room.

He calls out for Tessa. Nothing. From the office he calls Tessa's mobile. It rings in a coat pocket hanging by the front door. From the kitchen comes a querulous little voice.

'Tessa?'

'Mum, what happened?'

Dyllis stares, unrecognising. 'Tessa. Where's Tessa?' There's a rising note of panic in her voice.

'Mum, it's me, Stephen.'

Dyllis turns away and closes her eyes so that she can't see him.

Stephen struggles against a rising tide of panic. 'You're in our house. The vicarage. Mum, what happened?'

Carter's got the Mini. Outside it's dark as January.

'What is it?' Dyllis has opened her eyes again and now seems to recognise him.

'Nothing. Mum...'

'Tea. That'll warm you up. Where's Tessa?'

Good question. He fills the kettle and puts it on the hob.

'That thing'll take forever. I'm going to give you a new electric kettle for an early birthday present. Life's too short to boil water on a Rayburn.' Stephen's so relieved his mother's got over her funny turn that he laughs and goes to look for biscuits.

'In a Tupperware, in the larder,' orders Dyllis, reading his mind. And there he finds a box of buttery, crumbling flapjacks.

'Village shop do a fine line,' he says, offering Dyllis one.

She waves away the Tupperware. 'Tessa always gives me

a flapjack on a plate. And of course they're not village shop. Tessa made them, stupid.'

'Where is she?'

Dyllis snorts. 'Wouldn't surprise me if she'd left you, Stephen, for the all the attention you pay her. You know you're married to a saint?'

'Mum, we've had this before. She understands about my job.'

'That's just a euphemism for You. Now take the bag out of that cup before you can stand a spoon up in it and give me some milk. Tessa always makes a pot of tea, no matter how long it takes to boil a kettle.' Dyllis hugs the mug to her chest for warmth. 'I hope you've reassured her about what happened in London?'

'What happened in London?'

'Gavin sacked her!'

Stephen stares. 'She never said.'

'You never asked.' She reaches out and puts the tea down. 'For goodness' sake, Stephen. She's trying so hard to make this new life work for you and you don't even notice. Marriages need to be maintained, not taken for granted. Now, drive me home and then come back and make that lovely girl some supper. And talk to her.'

'I've leant the car to Carter Stoke.'

'Twit!'

'Stay, Mum.'

'I want to get back to my own bottle of whisky, if you don't mind.'

It's only six o'clock but the still-wintry night has clamped down over the village. Only a glimmer of moon behind a cloud silhouettes the church tower. Dyllis and Stephen struggle up the lane together, staggering like drunks: he's not used to helping, is no good at matching his pace to hers.

'Stop pulling me,' she protests, taking her arm away from him to feel her way up the hill alone. He walks beside her, hands stuffed deep in his pockets.

Rufus Stone and his doctor friend are off their heads. They drag Tessa round and round the kitchen table, ruthlessly waltzing to The Killers blaring out of an iPod with speakers. They're not rough with her, just stronger. It's as if they're partying in a parallel universe and Tessa's presence is that of an interesting foreign body whose language they do not speak. It takes her ten minutes to escape and after she's left she realises the precious bundle, including Dyllis' buzzing cushion, is still on the table. Dyllis can't exist without that cushion. Tessa looks back around the kitchen door. She's irrelevant to them now. Dancing around in flimsy fashion overcoats, Rufus Stone and his friend are locked in one another's arms, weeping with joy that they have found each other and swearing blood brother-style oaths that they'll never grow apart.

Tessa fetches the bundle with the nightdress and book and escapes.

The vicarage is black as the night around it. The back door she left open is locked. Through the windows she can barely make out cups on the table and the Tupperware of flapjacks.

Pulling her coat around herself she sets off for Dyllis' house, which she finds equally deserted. The doors are locked there too, which is really unusual. She feels in her pocket for her mobile and remembers it's in her other coat.

Now what? There's a light on at No. 3 Pratt Cottages. She knocks.

Carter comes to the door. 'Where've you been?'

Tessa's teeth are chattering. 'Can I come in?'

'Course you can. You all right? Your Stephen's been

looking for you everywhere. Dyllis had a turn. Couldn't tell him what happened.'

'Where are they?' He leads her back to the kitchen where ten-year-old Abbie, in a dressing gown, washed hair wrapped in a towel, feet in fluffy pink slippers, is eating beans on toast.

Tessa says, 'Hello.'

Abbie gives Tessa a sharp little smile. A television flickers in the corner with the sound turned down.

'Gone to hospital,' says Carter, putting bread in the toaster and opening another can of beans. 'He came and got the Mini back off me. Said the ambulance would take too long. What happened to old Dyllis? Her hands was wrapped up like a boxer's.'

'I should...'

'Best wait if I were you. Taxi'll cost you an arm and a leg. If you can get one. Vicar will phone, won't he?'

'My mobile's back at the house. And I didn't take my keys. He's locked me out.'

Tessa can see reflected off Carter's face Stephen's furious indignation that he found Dyllis in such a state. Well, let Stephen panic. Let him look at his mother's frailty and take on board that she needs looking after. Tessa sits on the edge of a wood-framed settee. She tucks her hands between her knees.

'She was run down by a mini-digger at the Old Rectory. I went back to find out... There was a doctor there who looked at her. But when I got back there he was off his head.'

'Is that Rufus Stone there, then?' Abbie's eyes gleam. Carter shoots Tessa a warning glance.

'Sorry,' says Tessa. 'I didn't think.

'He's lush,' says Abbie.

'Go on up and dry your hair, Abbie, if you've finished your tea,' says Carter, nodding towards the stairs. Abbie crosses her arms and sits back in her chair, not going anywhere.

65

'Go on!' he roars and this time Abbie jumps up quick enough, her bottom lip sticking out as far as it goes. As she turns onto the stairs Tessa hears a minute, mutinous, 'Not fair.'

'Grrrrrrrrrrrrr!' roars Carter, smiling now. And squealing like the little girl she is, Abbie runs on up.

'Where's her mother?' asks Tessa.

'Gone,' replies Carter, his face closing round that story.

Tessa stands up and brushes her skirt flat.

'I should leave you to it,' she says. She doesn't know where should she go. She's locked out of both houses. But it's too intimate being in Carter's kitchen without Abbie there. The room's too small. There's no room to put space between them. Nothing's happening and yet Tessa needs to escape.

'But I made you beans,' he says. So what else can she do but stay? He pours beans onto toast on a plate on the table. She goes and sits opposite him. Their knees bump and she jumps away, flushing. He doesn't react. Simply carefully rolls a cigarette and then chivalrously waits for her to put her knife and fork down before lighting up. Dextrous fingers on rough, calloused hands. She imagines they'll be cool, and dry to the touch. She swallows a few mouthfuls for the sake of good manners and pushes her plate away. The smell of tobacco smoke is bitter sweet in her nostrils. She's never smoked. She wishes now that she did.

'I'll get you back into your house after, if you like,' says Carter, nonchalantly offering to break and enter.

'Thanks,' says Tessa, primly.

She hears the Mini return and hurries down to ask after Dyllis. But Stephen's too angry to let her speak. He bulldozes her. And that Stephen can so misjudge her makes Tessa cold with fury.

She watches the accusations roll out of his mouth. He

doesn't ask what happened. Barking his wrong conclusions, he interrupts before she can explain.

Anyway, why should she have to defend herself? She's done nothing she need justify. Besides, he's too angry to listen to anything she might have to say.

Stephen's a spoiled little boy, she thinks. His mother spoiled him, and Tessa took over where Dyllis left off. He's good to strangers, people he works with, people he doesn't take for granted to service his life so he can be wonderful in public. This first time in their whole marriage that Tessa has not been there to calmly explain an already resolved situation, he's panicked, and is assuming the worst of her.

Eventually Tessa suggests, thin-lipped, 'Perhaps you'd better sleep in the study.' And leaving him open-mouthed that she should feel entitled to be the rejector, she drags herself upstairs to bed.

Next morning, she doesn't even wash for fear of an attempted reconciliation by the toothbrushes. She hates rows: her mother rowed constantly with her father in order to get his attention, in order to manufacture horrid sickly-sweet and usually desperate making up sessions. He left when Tessa was fourteen. Tessa's barely seen him since. He moved to South Africa where he lives now with his Xhosa housekeeper and a litter of new children. He used to send her postcards from time to time, never at birthday or Christmas, telling her of the birth of a new infant and signing himself 'Michael'. It's been some years since Tessa bothered to include him in her change of address list. Tessa's not a kiss-and-make-upper. When Stephen's ready, he can apologise if he wants. Tessa knows she sounds like a teenager: but being shouted at like a child has made her feel as mulish as one. Stephen can negotiate with Carter over the Mini. Unbreakfasted, Tessa takes her bicycle and flies downhill all the way to Stockford, arriving at the surgery breathless and exhilarated.

'Tessa Wilkinson,' she says to the doctor's receptionist. 'For my check up before you add me to the surgery list.'

'Ah, yes. We're still expecting a call from your husband.' The receptionist's eyes twinkle, as if to say 'Husbands!'

'I'm not his secretary.' Tessa knows she sounds rude, but he can organise his own appointments.

The receptionist sniffs. 'Well,' she says, 'the doctor's running late. I don't know how long you'll have to wait.' That'll teach Tessa not to join in with surgery banter.

The doctor's a wiry little woman, her consulting room hung about with pictures of her jumping out of aeroplanes, climbing mountains, white water rafting.

'You're very thin,' she says as Tessa steps off the scales.

'Nervous energy,' says Tessa with a puffy laugh. She hates having to put herself in the hands of authority figures who might tell her off, doctors included. She almost expects a comment next on how unattractive she is. Instead, the doctor leans forward and peers at her face.

'Have you always had slightly protuberant eyes?'

'They run in my father's family. Along with being skinny. I eat like a horse.'

'Children?'

'No.'

'And how old are you?'

'Not yet thirty-nine.'

'You don't want children?'

'They just never came.' However true, it still hurts to say it. The doctor starts scribbling on a pad of forms, her spiked, left-handed writing completely illegible from Tessa's side of the desk.

'I'd like to order a blood test, if I may. I think you might have an overactive thyroid.'

'I don't feel unwell.'

'No. But if you've always suffered the condition then you won't know how well you could feel, will you?' Tessa is taken aback by the blunt interest of the doctor.

'In London they used to weigh, measure, ask if all was well and chuck us out.'

'Thyroid's a pet subject of mine. You might be fine. Do you find you get tired easily?'

'How tired's tired? I thought I'd just been overdoing it, you know... It's been a... umm... busy year. And we used to live in London, which is tiring. I just think life's quite tiring. Isn't it?'

'Not necessarily... I think we might run some tests.'

Tessa's not going home yet to face the man who thinks she'd leave his mother in extremis and go partying. Instead, she points her bicycle towards the chilli farm, which she's been told lies on the way to the Bag Enderby Estate. Tessa's instructions are to go out of Stockford, past the showground, through a wood, up a hill, over the brow, and she can't miss the poly tunnels. The hill's so steep that she gets off to walk. This is freedom, she thinks, gulping at the balmy promise of spring in the air. She knows her mobile telephone's still in the pocket of her jacket in the hall. Stephen won't find her.

Daisy said to drop in any time so she dawdles her way, and rests on a fat rock, admiring the tall, silver trunks of the beech trees either side of the road, their thousands of leaf buds tinting the tree tops pink with promise. Later, the wood will be carpeted with bluebells.

The crumbling stones edging the road have furry handfuls of young foxglove leaves bursting out between the cracks. For now there are primroses, and patches of miniature, sweet-scented violets.

She leaves her bicycle and walks through to the edge of the wood. Here, the land falls away from her in rolling folds, like an unmade bed covered in a rumpled green quilt. There are the poly tunnels. The beech trunk she's leaning on is scarred with the rounded edges of an old carving. The intertwined letters S and K have been gouged into the silvery trunk, and round them a heart with an arrow has been drawn.

This must be a lovers' lane, she thinks, climbing back down into the road and cycling on, downhill now, to the red brick Victorian farmhouse with the field of poly tunnels along its north flank.

'There were rows of collapsing chicken sheds here.' Daisy shows Tessa her 'Empire', as she calls it with a self-deprecating shrug. 'So we had no problem getting planning permission. Bit of a risk, though. This area's better known for its cheese than exotic veg.'

The poly tunnels are hung with daylight bulbs and are astonishingly hot.

'Ground source heat pump,' Daisy explains as Tessa wipes enthusiastically welcoming Labrador-lick off her face with the sleeve of her jacket. 'I plant my new seed on Boxing Day. Luckily, you can be organic and still use lots of electricity for the lights. Heat and light...' She runs her hands through the thick green leaves of a plant covered with little white flowers. 'I keep the old chillies going as long as I can, but at some point they use too much energy to make too little fruit. Usually in about November we grub them all up and give the top layer of compost over for mushrooms, add a layer of horse shit, then put the chickens into the tunnels to dig the shit in and clear any pests. We crop for local delis and a growing list of restaurants. And we have quite a good seed catalogue coming. My ambition's to develop a new, sweetly hot chilli I can call Jelly Bean after my daughter. Here's the shop.'

They've come full circle to the shed next to the gate. Inside, a beaming, moon-faced girl of about twenty sits behind the till, hands in her lap, waiting with all the excitement treasured responsibility can bring.

'Hello,' she says. 'Can I help you?' Tessa can't help but smile back at her.

'It's all right, Jelly,' says Daisy. 'Tessa's a friend. She's come to help me write my book.'

Jelly claps her hands, delighted. 'Then you won't complain about how hard it is all the time. I'd help, but I'm even thicker than Mum is.'

'You all right here?' her mother asks. Jelly nods, seriously. 'Anyone been in this morning?'

'Just Pete, and I told him where you were. And I took two messages.' She holds out a pad on which careful note has been taken of names and telephone numbers. 'You didn't come through the shop,' she says to Tessa.

'I didn't see the sign.' Tessa's enchanted.

'I better check it hasn't got knocked over, then.' Jelly hops off her stool and heads for the door.

'Why don't you shut up shop and come in and have lunch with us in a minute?' asks Daisy.

Jelly shakes her head. 'Someone might come. You can bring me mine. You and this lady have business to talk about. I'll be in charge here.'

'She's in love,' explains Daisy as they cross the yard to the house. 'She can't bear to leave the shop in case he drops in unexpectedly. Which I doubt he will. I don't know what to do about it, really. Whether I should do anything. I'm sure he has no idea of her affection. I expect she hasn't even spoken to him. And if she has, he probably just thinks...'

'Who's she in love with?'

'One of the boys who work the fair that goes round at carnival season. He's probably long gone. They aren't local. He was nice to her when she was a bit frightened on the waltzer. She's my eldest. Then there's Jonathan. Still at school. A-Levels next term. Then God knows what. I'm sorry about the mess.'

They walk straight into the kitchen, a working nightmare of sports kit, half-cleared breakfast, a slew of bills. Tessa manages not to trip over a gigantic dog basket. Daisy reaches for a tray of eggs.

'Omelette do you?'

'Have you started this book?' Tessa pulls a chair out from the table and a cat jumps off it, yowling.

'Ignore her,' says Daisy. 'I got approached,' she says. 'I do food festivals from time to time, give talks and things.' She's chopping spring onions and a handful of light green peppers, grating cheese into a bowl full of whisked, bright orange-yolked eggs. 'I got over-excited, basically, and said I'd do a book and signed a deal and everything – the money was surprising! - and now the shit's hitting the fan because I find I have neither the time nor the intestinal fortitude to write anything down. I'm getting more and more stressed and the publisher keeps ringing and I keep lying about how far I've got.'

'Do you have any notes?'

The eggs, onions and chillies are tossed to sizzle together in a pan on the Aga. Daisy sits down across from Tessa and pours them both a glass of elderflower cordial from the jug on the table. 'God, it's delicious, this,' she says, draining her glass and pouring more. 'Ellen Wiseman makes it and freezes it and brings it to the farmers' market in the dog days of winter when all you long for is a taste of spring.' She stands and starts bringing plates and knives and forks to the table. 'And Jonathan's finished the bread again. He's like an eating machine. Sorry.'

Neither Tessa nor Daisy notice the lanky figure snake over the wall dividing the woods from the yard and into the shop. He emerges seconds later with a bulging carrier bag. He sneaks off the way he came.

Stephen checks the clock again. It's gone eight. There's been no word from Tessa since she stormed off this morning.

Stephen's making a list. It reads:

1 Move Mum?
2 Money?
3 Us?

He picks up the pen, scrubs at that last line furiously, until it can no longer be read, then goes the whole hog, screws up the paper and throws it in the fire he's lit in the sitting room.

The kitchen's full of the scent of his re-heated lamb stew. To make it up to Tessa he's mashed potato with cream cheese and black pepper. He's laid the table and opened a bottle of wine. He's not drinking for Lent, but there's no reason why Tessa shouldn't.

There's the clink of the gate. He hurriedly lights the candles he's put in the middle of the table, sits down again, stands... He may be good in an emergency but getting it right with Tessa on the other hand... Still, he shouldn't have taken his fear for his mother out on her. And Tessa doesn't know he's feeling fragile because he hasn't told her. And Rufus Stone is a bit of a touch paper for him. He still won't tell any of this to Tessa because he doesn't want to sound pathetic. But he must make it up to her if he's ever going to persuade her back to live in a city, an interesting one with culture for her and challenges for him. He saw a job in Bristol. She'd like it there. He's already emailed to register his interest.

'Hi.' He comes round the table and hugs her awkwardly because she's carrying a big box file and a supermarket bag filled with... 'Chillies?' She dumps the bag on the table with the box and shrugs off her coat.

'I've got to go to the loo,' she says, brushing past him. He takes the stew out of the oven. He pours her a glass of red wine recommended by April and holds it to give to her as she comes back into the room.

'I'm sorry,' he starts. She stands with her back to the Rayburn, sipping the wine and waiting. 'I'm really sorry. I've been so wound up with what's been happening to me. Mum says Gavin terminated your contract.'

'That's not enough of an apology, Stephen. You thought I'd get your mother beaten up and then abandon her so I could go to a party.'

'I didn't think that. But Rufus Stone...'

'Rufus Stone what?'

'OK. OK! I'm sorry. OK?'

'OK.' It's not. But Tessa has to agree to this truce in order to be able to tell Stephen about Gavin because then she can boast that she's already got a new commission from Daisy.

'Mum's insisting the nurses call her 'Mrs Wilkinson'. It's put all their backs up. They're keeping her in still. She had that turn.' Stephen ladles stew onto plates. 'Will you eat with me?'

Tessa pulls a chair out and sits down. She's too hungry to refuse supper.

'Talking of doctors, you've got to make an appointment to have a check up so you can be put on the surgery's list,' she says, wolfing the stew. 'I did mine this morning. The doctor said I looked tired and thin. She wants me to have blood tests.

What turn did Dyllis have?'

'Blood tests for what?'

'Just checking. To be sure.'

'Sure what?'

Tessa draws it out. His looking so worried proves he cares a bit. 'She was a bit vague. I'm having the test next week. Then it'll take a while to come back. She said she'd call me.'

SPRING

Chapter 7

To Lauren's six-year-old twins the camp in the wood is wicked. There's a fire with a pot hanging over it on a cast iron hook, and a van for living in, and a stream. And when Ryan goes off to get stuff to eat, their mum lets the girls curl up with her and they look at their storybook together. Lauren can't believe how good their reading is. Better than hers, she says, though that must be rubbish. They've never come across a grown-up who can't read. When she washes their clothes in the sink they cuddle up in bed to keep warm till the clothes are dry.

At night Ryan pulls a partition over and he and Lauren sleep on the bed that folds away into a box for sitting on during the day. The girls share a little mattress above the driver's seat. This morning, Trix found mushrooms growing out of a place where someone had a fire before and Lauren reckons they can eat them. Ryan's gone to get eggs so they can have them cooked together for tea. Of course they miss their Nanna a bit. But it's nice not to have her going on about clean hair and what people will think all the time. And Belle hates swimming and they've already missed that. At night they scare each other, imagining what the noises are. Ryan tells them not to be stupid. It's just the woods. And Lauren tells the girls not to listen to him: he's from a big town where the foxes are grey and live on rubbish so what does he know?

Lauren's loving this. Total freedom. Off the list. Out of the system that never gave her anything. She's missed two meetings with her probation officer and she doesn't give a shit. How will they find her here? The only problem is Carter's pick-up. She wants to get it back to him. Ryan says if she does that the authorities will be on to them right off. She's got to choose total freedom.

'We can't go on living off that spazzer at the chilli farm forever,' says Ryan, cutting Lauren a thick slice of Daisy's homemade bread and balancing a chunk of hard yellow cheese on top of it. 'We gotta find my mates. They'll know how to get rid of the pick-up.'

'Can't we stay here? I like it. I don't know your mates. We're happy as we are.'

'Stay here and we'll be found. We gotta sign on. Can't do that in your home town.'

'You could get a job at the cheese factory. Nobody knows you. Be lush here, just us, all cosy.'

Lauren spoons fat she saved from some bacon into the cast-iron frying pan. The mushrooms the girls found will make a feast. They sizzle. Ryan takes Lauren's face in his hands.

She loves being told what to do by him. He's only eighteen but has the confidence of a king.

'It's decided. We leave here tomorrow,' he says. 'I got mates got a camp near Coventry. We go there first and see how we do, right?'

Carter does odd jobs at Bag Enderby on Thursdays. It's the rough stuff Sir Charles employs him for. Carter mulches the borders in the spring and clears them come the autumn. He does the hedging, ditching, logging and, in the summer, mowing. He feels a right wazzock driving up with bits of equipment sticking out the back of Stephen's Mini, but until he gets his pick-up back, or the insurance pay up, he's stuck. And the insurance won't pay until the police have found Lauren, and the old pick-up's certified alive or dead.

At dinnertime he takes peanut butter sandwiches up into the woods. He loves this place. His mum used to bring him here when he was little to look for mushrooms. St George's mushrooms, if they came this time of year. He's got a plastic bag with him in case. Eyes down, shuffling through the leaf mould, he walks up to the place above the chilli farm where you can sit and look out at the view. He wonders where Lauren is. Stupid bitch. Like his mum, she's all knee-jerk reactions and no forward planning.

Tessa hates needles. She screws up her toes in their shoes until they hurt so she won't feel the pain.

'All done,' says the nurse and Tessa gingerly looks round. There's the phial filled with dark red. She doesn't mind that. She's told to hold a blob of cotton wool to the hole where the needle went in. She doesn't mind that, either.

'The results will be in by Tuesday, probably. If you ring around five. They'll tell you if you need to see the doctor again.'

She rewards herself for her bravery with a chicken salad sandwich from April's deli and cycles up to eat it in the place she found in the woods the other day.

'Oh.' She finds Carter Stoke sitting on the tree stump she'd had in mind for herself. 'Sorry. I didn't mean to...'

'Good place to eat, this.' He moves, lays his jacket at the foot of the tree with the initials carved into it, and sits there. He always looks as if he's secretly laughing at her. Tessa perches on the tree stump and tries not to look prim. She's glad of her boots, jeans and old jacket: at least she doesn't look too middle class mumsy today. She takes her hat off. Her hair escapes into a too-wild cloud. She fiddles, trying to tame it. She ought to just walk on, as if she'd never planned to stop here.

There are the shrieks of playing children down in the dell.

'Must be bunking off,' says Carter. He twists the lid back on his thermos and stands up. His hand brushes the carving on the tree.

'That was my mum,' he says, pointing at the K. 'Don't know who S was. I reckon she was a bit of a one for the men.' She sees him contain his hands in his pockets. Tessa stands too. She needs to be on a level with him. She stumbles on a tree root. He steadies her.

'Is your dad still around?' she asks, making polite conversation as if they're strangers looking for common ground at a party.

'Never knew him. Mum never told. "Just remember, you're a Stoke," she always said. There's been Stokes round here since forever. There's a Stoke Barton in Stockford. We might of been posh farmers once.' He chuckles.

'My father was a teacher.' Tessa feels she has to give something back to pay for her questions. She hears herself blunting the sharp edge of her accent on his account and thinks she probably still sounds ridiculous. 'He left.' She bites her tongue. She should walk away now.

But she can't. She and Carter stand side by side, looking out at cloud shadows scudding over the velvet sheen of new grass. His hands have escaped their pocket prison. Their fingers are millimetres apart. She's given up trying to tame her hair. Tessa rolls her hat up and shoves it in her pocket where she finds her lip gloss. She puts some on.

'Smells of strawberries,' he says. Then he reaches out and touches her lip, taking his finger back to taste it. Tessa's spellbound. But in the corner of her locked eyes there's the flash of little faces over the ridge edging a dell.

'Trixie!' roars Carter, thundering off, leaving Tessa to crash to earth alone. 'Belle!' he shouts. Suddenly there are two dirty little girls, their arms round him, laughing and dancing and swinging him round. For a second he looks back, thrilled. He waves to Tessa to come down to where he's being dragged by the girls towards a splashing stream.

Reeling, breathless, but still a good girl and not guilty of anything, Tessa carefully picks her way back through the wood to the lay-by and cycles purposefully away.

The job in Bristol's gone, but Stephen's seen another he likes the look of in a big parish in Leeds. He'll check it out before involving either Tessa (to whom he'll have to sell the move) or this PCC – who must be made to understand how precarious is their assumption that there'll always be a priest to take services for them. The Parochial Church Councillors waste their time arguing over whether they should sing hymns ancient or modern, and fuss about being asked to offer one another the peace before he's even read that Sunday's collect, when they should be panicking about how to get more bums on seats in order to warrant somebody taking a service at all. Even to Ellen Wiseman, who seems to Stephen to be an intelligent, wider-thinking sort, the slow closing up of the country churches of England is a blind spot. The congregations here are used to the word 'decline': Stephen needs to make them face the possibility of closure.

This evening, the Hindle Green PCC meets at David Tait's house. When Stephen was a child this was a tumbled-down piggery in the Tresters' yard of outbuildings. Now the place is very des-res, all box-hedged herb beds, and a slate reading 'Ham House' inlaid in the stone beside the front door.

Stephen refuses a glass of wine, accepts a trout-pâtéed biscuit and clears his throat. 'To the matters in hand, David.' Stephen nods at the other Hindle Green churchwarden (the first being Anna Trester, of course), this one an accountant working for the local firm of solicitors in Stockford. Stephen hopes that fundraising, and helping Stephen handle Anna effectively too, will be just up his street.

David Tait shuffles the papers in front of him. His wife

loves having the PCC to their house so that she can show off how pretty it is. He hates having to be public about anything. The only reason he's churchwarden is because he didn't know how to say no. He hates having to speak out loud, but Stephen says he must in order to stop Anna Trester steamrollering them all into spending the whole meeting discussing flower rotas.

'You've all got copies of the Quinquennial report. It seems the old firm weren't quite as beady-eyed as this new girl. She reckons we'll need about a hundred thousand to make the tower good,' he begins. There's a collective gasp: a hundred thousand!?! 'The tower is sixteenth century and has unusual, pre-Reformation gargoyles which need special treatment.'

'How can we go from having a perfectly sturdy tower one Quinquennial to needing to spend a hundred thousand on it the next?' protests Anna Trester.

Stephen interrupts. 'St George's has never had a competent archaeological survey. The architect I met the other day said if we applied for an English Heritage grant, then one of their people would come to have a really good look at it: you know, checking historical documents, paint analysis and things. Who knows what we might find?'

'Sounds as though you want to turn it into a tourist attraction,' snorts Anna.

'I want it to be economically viable. Otherwise one day you'll find you can't afford to keep the church open, you'll have lost your parish priest, and you'll only get a communion service in the village if you invite willing priests to take services in the village hall.'

David Tait shoots Stephen a 'do you mind?' look. Having been forced to stick his neck out, he'd like to be allowed to get through what he's prepared. 'The hundred thou's very ball park at the moment,' he continues. 'But while we're making good the tower we may as well try and get a faculty to put in a

few other twenty-first century essentials while we're at it.'
Stephen nods encouragement. 'Like toilets. And perhaps a kitchenette. And more effective heating.'

'Well, if people can't spend an hour a week in the cool...'

'Anna,' Stephen smiles benignly. 'We have a regular congregation of about fifteen in this parish, including children. I have it on good authority that the promise of heating would bring in at least another five or six.'

'But a hundred thousand. PLUS lavatories! There are fewer than two hundred households in Hindle Green. Are you expecting each one to stump up five hundred pounds for a church most of them only visit at Christmas?'

'I'm exploring the grant system. But don't you think, Anna, that the more people we get involved, even in the smallest way, the more people will feel as if the church is theirs to use?'

'Use in what way? There's the village hall.'

'The Church of England is an inclusive organisation, isn't it? And you need to make your church building pay for itself.' Stephen keeps his voice gentle, but tries to make his point clear: these people have no idea how close they are to losing their church altogether. He won't be here to help them keep it, but he can help them see what they're going to have to do to be able to ensure at least a monthly service in a church with a roof. 'St George's needs to become a venue, a draw, a place people are used to coming to for all sorts of activities.'

Anna narrows her eyes. 'It's all very well to say that, Vicar.'

'Tessa?' Stephen pushes open the front door and dumps the PCC file on the desk in his study.

'Up here,' she answers. She must be working.

'Anything for supper?' He pulls his boots off and goes to

find the sheepskin slippers she bought at Stockford market to keep the chill off their feet.

She shouts from her office. 'Look in the larder. There might be leftovers. Chicken stock. Make some soup. Actually,' she appears at the top of the stairs, the slightly distant, concentrated look on her face which she gets when she's working evaporating as she comes back to the real world, 'if you make soup, can I have some? I'm starving.'

'You're always starving.'

'I'll finish up. You cook and I'll be there in a minute.'

He heads into the kitchen with a smile on his face. He'd like to meet this Daisy person who's put a spring back in his beloved wife's step.

'I dropped in on Dyllis earlier,' she says, coming into the kitchen and hugging the Rayburn. She's wearing fingerless gloves, a cardigan over a sweater, her jeans are tucked into socks, and her feet are wrapped in sheepskin – but her lipstick's on.

You can take a girl out of the city… thinks Stephen.

'She won't even talk about the nasty turn she had the other day,' says Tessa. 'She was all brittle and said we should have her put down if we think she can't manage on her own any more. She has this whole spiel about my taking her out and leaving her to die of exposure beside Bag Enderby Tower. I hate it when she talks like that.'

Stephen browns a chopped onion in a knob of butter, adds a can of sweet corn, pours the chicken stock into the pan and reaches for a Green Farm egg. He doesn't want to talk about his mother's ageing: he's not ready for her to be one of the can't-manage old. Tessa peels herself away from the warmth of the Rayburn and goes to the larder for bread and butter and a glass of red wine for herself.

He can't talk about the Leeds job, either, until he's done

more research, worked out how he might pitch it to Tessa. So, 'Did I ever tell you about Kat?' he asks, gently stirring the egg into the soup to make clouds.

'Who?'

'Carter's mum.'

Tessa sits down at the kitchen table and covers her cheeks with her hands in case she blushes. 'What about her?'

'When I was a little boy I used to follow her around. The first great wrench of my life was when she left primary school and went to the secondary modern. I was streamed for the grammar. So was she, but her mum insisted, "Don't do nothing, do it?"'

Stephen chops a handful of spring onions for green garnish in the soup. 'By the time I was fifteen and she was seventeen she occupied my mind day and night.'

'You were in love with her?'

'Teenage crush.'

Tessa knows all about crushes. If Stephen were only her friend and not her husband she could laugh with him about her heart fluttering every time she sees Carter. It would be something they could talk about. But no matter how long it is since she and Stephen slept together, he is, still, supposed to be the only one she wants to do that with. And so she keeps schtum. And the silly pash she feels for Carter bubbles unchecked within her.

Stephen pours soup into bowls and scatters crunchy green spring onions on the surface of each. He sits down opposite Tessa and looks her in the eye.

Tessa, nervous of what he might see in her face, stands and fetches them both a square of kitchen roll with which to wipe their chins. 'Why are you telling me about this woman now?'

'It's living here. She's long gone. But I see her all the time. Glimpses of her. Flashes of red hair and taunting eyes.'

He laughs at the memory. 'Everything was always a dare with her. And if you weren't up for the dare she wasn't interested in you any longer.'

Tessa pushes away her soup and gulps at her wine. 'Stephen, you really know how to make a girl feel wanted.' How's she going to persuade him to try and have a baby with her when it sounds as though he's fallen in love with a ghost? No wonder they never have sex. Tessa's hair's not the flashing red sort. And she's never been any good at taunting eye action. Is that what he wishes he'd married? Has he actually, really, gone off her? Twenty... thirty years of not being fancied by her husband stretch out in front of Tessa. A lifetime of being good-mannered flatmates: the management of Dyllis' old age the glue that keeps them together. It's a hideous image.

Stephen can tell her about being haunted by Kat because Kat's not here. Carter's too real a threat to be mentioned.

When David Tait knocks, Tessa answers the door with her hair wrapped in a paint-splashed towel secured with a bulldog clip. She's wearing an old blue fisherman's slop and Radio 3 is blaring a *Goldberg Variation* from the kitchen so loudly that she waves at her visitor, runs through to turn it down, and then comes back, wiping paint off her hands onto the front of the slop.

'Hi,' she says. Then, 'Sorry. May as well have some music while I paint.'

He holds out his hand. 'David Tait,' he answers.

'The other churchwarden,' of course she knows who he is.

'Well, we have to get involved in our communities, don't we, or we won't have them at all?'

Unsure whether to take this as a question, an accusation, or the preliminary to a rant, Tessa does what she's learned helps every situation in the country and asks the fellow if he'd like a cup of tea.

He thanks her, but no. 'I won't take up too much of your time now,' he says. 'But I would like to be able to prevail upon you later.' He explains that he's collecting a fundraising committee for the church tower. Tessa likes his earnest enthusiasm.

'Of course I'll help,' she says. 'When do you plan to meet?'

And because she's outside, and because it's perfectly normal, given the subject of the conversation, she glances up the hill to St George's and on, past... What's that? Parked round the side of No. 3 is a traveller's lorry. And in the lane there's Carter's pick-up. Lauren must be back.

'Well, would a regular first Thursday suit?' asks David Tait, fiddling about with a clipboard she hasn't noticed before. 'Do you have an email so that agendas and so on can be sent to you? Will you mind meeting in the church the first time? It'll be cold but I think it important that the committee...'

Up the hill Tessa can see Carter, standing on his doorstep, talking into the house.

Distracted, 'I'm sorry, I must get on,' she says. She reaches into her bag in the hall and finds him one of her cards: old address, old telephone number. 'All my contact details are there.'

But before she can escape, Carter's swung into the cab of the pick-up. The lawnmower in the back is jaunty as Daisy's Labrador. Spring has sprung. Tessa turns back to the churchwarden and gives him a false smile, 'Bye then.'

She has no idea what he was saying and realises too late that she's actually shut the door in the man's face. Telling herself to stop getting her knickers in a twist about a touch so brief it's possible she imagined it, she stomps upstairs to continue stripping the Peter Rabbit frieze and see if the ceiling of her office is ready for a new coat yet.

And that's where Carter finds her: on a stepladder, testing the tack of drying paint.

'All right?' he says. And she flushes, wobbles and slips, holding on for dear life and cracking her chin on one of the steps so badly he can hear it. There's a nasty graze. Carter takes the shred of spotted fabric he wears around his neck and holds it to the pearling blood.

'I wanted to talk to you. I'm so glad you came.' She must keep talking. 'Will you help me build a vegetable garden?'

'This where you work?'

She takes the strip of fabric from him and looks at the blood on it. He examines the room with, she thinks, some disappointment.

'Did you expect an ivory tower?'

He grins at her and his teeth are very clean in his outdoorsy face. 'Didn't think you'd be the sort to do your own decorating.'

'I started the wrong way round. Should have painted first, taken on commissions after.' She can't help the pride in her voice when she says commissions.

He flicks at a hanging end of the Peter Rabbit frieze, then rips it off the whole wall in one, smooth movement. 'I like decorating,' he says.

'Don't you have to work?'

'Too boggy for mowing.' He pulls at the frieze under the window. Tessa holds tight to the stepladder. There's lip gloss in her pocket. If she put some on now would he touch it again?

It was guilt that made her so accusing of Stephen last night. Did she ever drool at the idea of Stephen like this? She doesn't like to put them together in the same thought.

The hiatus is broken by the telephone.

'Tessa Wilkinson? We have the results of your blood test. Doctor wants to see you this evening if possible.'

'Yes...' says Tessa, relief and disappointment battling within her. She'd forgotten all about the blood test.

Waiting patients still sit in the bay window of the Georgian house which has been home to the doctors of Stockford for nearly a century. Tessa stares idly out of the window. She can see April's deli, and the healthfood shop where she bought the ill-fated oranges. And there's Stephen's immediate boss, the rector, apparently having an altercation with a policeman.

She stands to peer more closely through the surgery's net curtains.

They're manhandling him! Whatever can be going on? The rector lashes out and thwacks a policewoman so hard on the nose that she cowers, bleeding into the gutter. There's shouting. The second policeman has the rector's hands behind his back and is handcuffing him. Tessa can't see now because of the crowd that's gathering. She goes to open the surgery door.

'Shame,' she hears someone say as the police car revs off down the high street with an obliging flash of blue light and whoop of siren for the gossips to take home and discuss.

'Mrs Wilkinson?' The doctor calls from her consulting room door.

Tessa spends the whole appointment wondering what on earth could have happened, fretting to get home and tell Stephen. She's given a prescription and realises she's heard practically nothing of the doctor's diagnosis. All she knows is that she has an over-active thyroid, she's to take some pills, and come back for another blood test in a few months' time.

'Fine,' she says, hoping the doctor doesn't realise how little attention she's paid.

The ride back to Hindle Green is a real lung-buster. Tessa throws her bicycle down on the grass at the back of the house.

Bursts into the kitchen, panting with the news that the rector's been arrested.

'Oh!' she says. 'Oh, I'm sorry.'

'Tess, you remember Caroline Matthews, the rural dean?' Tessa's news has already been broken by the all-knowing organ of the Church of England. The woman wears her dog collar tucked under the collar of a Liberty print shirt. She pushes back her chair. Her kiss hello is calm as oil on water after a shipwreck of a day.

Tessa leaves Stephen and the rural dean alone. She knows Stephen can't take the dean into his study because he hasn't lit the fire in there for days and it's too damp and cold, whatever the dean would probably say about not minding a bit.

So Tessa says something about painting her office and retreats upstairs.

Stephen closes the kitchen door to keep the warm in and concentrates on what he's being told.

'Len's been working so hard,' says Caroline. 'We've been thinking for a while that he might like to retire. And now there's this financial crisis...'

'You can't close St Peter and St Paul in Stockford.'

'No, but we could amalgamate the job with your three parishes. We'd have done it before, but Len...'

'That would be a big job,' Stephen says, frowning. 'For someone.'

'We'd have to advertise for applications.'

'Of course.'

'But would you be able to take it on while the prosecution takes its course?'

'Len's well liked in Stockford,' says Stephen, keeping his face bland. He's going to be under pressure to take this job. He doesn't want it. He doesn't mind helping out in the short-term. But he wants the bigger challenge of an inner-city parish with real deprivation, and hopelessness, a place where he can make a measurable difference. 'The people will stick by him.'

'Don't you believe it.' Caroline accepts more tea. 'The charges will be all over the *Advertiser* with WI embroidery to boot by Friday, you'll see. Will you mind helping out? It'll mean extra services. And a lot more community work.'

'And youth club committee meetings,' Stephen says wryly.

'Ha ha! Given the current circumstances perhaps we should let those lie for the moment?'

'But if the grants aren't used then the council and the other charitable trusts might allocate the money elsewhere.'

'Won't you have enough on your plate with St George's to worry about?'

'I love a challenge,' says Stephen, slugging the end of his tea and standing up as if he's going to head off right now, into the gathering evening, to build Stockford's youth club with his own bare hands.

'I hope you'll want to apply for the new job, once it's formalised and advertised.' The rural dean smiles winningly.

Stephen smiles back. 'Sorry. I'm still after getting back to a city parish.'

'Life here not exciting enough for you?'

Tessa's balanced on her stepladder, rolling paint onto the office ceiling, and doesn't look down when Stephen comes in. 'What did she say?'

Stephen takes hold of the ladder and it wobbles. 'You shouldn't do this on your own.'

'Don't!' says Tessa. 'Go on, what did she say?'

'She wants me to take on Stockford, short-term.' Stephen changes the subject quickly. 'This looks fantastic. You got the frieze off all in one go. I would have made a right hash of that.'

'No! What did Len Fox get arrested for?'

'Oh... Arson.'

'What?' Now Tessa looks down.

'Apparently he burnt the youth club down.'

'Why?'

'Perhaps he couldn't bear the way all the planners and the listed buildings people made it almost impossible for him to turn that barn into what he wanted. I can see his point.'

'And so long as this takes to sort out you're to take all the Stockford services too?' She's down the ladder now, hands on hips, looking Stephen straight in the eye.

'You do understand?' he says hopefully. 'I'll have a lot on. You won't be lonely?'

'Just don't steal my bicycle again or I'll be forced to make new best friends with Rufus Stone.'

Stephen's serious. 'Tessa, I don't have any choice.'

'I wouldn't mind if you were throwing yourself into this place because we're going to stay. But what's the point if you're going to be trawling around looking for a job elsewhere all the time? I want to put down roots, Stephen.'

'But when will you understand that the bucolic dream is just that? It's a dream, a fallacy. Believe in it and you will be disappointed.'

'I don't know what you're frightened of. Why can't you just allow this to be real? Allow yourself to enjoy your job and live in a lovely place.'

'Opening endless fêtes worse than death.'

'You've just come in here all shifty because you think I'm going to tell you off for working too hard and now you're snooting at the job. If you want to stay then by all means, do it, give it your best. I just don't see the point of slaving at something you look down on and are planning to leave as soon as you get the chance.'

'You will get bored, Tessa.'

'I WON'T!'

This evening there are storm clouds gathering all over the village. Up the lane from Tessa and Stephen's stand-off in her office, there's a Stoke family meeting in the kitchen of No. 3 Pratt Cottages. Carter's tightening the fists he's hidden in his armpits while he listens to the stranger whine.

'The girls'll be all right. I'll make sure of that.'

'How? Begging and stealing your way around the place? And what about schooling?'

'You sound like a social worker,' says Lauren from where she's sulking, smoking in the corner, allowing herself to be fought over. She wants to stay. She wants the girls. But she doesn't want to lose Ryan. Being torn like this makes her mulish and unable to help anyone, least of all herself.

'It's not right for children to live in damp caravans with no school!' Carter thumps the table. 'I don't know who you are, Ryan, but if you want to make a family with my Lauren and her girls then you make it here. You prove you can be the girls' dad and maybe they'll be allowed to come back to live with you. Find work. You too, Lauren. I'll take you both to the cheese factory tomorrow. There's always work there. Right now I'm taking these girls back to they Nanna.'

'You dare!' Ryan makes the mistake of putting himself in Carter's way. Carter grabs the little upstart by the scruff of his scrawny neck and throws him so hard his head cracks on the arm of the wood-framed settee. Lauren screams. Abbie has her grown-up ten-year-old arms around Trixie and Belle where they're sitting, watching, at the bottom of the stairs, silently flinching and chewing their bottom lips.

Before Ryan can right himself, Carter has a twin tucked

93

under each arm. Lauren's screaming.

Abbie puts herself between Lauren and the front door. 'Leave him go.'

Carter's face as he jams the pick-up into gear and roars it up the lane to the T-junction is a mask of brute strength exercising responsibility.

But after he drops them off at their Nanna's, delivering them, like parcels, without a word of explanation, he returns to Hindle Green the back way, taking the pick-up through Green Farm's yard and up the track edging the Old Rectory meadow, leading to the woods. He gets out and sits on the stile overlooking the village. The smoke from his roll-up smells bitter in the air. He wants his mum home to take charge. He needs a break. To be a lad allowed to roam free off the leash.

Chapter 8

Tessa's woken by hammering. She rolls towards Stephen's side of the bed. It's cold. Good thing she's got daydreaming about Carter to distract her from real life. She wasn't naïve enough when she married Stephen to think it would be all fairytale. But she never anticipated that there would come a day when there was no sparkle at all to keep them going. She snuggles under the duvet and listens to the hammering as it goes on and on. She shuffles her feet into slippers and pulls Stephen's father's camel-coloured dressing gown over her pyjamas. She turns the threadbare cuffs back over her wrists. The clock reads 6.45 am.

Downstairs she pads about, boiling the new electric kettle Dyllis has given them, stirring porridge, taking the pill she has to before breakfast. It's not until then that she thinks to open the curtains.

And then the back door.

'Carter?'

He stands up from the long, narrow box he's making. Next to the shed are another three boxes, already arranged in a row.

'You'll need six raised beds in all,' he says. 'You got double rotation then. Reckon you'll be growing just for you and the vicar or surplus to sell?'

'Carter, it's not even seven o'clock in the morning.'

'May as well get on,' he insists. 'While the weather's clear.' And now he stops shuffling and looks at her. His eyes are so tired they look bruised. His face is haggard. His mouth's set in a recessive line, his chin drawn back against his neck. He looks as if he thinks he's going to be told off.

Instead, 'Tea?' she asks him. And he clasps his arms crossed tight across his body. 'All right.'

Tessa pours him a cup. She folds her pyjama trousers round her ankles and tucks bare feet into wellies. She makes a path of footprints over his on the springing, wet lawn.

'Quite a system you've got going here,' she says. His hands are white with cold. There are spots of red on his cheeks. His hair curls damply. 'What's a raised bed?' He grins at her. She knows he feels better when she plays the ignorant townie. Whatever's happened up at No. 3, he needs to feel altogether more confident before he'll tell her anything.

'I've put them wide enough to mow between,' he says. 'We'll cover the grass with cardboard and fill them with compost and there's your vegetable garden.'

'Where do we get the compost from?'

'Stockford Recycling Centre. All that food you throw away comes back as black gold to grow your tatoes in.'

'Is it free?'

'Twenty quid a tonne. You need about a tonne a bed. I can fetch it in the pick-up for you, if you like. Save a bit on the delivery.' Tessa wonders where she's going to find a spare hundred and twenty quid. Carter's knuckles are grazed. One of his eyes is really bruised.

'You been fighting?' The question's out before she can stop it. And his face doesn't close in on itself as she thought it would. Instead, he stares out, over the roof of the vicarage, at the wide valley and Stockford's church tower visible, just, beyond Sink Wood.

'I done the right thing,' he says, simply. 'Not always what people want. But it were the right thing.'

'Those girls?'

'I took 'em home to they Nanna. Their mum's boyfriend didn't take kindly to me doing that.'

'Where's your sister Lauren and the boyfriend now?'

'No. 3.' He nods up the hill. 'Just 'cos they fight me don't mean they're too grand to sleep under my roof. He says there's something wrong with his van. Can't go till he gets it sorted. Old shit heap, drove here all right. They slept in my mum's room. I reckon I'm stuck with them now. They won't get jobs. They'll live off me and complain about how life's done them down all the time. And I can't do what I really want because of little Abbie.'

He sniffs, wipes his nose on his sleeve, hands Tessa the empty teacup. 'Thanks for that.'

'How old is Abbie?'

'Just ten.' Carter flashes her a wide grin. For the first time, Tessa notices that he's missing a side tooth.

She wonders how much he'll charge but daren't ask for fear of sounding wrong.

'I'm only setting you up.' Tessa blushes. 'Like a favour.' She won't ask about money then. She's mesmerised by the gap in his teeth. 'Most of the stuff is left over from other jobs,' he continues. 'If you don't mind it being a bit... you know...' Tessa wonders if she's being asked to be a receiver of stolen goods. 'Second-hand,' he finishes.

Tessa looks at the old scaffolding boards he's made the raised beds from and decides to just allow it all to be. She's a vicar's wife, standing in her garden, in her dressing gown, at seven in the morning, with a man she can hardly stop herself from touching, who isn't her husband. The whole situation makes her want to giggle. She'd better get inside and eat her porridge before Anna Trester sees.

'Have you had any breakfast?' she asks, hoping her voice sounds both ordinary and innocent.

It's as if Tessa's tiptoeing around herself. She might take fright at any moment. This is wrong. What she wants to do is wrong. When did this fantasy involving Carter become so real?

Carter eats his porridge with a swirl of dark brown sugar on top and a slosh of cream. She eats nothing. And now they've come to a speechless moment where someone has to make a move or they might miss the opportunity forever. She reaches for the bowls, hers full, his empty, and would have put them by the sink. But his arm snakes out and catches her round her waist. She jumps, as if bitten, turns, looks at him. He doesn't let go. His other arm joins the first and pulls her towards him, so that she's trapped between his legs. Giving in, she can no longer fight the smile she's been hiding all morning. It flowers on her face as he pulls her towards him, pulls her down so that her hair hides her shame from the real world. Her giggles are infectious, and their first kiss is snatched between bouts of helpless laughter.

The curtains in the front rooms of the house are still closed. She should be sanding the wall where the Peter Rabbit frieze was stuck. Instead, Carter's breath is hot on her neck. Does he do this to all the women who move into the village? Tessa doesn't care. Stephen's not here. Stephen's never here. His priorities are elsewhere. Stop thinking about Stephen! Enjoy the moment. Come on, Tessa.

But there's the growl of a car parking outside the front and the screech of a handbrake being applied with force.

Carter pulls away. Tessa leaps back, pulls Stephen's dressing gown tight about her and re-knots the sash. So much for daydreams come true.

'Shit!' says Carter. 'Got a bloody funeral, ain't I? Gotta hide the digger round the back of the church. Mind you, he'd have liked it. Loved the smell of hydraulic fluid, that old man did.'

'You're the village sexton?'

Carter pushes a hank of hair off Tessa's face and for a second kisses her hard. 'And you're too distracting.'

Rufus Stone's black Lexus snakes its way between the parked cars jammed along the road past the church. The builders had better have got on or he'll fire them. He's on a detox and a detox always makes him ready to pick a fight. The stereo is deafening. A group of black-clad mourners at a graveside turn to stare as he passes.

Rufus needs to be out of London and away from temptation. He's told them all to keep away. Including that fucking Joseph! Bastard! Stupid, short-sighted, BORING!!!

There are no builders in sight. The Old Rectory is deserted but for two women sitting, heads together, in a VW Polo outside his front door.

'Hi! Hi.' Rufus climbs out of the Lexus and flashes the women his devastating grin. Apparently unmoved, they shake hands politely.

'Amanda Davis, architectural surveyor,' says the more film star of the two, her platinum-blonde, carefully rumpled hair kept off her face with a diamanté-encrusted clip. 'And this is Hannah Riley, conservator from the planning office.'

'Come in, come in.' Rufus unlocks the front door with a flourish of the old iron key and ushers the women inside. 'I'll make you some coffee,' he suggests. 'While you explain why you have the right to order my builders off site.' He smiles to show them he's not being that aggressive.

'You may not be aware, Mr Stone, but without listed building consent you aren't supposed to start work on a property.' This woman's clearly not the ditz she's made herself up to be. 'While we appreciate that your London architects have submitted a vague plan, the conservation department won't be in a position to grant permission for any changes you'd like to make to this house for months. A detailed archaeological survey of the building needs to be done first. Areas which need special conservation must be identified. You can't just put in a new kitchen without us looking first.'

'But without a new kitchen I can't move in.'

'If their houses are of special historic interest, people often rent in the area while works are carried out on their own property. What do you know about this place, Mr Stone?'

Rufus' detoxing hands shake as he puts coffee cups under the spouts of his state-of-the-art espresso machine.

'Was it a Mrs Wilkinson who reported me to you?' he asks the more amenable looking of the two girls: Hannah, with her flat, mousy hair and delicate silver jewellery might be the sort he can fell with a careful flick of an eyebrow.

'May we have a tour?' she asks, blushing.

He stands and opens the door to the parlour. 'Be my guests.'

This is sooooo crap, he thinks. He should be rewarded for being brave enough to break up with Joseph, not punished by over-qualified women invested with county authority.

Tessa needn't have panicked. Hours later, long after Carter has finished back-filling the grave with a mini-digger from the hire centre in Stockford, there is still no sign of Stephen at the vicarage. By now, Tessa's guilt-driven mad clean of the kitchen is long finished. Her mind still whirring, she's put the first layer of apple-green paint on the walls of her office. And now she needs to escape. She needs to grow up, reject temptation, realise the error of her ways, decide to tell Carter firmly but kindly that he'd do much better to look out for somebody closer to his own age. And she needs to not see Stephen while she persuades herself of all of the above – or her husband's distracted disinterest might persuade her that her resolve is pointless.

Stepping out of the house, Tessa sees Stephen's Mini hove into view from the direction of Stockford. She turns right and, lost in her own march, is almost run down by a car pulling out of the drive to the Old Rectory. The women in the car have no time to apologise before they're borne down upon by Rufus shouting.

'What are you doing? Isn't it enough that you constipate my restoration of this glorious building without murdering my innocent guests to boot?' Rufus has grabbed Tessa's elbow and is pulling her up the drive. 'Leave those harridans. They're only off to bother the poor vicar with some can't-do, won't-dos re: his crumbling church tower. Besides, I owe you an apology,' he says. 'Or perhaps I should apologise to your mother.' Tessa's taken aback. This is not what she expected.

'Mother-in-law,' she hears herself say.

'Well, I'm sorry if we were slapdash. She all right?'

'Much recovered.'

'Come in,' he says. 'I'm lonely. And those two witches have just told me off like I'm some naughty schoolboy. They've stopped the builders. It's outrageous! Please come. Please! If I don't have company, I'm bound to fall off the wagon and I can't afford to do that now. I'm up for a Bond baddie next week. And they say Deborah Broccoli doesn't take kindly to anyone who doesn't look as clean living as a stick of organic celery.'

At least he's honest, thinks Tessa, too curious not to follow him up the drive. And his eyes aren't all over the place, and his breath smells of nothing more dangerous than coffee. Perhaps he'll be in the market for a gardener, she thinks. If she were a different kind of woman then she and Carter could have trysts in Rufus' garden shed. She almost bursts out laughing at the idea and when Rufus turns to look he asks, 'What happened to you? You're beautiful.'

He rattles the espresso machine again and asks, 'So what's it like round here, then? All posh plumbers, or country ladies asking with whom you hunt?'

'Do you really want to get involved?' Tessa holds her hands behind her back, absorbing heat from the open fire with which he replaced the old range before those 'harridans' could stop him. 'I could get you co-opted onto the fundraising committee for the church tower if you like.' How can she be making mild chit-chat with Rufus Stone after what she's just done?

'So I could endow the Rufus Stone memorial church toilet, you mean?'

She laughs. 'There needn't be a scatological connection. Show your self-deprecating side by sponsoring a gargoyle. Just allow me to add your name to the list of committee members and we'll raise all the money we need if people think they might get a glimpse of you at the next fundraising barn dance or whatever.'

Tessa sips the coffee he gives her – it tastes of London.

'What other hot activities?' Rufus arranges himself in one of two leather armchairs he's installed in front of the fire. He crosses his legs carefully. The shine on his hand-made shoes is blinding.

Tessa perches on the arm of the other chair. 'Not much you'd call hot.'

'Don't tell me it really is cow meditation that's given you such a bella figura.'

'I'm planning a lot of vegetable gardening. Even now my seed potatoes are growing knobbly little green shoots in egg boxes on the window sill in the larder. It's called chitting.' Rufus looks totally lost. 'Or you ask around for a gardener.'

'Are you all right?' asks Rufus. She's choking on her espresso.

'Sorry, went down the wrong way,' she lies, wiping streaming eyes. Emergency subject change. 'Do you remember me?'

Rufus shakes his head. To be fair, their non-relationship had been more than ten years ago, just at the beginning of his vertiginous rise to fame. 'Your face might be familiar. Did we..?'

'You took me to dinner a few times. We were what you called 'papped' together. In the end I decided you weren't really interested. Though you got surprisingly possessive when Stephen hoved into view.'

'Stephen?'

Tessa forces her face to stay neutral. 'You'll meet him. He's the vicar those women went to see about the tower. The man I married.'

She remembers Stephen screeching to a halt, come to fetch her from the gallery where she'd gone to an opening with Rufus - a knight in shining bicycle helmet. He'd shaken Rufus' hand, then taken Tessa's, smiled at the general company and asked if he and Tessa might be excused. Then he'd taken her outside and kissed her in front of everybody, bending her over backwards as if he were an exaggerating romantic lead. She'd laughed until she got a stitch, and then been perched on his bicycle crossbar and taken off to an unfashionable pub round the corner where he'd plied her with pork scratchings and warm gin and tonics while persuading her to go home with him.

That night he cooked moules marinières for her and afterwards she slept in his bed while he slept on the sofa. One of the most erotic experiences of her whole life was the six months she spent not sleeping with Stephen before they married. The expectation was so high on their wedding night that by rights it should have been a disaster. Instead, she'll never forget a lovemaking so tender, and yet so biting sharp... Now she tries to remember when they last made love. Last year? Before they left London, definitely.

It is days until Tessa sees Carter again. Days and days, in which more dead are buried, Lent gallops towards its close, Stephen leaves the marital bed before Tessa wakes and returns too late to eat supper with her. This is it, she thinks. She's going to spend the rest of her life sharing a house with a man she never sees. She'd hoped so hard that a move to the country would make things different.

She could force the issue: make something give, manufacture a straw with which to break the camel's back. But that's not what she wants. Instead, she makes a proper wifely effort with a swirly Indian cotton skirt, swept-up hair, lip gloss, scent. She lays a pretty table for supper: those napkins, candles, crusty bread, her newly-perfected carrot and coriander soup, a round of Ellen's fresh goat's cheese and primroses and tiny violets arranged artfully in an egg cup.

She falls asleep waiting. He doesn't arrive home until a quarter to ten. But still determined to make an effort, Tessa stirs up the soup and scatters green coriander leaves on top of a spoonful of yoghurt as garnish before grinding black pepper with a flourish. Stephen only grunts in recognition of her efforts and bends low over his bowl, slurping, in between tearing off chunks and chewing his bread with his mouth open. He doesn't tell her about his day. He's making a list for tomorrow.

Tessa tucks escaping tendrils of hair behind her ears and sits down next to him. 'Have you put in for the English Heritage grant for St George's yet?' she asks. She's not looking for an excuse. She wants him to include her.

'David Tait's in charge of that,' says Stephen, wiping the bottom of the bowl with a crust of bread and pushing his chair back. 'You better ask him.' And he's off. The kiss on her head as he passes is like an absentminded pat for a dog. Stephen closes the door to the office. This is not new behaviour: when Tessa's working hard and happy, she's much nicer to her husband; when Stephen's under pressure, it's as if Tessa barely exists.

She sits alone in the dark sitting room, looking out at a sky glinting with stars. What should she wish? There's the rumble of a diesel engine and Carter's pick-up zips past.

In his office, Stephen sits in the dark too. He knows that he's failing his wife. However many years he may have spent advising other people how to save their marriages, he realises now how easy it is to tell someone to do something when you don't have the same problem yourself. How glib he must have sounded, how smug, how over-confident. He wants nothing more than to be held by her and understood. But he's so terrified to tell her what's going on with him that he's driving her away.

And suddenly it's Holy Week. Stephen's taking services in the cavernous church in Stockford, as well as around the benefice. The churchwardens have crisply-ironed surplices ready in every different vestry, flower ladies are bringing in the buds of their scented narcissi to stand in buckets in sunny front porches so that they'll open in time for a feast of decoration on Saturday. Anna Trester has ordered white lilies for St George's: she'll charge them to the PCC. Being a good wife, Tessa washes and irons Stephen's black corduroys, and hopes he won't rescue anyone from a muddy ditch while wearing them.

Maundy Thursday. Wearing those corduroys, Stephen's downstairs making tea before Tessa's out of bed. Up the lawn, six raised beds are arranged beside the shed, filled with black compost. On the larder windowsill there are egg boxes full of greenly sprouting seed potatoes ready for planting. Stephen won't have time to help Tessa plant them. He says, 'Wouldn't it just be easier to buy them?' He doesn't see the point of planting and watering and waiting. With the added responsibilities of Stockford, Stephen won't have time to grow anything this summer.

Tessa's life is fuller than Stephen thought it would be. Which is a relief. It transpires that Len Fox has not been quite on top of things in Stockford. The churchwardens have been squabbling. The youth club didn't have the funding in place that everyone had thought, and there are worrying gaps in the paperwork. Old Jack Trester gave the barn to the parish of Stockford in exchange, it seems to Stephen, for permission to build 50 houses along the south edge of Sink Wood. Jack had been such a force locally that the difficult questions weren't asked until after he died. Mrs Trester insists the barn's been in Trester possession for so long there've never been any deeds.

Mulling over the problem of the ownership of the Black Barn, Stephen's way to St George's is blocked by somebody parking an enormous black car. Out of it steps Rufus Stone, who turns, bares his blinding gnashers and offers his hand, 'Long time no see, eh?'

Doing the 'Good Vicar', Stephen shakes the film star's hand and ushers him through the lychgate and up the path to the church.

'Almighty God, unto whom all hearts be open, all desires known, cleanse the thoughts of our hearts...'

There is a special calm to the said communion service. Apart from Rufus, the tiny congregation knows the words off by heart. 'We are not worthy so much as to gather up the crumbs under thy table. But thou art the same Lord, whose nature is always to have mercy.' Stephen lifts the host high while he tells the story of the Last Supper.

It is the betrayal that he finds most horrible. Betrayal is so purposeful and therefore vicious. Pontius Pilate didn't know Jesus from Barabas and wouldn't have cared which of them was crucified. Judas Iscariot, though; old friend and confidant, a man who'd been with Jesus throughout his ministry... Stephen has often thought that to forgive Judas must have been the hardest part of what Jesus had to do.

The communicants kneel upon a strip of canvas, embroidered in cross-stitch with olive branch-bearing doves by Anna Trester's mother-in-law before the Second World War, holding their hands out for slivers of wafer. The communion wine tastes like stale, sweet sherry. People walk back to their seats, and kneel to make their own prayers while Stephen pads quietly about behind the altar, tidying the Last Supper away.

Afterwards, Stephen makes sure to beam the light of his charm on Rufus, who expects nothing less than such attention and beams beneficently right back.

Good Friday. Food is becoming a passion for Tessa. In the three months since she's moved into this vicarage, she's developed quite a repertoire. She bought a coffee grinder in the charity shop and now that the coffee taint has worn off, the scent of whizzed up toasted spices for parsnip soup fills the kitchen with a mild scent of curry, an exotic touch to Ladybird Book Hindle Green.

This Good Friday morning, Tessa's tackling bread for the first time. Ellen has sworn it's simple. Tessa's done everything she was told. The mixing bowls were warm from the back of the Rayburn. She ground the Maldon sea salt so chunks of it wouldn't kill the yeast. She mixed the yeast with warm water and a spoonful of Ellen Wiseman's honey before turning it into the flour she bought from April. Dyllis' dog-eared copy of Constance Spry says that bread should be kneaded until the mixture pulls away from the sides of the bowl when you turn it. Left to rise, the mixture bubbled up spectacularly. She knocked it back on the flour-scattered kitchen table and shaped it into a tin. And now it's risen a second time she's putting it into the top right of the Rayburn, splashing an inch of water onto the floor of the oven to help the door seal tight.

She washes up, watching the clock tick the forty-five minutes she's been told she must wait.

And now the room smells like a baker's. The perfect loaf sits on a cooling rack. Tessa has had to fight the urge to photograph it. The kitchen door opens and boots are shucked off. Her womb flipping, Tessa doesn't dare turn to look.

'What do you think?' she asks, still admiring her handiwork. Arms encircle her waist from behind, imprisoning her, and a head rests on her shoulder; the bakery smell mixes deliciously with bonfire and grass cuttings.

Carter Stoke says, "'f I help you plant your 'tatoes will you give me a nibble?'

The marital bed should be sacrosanct. But when there's mud under her fingernails and her hair's damp from planting in a spring drizzle, Tessa can't resist violation. If she's going to do this, then she's going to do it properly. No uncomfortable shifting in secret corners. Carter lets her take the lead and, her heart pounding with the madness of it, she pulls him up the stairs behind her. He stands in her room and she pushes his jacket off, lifts his shirt from his belted jeans. She bites his mouth. And then he grabs her.

At the vigil kept in Stockford Church throughout Good Friday afternoon, Stephen looks up and is astonished to see Tessa tuck herself into one of the back pews. She doesn't kneel when the rest of the congregation do, or stand. She just sits and watches, looking pale, stunned. It crosses his mind that she might be there to tell him somebody's died. He cannot know that she's come to ask a God she doesn't believe in how she should handle guilt, enforce resolve, focus on a marriage in which Stephen is always elsewhere.

That's the thing, suggests the bad angel on her shoulder. *It's as though Stephen's having an affair with his job - so why shouldn't you find some happy distraction?* Tessa buries her head in her hands. She lost herself this morning. Now what?

Chapter 9

First thing Saturday, there's an imperious knock on the vicarage door. Innocent Stephen's dozing in crisp, clean sheets, which Tessa hurriedly flung onto the bed after Carter left yesterday. Tessa took Stephen a cup of tea earlier. She didn't wake him. She left it on his bedside table. Needing to escape, it's her turn to be up early.

She can't believe he hasn't noticed the change in her. Doesn't her rabbiting heart betray itself in the high flush in her cheeks? Isn't it as though she has a big sign reading 'UNFAITHFUL' branded on her forehead? She oughtn't see Carter again. But she went to the service in Stockford yesterday afternoon and Stephen looked straight through her. His God said nothing. Let down, she slipped away before the service ended because she had no idea what, if anything, she would say.

Now she hurries to the front door, finger to her lips. 'Sh!' she says, opening up to Anna Trester, who stands there in wellies with a basket on her arm, brandishing a pair of secateurs.

'I need your daffs.' Mrs Trester takes no notice of Tessa's shushing finger. 'We can't have the parish where the vicar actually lives outdone by the efforts of people like Ellen Wiseman at Pendle. Not that we will, of course. Her arrangements always look like nothing more than a hank of grass and weeds she's dug out of a hedgerow. Still...' Tessa realises Anna Trester's waiting to be invited in.

'Wait a minute.' Tessa fetches her own boots from by the back door. She shows Anna Trester around the side of the house, up past the freshly planted potato bed, to where three fruit trees are skirted with daffodils big enough to wear as ballroom dancing dresses.

'Oh, very good,' says Anna Trester, getting over her disappointment at not being invited to have a look at Tessa's Saturday morning kitchen. 'You've got the really common ones. Our wild daffs aren't brash enough to make a big splash on the window sills. These vulgar cultivars are much more the thing for a church display. Have you any scissors? Be so much quicker if I just cut chunks at a time. You don't want to look at them, do you?' The hatchet face splits into a laugh. 'Of course not.'

'Why don't I pick some for you?' Tessa asks. 'I could bring them up and help decorate the church. If you like.'

'Never turn down the offer of help!' Mrs Trester's laugh is a rusty saw. 'I'm going up there now. Would you bring us some of your flowering ivy berries too? The yellow of the daffs shows up so much better against some dark green, don't you think? Though who am I to tell you? After all your years as a vicar's wife I've no doubt you know all about what looks good and what doesn't on a thirteenth century windowsill. Or were your previous livings always ghastly gothic revival nightmares?'

'Always.' Tessa feels a sort of anthropological liking for Mrs Trester. She's as curious about what drives a woman to become the stereotypical village dragon as the dragon is about Tessa. They're quits.

'I'll see you up there,' Tessa says, smiling. 'After I've given the vicar his breakfast in bed.' With which she can't help but give Mrs Trester a naughty wink before she marches down the lawn and through the kitchen door without a backward glance.

Dear Rufus, Tessa types. Stephen sleeps on. He can get his own breakfast when he surfaces. Before she looks Stephen in the eye, Tessa has to decide how she feels about this: what she's going to do about it – she can't even allow the word 'Carter' into her mind until she does. Fluffy banter with Rufus will stop her descending into a slough of uncertainty. *Off to do Easter flowers at St George's. If you're still trying to keep yourself out of trouble, come along and make my day watching the dread Mrs Trester meet you. I can't decide if she's likely to pull rank or fawn. PLEASE come, just for my amusement.* With a feverish flourish she presses 'Send'.

Tessa wants the company of somebody else who knows how to be ruthlessly badly behaved. He might give her courage. Help her banish the guilt...

She's never done anything like this before. She's not the unfaithful sort. With her back to the house, hacking at the ivy bunching along the back wall of the garden, and picking only one in every ten daffodils for Mrs Trester's display, Tessa, remembering yesterday, finally allows a grin on her face as wide as a tiger's. Being wicked is a feeling she never thought she'd enjoy so much.

For the walk up the hill to St George's, she can't resist brushing her hair and piling it up on top of her head so that the back of her neck is bare. She cleans her teeth. She sashays along, swinging her basket.

'Mrs Trester...' Rufus Stone is unctuous as he bends over the churchwarden's hand. Tessa thinks the old bat might hyperventilate. The other flower ladies stand about, an appreciative audience, respectfully watching the show unfold. 'I brought a contribution.'

The windows are mostly finished. Unadorned during Lent, the pale stone sills are now bursting with arrangements of daffodils, catkins and pussy willow embedded in dark green ivy. Beside the altar a stand of lilies leans rakishly, orange stamens threatening to stain Stephen's vestments tomorrow.

There are painted eggs hanging on branches of contorted willow in a jug on the oak bench in the porch. Only the little replica garden built into the bank by the lychgate, with its miniature stone cave and budding primroses, waits to have last year's goose grass pulled away from it and three new crosses jammed into its tiny hillock.

Rufus presents Mrs Trester with an armload of lilies and cellophane-wrapped tulips. 'Am I too late?' he asks, looking about him. 'You are clever.' He's childishly pleased. 'I could take these back...'

'Oh no!' A flurry of activity, of dusty vases rootled out of the vestry cupboard, of brisk wiping with damp cloths. 'If we move Amy's painted eggs... Amy, will you mind? Then I'll put *my* lilies in the porch, and yours can go by the altar, Rufus.' Mrs Trester calls him Rufus coyly and looks up at him through her six sparse eyelashes to see if he's noticed.

'Phew.' Rufus slumps into a pew. 'Wouldn't do to get in trouble with the vicar's wife for not pulling my weight now, would it?' He winks at Tessa: it's all she can do to keep a straight face.

Now, when Tessa's with Stephen she finds herself being extra solicitous – clean towel for his bath, cooked breakfast on Easter Sunday, a chocolate egg from April's shop – all of which she gives him because she feels sorry for his unhappiness at being banished to the country, and guilty for her own secret joy. But the princeling, only boy child that he is, accepts her kindnesses as nothing more than his due: he eats the bacon in his fingers while putting the final touches to a new Resurrection sermon which he'll give three times before lunch today.

She and Stephen are invited to Ellen Wiseman's for Easter lunch. They pack Dyllis into the passenger seat of the Mini and after church they drive through lanes where the cow parsley foliage is already a foot high. Ellen's provided home-grown spinach and pork terrine, followed by a leg from one of last year's lambs, with roast potatoes and sweet, buttery, peppery purple sprouting broccoli. For pudding there's home-made raspberry ice cream and meringues drizzled with honey.

Tessa feels daunted yet inspired by such industrious use of Ellen's home produce. She's realising that it's maintaining the constant production that's hard work. You don't just plant things and leave them. But what an achievement to be able to eat like this all year round, thanks to your own hard labour.

'Did you go to college to learn the gardening?' Tessa asks as she takes the dripping plates from Ellen and wipes them dry before returning them to the rack on the dresser. Dyllis and Stephen are both ensconced on a sofa by the fire. Stephen snores so gently only Tessa is irritated by it.

Dyllis doesn't sleep. Instead she watches Tessa from beneath three-quarters-closed lids. The girl's happy, thinks Dyllis, if a little hyper. Or is it just that she's eager to please? This busy enthusiasm for country life suits her. Dyllis wishes the condition were catching, that Stephen would come down with a good dose of contentment. He fights everything that comes his way, over-complicates every situation, looks for trouble, finds it, dives in to mix it up. No wonder he always has black bags under his eyes. He lets himself be held to ransom by his job, thinks Dyllis.

Dyllis' eyes snap open. Tessa looks more than happy...

'I just picked up the gardening as I went along,' replies Ellen, wiping her hands on Tessa's dishcloth. 'It becomes an obsession if you let it. And I discovered I could make a living at it. So why struggle doing anything else when you can get paid to be outside all day with your hands in the earth. Would you like to see?'

And Tessa's taken on a tour of recycled plastic-bottle

cloches, under which baby salad peeks through crumbed baked egg shells - 'Keeps the slugs off' - and long lines of hazel pea sticks - 'I'm a bit ahead with them. There won't be peas to plant out for a month yet. But the broad beans are flowering already. Stick your nose in there.' Tessa bends, waits for a bee to buzz off, and inhales a scent which makes lime blossom fade into insignificance.

'Wow,' she says. 'And you're not lonely working all on your own?'

Ellen grins. 'With this zoo to look after?'

It's after Easter that the grass seriously starts to grow and Carter's workload expands to fit the hours people want him. He starts his day at five thirty with tea and toast, filling a thermos flask with more for later. Until this year he's worked because there's been nothing he'd rather do. He loves the security of money in his pocket, is constantly conscious that it is to him that his sisters come when they can't cover their own costs, that in the absence of his mother he's fully responsible for Abbie, whom he dresses in new clothes and gives generous pocket money to and who thinks the efforts he makes on her behalf are nothing less than her ten-year-old due.

Before she left them Kat said, ''f you're in trouble, go on the social.'

'Why you gotta go, Mum?' Abbie wailed like a four-year-old being left for her first day at school.

'Because I gotta put right what's wrong.' Kat was magnificent in her determination. 'One day you'll understand and you'll be proud of your old Mum.'

Carter would never go on the social for fear of having to compromise somehow in return for the handout. And he has a healthy liking for money so during the summer he works every hour he can.

But now he makes time for Tessa. The vicarage has a magnetic appeal for him. He gets to know Stephen's schedule backwards. When he's with Tessa his responsibilities melt away and for the first time in his life he's just a young man indulging his lust.

Tessa's like a chocoholic where Carter's concerned. When he's not there she's determined this affair must stop. But like chocolate stashed in a drawer, it's as though he calls to her – all the time. And her stabs of guilt are blunted by Stephen's lack of interest. She knows she shouldn't blame Stephen for her inability to resist Carter. But Stephen gives her no reason to fight her lover off. Besides, it's not impossible that there's an altruistic side to their love-making: they're making each other so happy that the happiness rubs off on the people around them.

She laughs at herself and says, out loud, 'Excuses, excuses.' Then she puts in a word for Carter at the Old Rectory where Rufus gives him a job which comes with a shed of his own, equipped with a kettle and a teapot. Tessa finds an old sofa at a charity shop in a town twenty miles away when she goes to help Daisy at a food festival.

At the shed there's the growl of the reversing pick-up. Rufus has gone to London for the day. The garden at the Old Rectory is walled. Tessa has no need to hide. She pushes her hair off her face and steps out into the spring sunshine to help unload. A white shirt is tucked into her flowing, Indian cotton skirt and her waist is lightly cinched with brown leather. On her feet are grass-green suede clogs. She's shaved her legs. She's put on weight since she started taking those pills for her thyroid. Her face has filled out, and her breasts. She looks... feels... twenty years younger. It's her thirty-ninth birthday today. Stephen's forgotten. They're not usually big birthday people. He knows she doesn't want to be reminded she's getting older. Not long ago she would have been drowning in a depression caused by the onrushing threat of being forty.

But thanks to Carter, today she doesn't care – that Stephen's forgotten, that she's thirty-nine, even. She's even more or less stopped feeling that throbbing ache caused by the lack of her own child. Being with Carter makes her feel young enough to have years of childbearing potential in front of her. She smiles widely at her lover as he rolls the sofa towards her down the open back of the truck.

It's too heavy for her. He leaps down and takes it, kissing her for being a woman he can be strong for. He lowers the sofa through the shed door and pushes it until it's almost jammed under the potting-up bench.

'It's not going to fit!'

Carter rolls it onto its side, tugs it round, flips it back onto its feet and shoves it against the back wall.

'It's too jammed in,' says Tessa. 'I hate furniture squashed into corners.'

'You don't know you're born,' says Carter, scooping her up into his arms and dumping her unceremoniously onto her back. 'It's not like I'm gonna be having Mrs Trester round for tea parties now, is it? Just remember what this is for!'

Until the conservation officer came round, Rufus wanted to rip out the ancient wainscoting and install stained-Perspex panelling in the kitchen. Now he's on a historical bender, loving the wind-whistling master bedroom for the loose-leaded windows, not minding when he smashes his designer china because the sink was carved from solid stone two hundred years ago. Other than a state-of-the-art espresso machine and a gigantic black fridge, his grandiose modern ideas seem to have gone down the plughole.

The truth he keeps to himself is that the last three jobs he

117

went for, he didn't get. So he has no money coming in with which to appeal to the planners or bring in specialist builders. Rufus suspects foul play by his erstwhile agent and lover. He's still too angry about their split to get himself new representation. What he'd really like is for somebody to offer to take ten per cent for getting him wonderful parts in films which will be both critically acclaimed and commercially successful. But he's too sulky to go cap-in-hand himself. This is why he's home alone at the Old Rectory and, while not yet quite broke, is learning to like the rhythm of sweeping his own kitchen floor. The house is weather-proof enough to live in for the summer and Tessa makes a good substitute audience.

To keep her close, he commissions her to research the house for him.

'There are hundreds of years of history in these ancient dressed stones,' he says seriously. 'I want it recorded for posterity.'

He's invested in a tiny specialist hammer with which he's testing the plaster.

'This part of the house isn't old enough for priest holes,' says Tessa.

Rufus ignores her and keeps on tapping. 'The skill is,' he says as they explore an attic bedroom where a mouse-house eiderdown still hugs the skeleton of a plain, black-painted, wrought iron bed, 'not to restore, but to conserve.' In the spirit of 'If you can't beat them, join them', he's now a paid-up member of the Society for the Protection of Ancient Buildings and has become an instant aficionado. 'If we find anything of any major interest then the question will be whether we reveal it, or just identify it, X-ray it, document it in our book. I'm not going to install central heating. It'll dry the house out.'

'Are you going to pay a log man to keep fires burning through the winter, then?' Though he didn't get the Bond part,

Tessa's under the impression Rufus must still have money coming out of his ears. He just doesn't have much to do. Tessa thinks the house is replacing his love affair with cocaine. It's going to be a much more expensive habit.

According to Amanda Davis, the part of the Old Rectory Dyllis refers to as the lean-to on the back, with its three-foot stone walls, the kitchen, the bathroom, the scullery and various larders and pantries, are all that remain of a fourteenth century hall house. The drawing room, dining room and study, built from warm, red brick softened by ancient lime mortar, are Queen Anne.

'Living here's like permanent posh camping,' says Rufus, skidding back down the slippery elm stairs in a pair of ironical pink tasselled loafers. 'I might not do anything to the house at all. Roughing it's the zeitgeist, no? The fire draws well because of this ledge,' he says, inviting Tessa to blind herself looking round behind the smoke at the arrangements in the kitchen chimney. 'Good place to smoke hams.'

'I should introduce you to Ellen Wiseman,' says Tessa, opening the kitchen door to let in some heat from the sun-warmed yard outside – though she won't: she's keeping Rufus to herself for the moment.

There's a huge bunch of red and yellow striped parrot tulips in a shop-delivered vase on the table; not all of Rufus' London friends have deserted him. Tessa bought some of the first of Ellen's broad beans at the farmers' market that morning and starts podding them into a bowl while they talk.

'Very Vermeer,' says Rufus, making them coffee.

'She keeps them under plastic all winter to get a crop so early. Also, her vegetable garden's stone walls work like radiators for the young plants. And they stop wind rock.' Tessa laughs. 'I love pretending to know what I'm talking about when it comes to gardening.' She sips the coffee. It's so strong it almost makes her gag. She puts her cup down and begins to tell Rufus what she's uncovered about his house so far.

'Once upon a time,' she says, 'there was a priory in Hindle Green. And I think this house was part of it. But the plague came and killed the village off during the fourteenth century...'

Later, leaving Rufus to update his Twitter feed with imaginary plague pits in the garden, Tessa slips round to the potting shed. No sign of Carter.

'What am I doing?' she asks out loud.

Tessa tries to rationalise her situation like this: Stephen's busy. She thinks he wants her to be happy. They never have sex. She clearly can't get pregnant. So must she push away this cheerful young man and his opportunistic attentions? Can there really be so much harm in her friendship with Carter Stoke? OK... affair. AFFAIR. Yes, she's having an affair. And yes, she feels guilty, and no, she doesn't want a divorce. But the fling with Carter is an exciting bubble of unreality, perhaps even the secret to keeping the humdrum of her marriage going.

When she married Stephen it was as if she was playing at being grown-up. She remembers how proud she was of the serious diamond engagement ring, which Stephen's father had once given Dyllis. Now she's nearly forty, it seems she's fighting age by turning child again, amused by virulent, plastic cocktail rings and playing with Carter while the bread rises.

Can't she get away with it for a little while?

Tessa's under no illusion. This country idyll can't last forever. It's only a matter of time before Stephen drags her back to the grit of an inner city parish. And she'll go with him because that is real life and nobody gets to live a fairy story forever. In her heart of hearts she agrees with Stephen: life cannot be perfect – after all, what has she done to deserve the dream? And so she must not waste a minute of the time she has in Hindle Green. She feels driven to make the most of everything from growing her own potatoes to rolling about with Carter on the sofa in his shed.

And she knows the vows she made on her wedding day as well as the next person: but why should she carry on forsaking all others when it seems that Stephen's long forsaken her for his real true love, the Church? Did he marry her because he thought he ought to be married? No, he's not ambitious enough to marry for the sake of his career. And he clearly doesn't care about having children. So what are they doing together?

Perhaps it's Carter she should be worried about. Stephen's a big, grown-up boy who, if push came to shove, could look after himself. Carter's the one made fragile by youth and inexperience, incarcerated in a life caring for younger sisters. He should be travelling the wide seas, lying about on beaches getting stoned in the moonlight, scattering his wild oats on more fertile ground.

Tessa leans on the warm stone wall between Rufus' garden and his orchard meadow. There are lambs bouncing about, the cow parsley's almost in flower, the air smells damp and rich and fecund.

Tessa can't maintain the guilt. She's numb to it already. She doesn't really want to rationalise anything. It's as if each encounter with Carter is one in which she steps into a dream world where her non-relationship with Stephen becomes irrelevant.

'We'll have to find you a greenhouse.' Carter puts half a tray of lettuce seedlings, his excuse for this visit, onto the kitchen table. Does curtain-twitching Anna Trester wonder if there isn't something going on? Tessa will have to tell him to be more careful, not drop in so often, in broad daylight, confidently marching round to the back of the house as if he owns the place. His shirt sleeves are rolled above his elbows, his trousers held up by a black leather belt with a brass buckle. Tessa pops today's loaf onto the shelf in the top oven of the Rayburn.

'Three quarters of an hour,' she says, one eyebrow raised. 'Unless it's tea you're after.'

Carter grins at her. 'Not that kind of thirsty.'

He snaps open the clip holding the cloud of hair off her face.

'Anybody home?' Stephen's voice calls from the front door.

Tessa's hands shake as she re-fastens her hair. She shoves her bare feet into her clogs. She tells herself to calm down: if she doesn't answer and she and Carter make no noise, the chances are Stephen will just disappear into his office. He's so focused on his work it's possible he could walk into the kitchen and not even notice if Tessa and Carter were snogging by the Rayburn.

Tessa doesn't get a chance to test Stephen's observance. Carter's already crashed into the table as he hurries to put his boots on. He's caught on one foot looking shifty when Stephen comes in.

'Just the man,' says Stephen, smiling, slamming his work bag onto the kitchen table and shrugging his jacket onto the back of a chair. 'Any tea, Tess?' he asks. She hurries to do his bidding because it means she can turn her back and hide her face. 'Got five minutes, Carter?' Carter stares dumbly. 'I've been on to the social worker who's looking after the case of your nieces. Seems, now that Lauren's in a steady relationship with somewhere safe to live, the social worker reckons there might be a round table discussion about giving her greater access to the twins. That's great, isn't it?' Stephen accepts a cup of tea from Tessa with a 'Thanks, Love.' He heads back into his office, Carter obediently following. Tessa feels as though she's a prop in a play Stephen's starring in: she has the part of cheerful tea-making wife who doesn't mind being absentmindedly referred to as 'Love'. She feels as though she's supposed to turn now to an imaginary audience, shrug elaborately and say 'Men!'

Stephen pulls into Ellen's yard. No sign of her. He slams the door of the Mini to draw attention to himself and then calls into the house through the open door. The spring sunshine bounces warm off her flagstones. Turning round again he spies her, dressed apparently as a spaceman, bending over some boxes at the other end of her orchard.

'Hi!' He shouts and waves and starts walking towards her.

She puts a hand up to stop him coming closer and he realises she's working with opened bee hives.

Stephen stops a few metres away, and waits. A cloud of bees weaves around Ellen, bouncing off her veiled helmet, crawling over her head. She takes no notice. She removes the lid from a second box, lays it carefully on the ground and, one by one, begins to pull out and examine wax-filled frames.

'I'm looking for the queen,' she says. 'She should be laying. And then they can have Graham Wilson's rape blossom from over round the back of Stockford. Do you know him?' She talks quietly, concentrating all the while. 'There,' she says, peering closely through the black veiling of her bee suit's hat. 'Brood. She must be around somewhere.' Frame by frame, she goes through the box while Stephen stands to one side. The bees are interested in him too, but not aggressively so. One or two of them land on his arm and seem to check him for anything useful before flying away.

'If you were a nectar source they'd come home and do a little dance to show their sisters where to find you,' says Ellen, looking up briefly. She puts a tray of white, crunchy-looking stuff back in the hive and replaces the lid. 'Sugar fondant,' she explains. 'Keeps them going till the good nectar sources really open up. We steal their honey, you see.' She unzips her veiled hood and shakes it off as she walks away from the hives, a smoker in one hand and a hooked tool in the other. 'They'd die off completely if we didn't feed them in the spring.'

'We've got a vegetable garden now.' Why Stephen should feel obliged to mention Tessa's hard work in the face of Ellen's industry... 'Well, Carter Stoke's made us some raised beds.'

'You'll want chickens next,' says Ellen, grinning. 'I've got some nice young pullets for sale. Long as the fox doesn't get them. Or my neighbour's cat!'

'Promise not to lumber me with a cockerel!' laughs Stephen.

Ellen pulls off elbow-length leather gauntlets and tucks them into the pockets of her bee suit. 'Tiberius just caught you unawares. What can I do for you?' She needs to get on.

'Well, I wondered if I could ask you to do a little subtle research for me?'

'Subtle?' She kicks off her boots in the porch and leads the way into her kitchen. On the table are the remains of a hurriedly eaten breakfast. 'Sorry about the mess. Fridays are always a bit of a rush because of the market.' She reaches for a list leaning against a jug of sweet-scented late narcissus.

'I don't want to put anybody's backs up, and the Stockford Rotary Club have already done some of this work, but I'd really like someone to start from the beginning, without prejudice, so to speak.' Ellen waits for more. 'We've got to get to the bottom of this ownership of the barn that the Tresters have given to be a youth club. I don't want to get the town council on it. It seems nobody has the ability to remain un-partisan. I wondered...'

'Isn't this the sort of thing Tessa would be brilliant at?'

'Tessa?'

'Surely this is just up her street?'

Ellen doesn't like to push the vicar out but there are lettuces to plant, the sweet corn patch to mulch, wonderfully early broad beans to freeze, and holes to dig for the concrete footings of the second-hand poly tunnel she's found in the back of the *Advertiser*. Ellen stands by the door, not offering tea. For some reason Daisy's insisting she go to lunch with her today. Since when were any of them ladies who lunch?

Feeling friendless, pointless, surplus to requirements, Stephen drives the Mini up to the tower on the Bag Enderby estate and parks there. He walks round to the viewpoint and the bench in memory of a man and his dog, burglar-proofed by a concrete plinth. The rural dean's always sending 'round robin' emails to the country clergy, reminding them to make time for themselves. He switches off his mobile and sits. The church year stretches out before him: Whitsun and then the long haul towards Advent. In the far distance he can barely see the crumbling tower of St George's through the haze.

He ought to be calling David Tait. He ought to be checking with the social worker about the twins. And yes, Tessa would be exactly the person to ask to research the ancient history of the Black Barn.

But he can't talk to Tessa. He can't look her in the eye. He knows she's trying hard to make things right. But the greater her efforts, the more curmudgeonly he becomes: she makes special supper after special supper and he runs away after each for fear of an intimacy which will reveal his weakness.

Life has rendered him unsexed. And if required to perform he wouldn't be able to pretend otherwise.

His face sets around eyes squinting into the sunlight. How do you tell your wife that being stabbed by some girl in London, and then moving to a job you didn't want, has rendered you rudderless? 'Unmanned' is the word that follows him around like Kat's shadow, jeering at him, bullying him.

He knows he should tell Tessa, but she's being so good at not asking, not prying, so good at making the most of her new life. He's excluded her and she's just made new friends and new interests and is leaving him to come back to her when he's ready. He isn't taking her for granted, but she must think he is.

He checked the C of E vacancies' listings again this morning. Nothing to get his teeth into: just more part-time jobs in villages called things like Smuggly Yummerton and Dave Sub Transit. Sooner or later Len Fox will be out of prison and retired, Stephen's current job will be wrapped up with the rectorship, and he'll be let go. They'll offer the position to somebody who says they want a country Living.

He drives back to Stockford and installs himself on a high stool in April's delicatessen.

April gives the vicar her wicked grin. 'You look like you need a double cappuccino with extra chocolate.'

'I'm using you as a displacement activity.'

'Saw Tessa yesterday,' says April, handing Stephen a smooth, bitter coffee. 'She was talking about your new vegetable garden. Saying she never knew how exciting it could be to watch seeds germinate.' Stephen doesn't even know what Tessa's planted. 'She said she's got some Cosmos seedlings. She's going to have a cuttings border for the church.' Stephen doesn't know this. 'I bet she's excited about her lunch today.' What lunch? Stephen finishes his coffee and slaps the change he owes onto the counter.

'You know more about Tessa's life than I do,' he says, unfairly irritated by April's superior knowledge.

'You should ask her out on a date. That's what finished my marriage. We forgot to talk to each other.'

Chapter 10

The house is tidy. There's a fresh loaf on the bread board and folded washing waiting to be ironed on top of the machine. Tessa's desk has carefully squared piles of notes on it. There's a letter starting *Dear Mr Stone*, on the headed paper designed for St George's fundraising. The laptop's open but dormant.

There's no sign of Tessa. And nothing to say where she's gone or when she might be back.

Stephen puts the expensive bottle of Sancerre April sold him into the fridge. April's marriage might have ended because she and her husband forgot to communicate. Well, on this beautiful evening, Stephen and Tessa will sit at the top of the garden, under the fading blossom of the fruit trees and drink wine, and talk to each other.

If he and Tessa have a picnic rug, he doesn't know where it's kept. He takes a pair of scissors from the drawer and heads up to the decimated daffodil circles but finds, upon closer inspection, that among their drooping, pigeon-pecked heads there aren't any left worth picking. There's a row of frothy fronded leaves planted down one side of one of the raised beds. Are they carrot tops? Tessa's beds of spring lettuce, and the first curls of some other seedlings he doesn't recognise feeling their way up wide-spraying hazel sticks, are still blanketed by horticultural fleece.

She has made this place her own, he thinks. She fits the life she's created for herself as if she'd stitched it on to herself by hand.

In the meadow there are cows just back from evening milking. Their accusing eyes stare at Stephen over the wall.

Stephen heads back to the house, opens the wine and pours himself a glass. He turns on the radio and, standing in the doorway to the garden, listens to confirmation that he lives in a world populated by the greedy, the selfish, the thoughtless and the smug.

He pours himself another glass and doesn't telephone his mother to see whether she knows where Tessa might be. He's in no mood for a lecture. At last he thinks to check the wall calendar Tessa bought from the charity shop. Today reads: 'lunch Daisy. 7.30 Movies w girls, Pendle.' He puts bread to toast on the Aga and reaches for the Marmite.

Ellen buys April, Tessa and Daisy glasses of April's house white from the makeshift bar at the back of Pendle's community hall. The film club is showing Rufus' most recent work. It's an English romantic comedy about a man having a mid-life crisis with a male lover, complicated by an attractive au pair and a wife who's having an affair with her seven-year-old son's primary school teacher. Rufus is very good in it: gorgeous, earnest and foolish in just the right quantities. The audience laughs heartily at his mishaps and each sheds a tear when he and his wife are reunited at the end, making the gay-romantic-supporting role godfather to their kiss-and-make-up child.

Afterwards April's invited Tessa and the others back to her place for pizza.

'What's Rufus really like?' April throws a cloth over the table in the flat above the shop.

Tessa pops the cork from a bottle of Prosecco. Duralex tumblers fizz with bubbles as she pours.

'He's really very nice,' says Tessa, passing the glasses around.

'That's not enough.' April's flipping pizza dough into rounds and laying them flat on floured baking sheets. 'Come and make your pizza, Tess.' Daisy and Ellen are already arranging theirs, scattering slippery black olives over the last of last summer's tomato sauce and some of Ellen's goat's cheese.

'I went out with Rufus for about ten minutes around the time I met Stephen,' says Tessa.

'Oooh!' say the others.

Tessa giggles. 'Rufus took everything, especially everything to do with himself, terribly seriously. He was exhausting to be with. Stephen was such a breath of fresh air. Matter of fact. Honest. He has no ego, really. You can be with Stephen and be free at the same time.' All this is true. It gives Tessa a pang. She goes back to the subject of Rufus to avoid thinking about Stephen. 'Rufus, now, he's sort of... I don't know.... he's like a very rich puppy, all enthusiasm and inability to concentrate. I think he's been horribly spoiled by his success.'

'But why's he spending so much time down here on his own?'

'God knows!' says Tessa. 'He's in love with his house, I think. Though I expect he'll get bored with it soon enough. It was fantastic when he came to help Mrs Trester with the church flowers dressed in a pink satin-lined leather coat and silver trainers.'

'I wish he'd come and help at Pendle,' says Ellen with a salacious grin.

'Well, if you weren't such a happily married woman,' says April, cocking an eyebrow at Tessa as she slips the pizzas into her wide, caterer's oven, 'I might suggest he was worth a bit of attention, don't you think?'

'Not Rufus!' Tessa laughs, not minding that she's blushing because with Rufus they've got it helpfully wrong.

'You should give a dinner party,' says Daisy. 'Then we could all meet him and make up our own minds. Sit April and Ellen either side of him and let them work their charms - see what happens?'

'Not me!' says Ellen. 'I'd have to get drunk to stop being too shy to talk to him and then I might end up dancing on the table and really letting the side down.'

Daisy says, 'You'd have to invite Gormless George, of course. But factor in that he probably wouldn't come.'

'Who's Gormless George?' asks Tessa.

'Your husband isn't gormless,' says April, putting an arm around Daisy's waist. 'He's just a proper, un-reconstructed, old fashioned Sloane Ranger. Could you invite Carter Stoke to this dinner, too? I'd rather sit next to him.'

Tessa screws her toes up in her shoes and looks April straight in the eye as she laughs. Ha, ha. And deftly changes the subject. 'We should be raising our glasses to your smallholder's manual, Ellen.'

Late that night, Tessa unlocks her bicycle from a downpipe outside the surgery opposite April's. Further up the road is the municipal car park where she can see shadowy movements. Nosy, she cycles slowly up the lane so she can get a better look. The party's based around a bench parked to one side of the bus stop. There's that boyfriend of Lauren's. Some of the kids have cans of cider. Nearly all of them are smoking. White faces look up at her in the moonlight. There's Abbie.

'Evening,' says Tessa, before cycling back to April's and hammering on the door. She leaves the bicycle leaning against the shop front and hurries inside. 'Can I borrow your phone?' she asks, reaching for it before permission's given.

Tessa doesn't have to search for the number. When the phone is answered at the other end she doesn't introduce herself. Little explanation's needed before Carter Stoke's pick-up is cornering into the car park and sharp words are exchanged with Ryan. Abbie's scooped up into the safety of the cab. Tessa's bike is thrown into the back and she, with a

'Thanks again,' and a wave to April, climbs up to sit beside Abbie and cadge a lift home.

April, standing in the window of her upstairs sitting room, wiping glasses, sees it all and doesn't judge.

'He's got to go!' roars Carter.

Lauren's backed up against the wall of the kitchen at No. 3, her arms crossed over her t-shirt. A cigarette shakes between her fingers.

Carter is jabbing at her face. 'I won't have him turn Abbie. She's a good girl. Till you come back she was doing well at school. I had no trouble with the truancy officer. Nothing. Now! What's she doing out at midnight with that Ryan?'

Lauren flinches. ''s just a party, Carter.'

'What, in a car park on a Tuesday night?'

'Exams don't matter till Year Ten.'

'Won't do no good if she can't read the questions.'

'He don't mean no harm.' Lauren tries wheedling. 'Give the girl a bit of excitement.'

'Dealing's no harm, is it? You went inside two years for it. Your kids can't live with you 'cos you did it. Your friend died of it. Dealing's no harm? How stupid can you be, Lauren? Abbie's ten years old. Ryan's gotta go.'

Carter wanted to keep the family together at all costs. But he knows you cut off the cankered branch to save the tree. 'And if you're not prepared to live without him then you better go too.'

'Mr Responsible. Mr Perfect!' Lauren's face is twisted with fury and her eyes bleed disappointment. 'You can't chuck me out. It's Mum's name still on the rental for this place. I got as much right as you to live here.'

'*He* don't, though.'

132

And all the while Abbie sits at the bottom of the stairs, picking at the skin around her nails. 'But the social worker said she'd let Lauren see Trixie and Belle more because she was with him,' she says.

'I'll talk to that social worker myself,' says Carter. 'And you, Trouble, can get off to bed. It's a school day for you tomorrow, whatever you might think.'

Stephen's about to email the contact he's been given at the County Records Office when Carter knocks on the front door.

'I don't know if Tessa's here,' says Stephen, holding the door wide. Carter's not carrying any gardening kit. He usually comes to the back, anyway, and more or less lets himself in. Today he's twisting his beanie in his hands and is wearing clean trousers.

'I need to talk to you, Vicar, if you're not too...'

'Not at all.' Stephen leads the way to the office. This time he lets Carter sit the other side of his desk. He's learned that country people like a bit of formality.

'So?'

Carter feels no disloyalty. To him, it's as if Tessa has nothing to do with Stephen. They live in the same house but never see each other. She's a single woman, in Carter's mind, free to do whatever she wants. Stephen's the vicar, and he's good at his job. Which is why Carter's here.

'I got to explain what's going on with my Lauren. You said the social worker agreed to a...'

'Round table discussion...'

'Yeah, whatever, now she's settled with that Ryan and that.'

'Well, the social worker's satisfied she's much more stable, and might easily allow her more access to the twins. The episode earlier in the spring when she took them off for a week or so won't have done her any favours in the short-term. But it's really important to keep the lines of communication open so that if and when the time comes for the girls to be allowed back to live with their mother, everybody's said their piece, and hopefully everybody will understand what's going on.'

'Well, you better put the social worker off,' says Carter. He looks straight at Stephen. How can he ignore Tessa? How can he not be hypnotised by the lights in her eyes? There's something monkish about the man, thinks Carter. He and Tessa never had children. Perhaps he doesn't really like women?

'That Ryan don't live with us no more,' he continues. 'And I put Lauren on notice that if she wants to keep seeing him she don't live at No.3 neither.'

'Where's Ryan gone?'

'He's sulking in that rust bucket van he got parked out the side. I caught him dealing and using our Abbie as bait. He's no more'n scum, that man, and if I can get rid...'

Tessa pops her head round the door, surprising everyone.

'Just off,' she says. 'Oh!' She stares at Stephen and Carter like a rabbit caught in the headlights. 'All right?'

They stare back. 'Fine,' they say in unison.

'Bye, then.' In her hurry to get out, Tessa trips in the doorway, recovers her balance, and runs into the kitchen.

Carter starts up. 'I gotta go.' Maybe he shouldn't be asking the vicar for help.

Stephen's flustered. 'Yes. Your mother... Kat. She could help. Do you know where she is?'

'Yeah – but...' says Carter with a shrug. 'She won't wanna come back yet. She only just buggered off.'

Again, thinks Stephen.

Tessa waits for Carter, leaning her bicycle against his pick-up outside No. 3. She's got nothing to hide. No reason not to speak to him. What she has to say will only take a minute. She won't be late for Ellen. She's decided. She can't do this. It's wrong. Stephen might be difficult and absentminded and not care whether she's there or not but Tessa promised to stick with him through thick and thin. The affair's got to finish. She'll encourage Carter to go away, travel, broaden his horizons, get an education at the university of life.

He comes up behind her and pinches her bottom. 'Oy!'

She whips round. 'Don't!'

Grinning widely, he pushes her up the path toward the door to No.3. Tessa fights him. She hisses, 'Somebody will see!'

Carter stops, looks around. The village appears completely deserted. Kissing her again, he reaches behind Tessa and turns the key in the lock, pushing the door open, pushing her inside.

'But Dyllis!'

'Got taken into town by the community transport people.'

'Stephen...'

'He's not watching out for you.'

'Carter, stop it. Stop. We've got to stop...'

But her protests are ineffectual, already only half-meant. She's protesting while hooking a leg around his waist and letting him hoik her onto the kitchen worktop. This is scandalous, and hot, and wet, and his hands are cupping themselves around her buttocks inside her jeans. 'Stop!' She's moaning and kicking her shoes off and burying her head in his neck.

'You can take them now, if you like.' Ellen deftly catches a pair of scrawny, grey-feathered pullets. 'I'm sorry they're not very sweet to look at. But they should grow up as handsome as they'll be good layers.' Tessa tucks one new friend under each arm.

'What do I feed them?'

'Pullet feed from the farm shop. Other side of Daisy's. On that industrial estate near the motorway junction.' Ellen remembers that Tessa doesn't drive. 'I think they have a delivery service. I'll get you the number.'

The women walk back up the orchard. Ellen finds a cardboard box to which she adds a handful of straw. Tessa carefully puts her chickens into the box. Ellen, businesslike, closes the lid.

'Carter's bringing you up the hen house from the Old Rectory?'

'He says it's perfectly serviceable. Rufus is chucking money at his livestock. His are to be rare pedigree something-or-others and they're to have state-of-the-art accommodation with strip-lighting, if you don't mind.'

'For a man you say doesn't know where his next crust's coming from, he's really throwing the cash about.'

'I think he gets royalties from adverts and things. Money we'd consider riches and he thinks isn't enough to live on.'

'At this rate Carter's going to have to give up all his other jobs around the place and work full-time for Mr Stone. Where are you going to put your hen house?'

'Under the apple trees at the top of the garden. Carter's got some leftover electric fence from somewhere he says will protect them from the fox.'

'I wish Carter Stoke would give me some of his leftovers. Come on, admit, he is quite the *Lady Chatterley's Lover* type.'

Tessa changes the subject fast. 'I think *you* could do a brilliant smallholders' book. With my help.' Tessa laughs, a little nervously, not liking having to sell herself.

Ellen jams a straw hat onto her head and grabs a hoe from her front porch. Its sharpened blade gleams. 'It's all very well getting excited about writing books when we're all pissed at April's and the evening is long and we're just talking to amuse ourselves. But seriously, I don't have more than about fifteen spare minutes a day. And during those fifteen minutes I like sitting down and doing nothing. The idea of writing a book feels like school work to me. And I was crap at that.'

Tessa's disappointed. She needs to line work up for herself and thought the idea of a smallholder's manual is just the thing to get onto after she finishes Daisy's chilli book. 'But I'll do the bulk of it,' she protests. 'You just give me the outlines and I'll fill in all the words.'

'Tessa, you've never gardened before, have you?'

Tessa holds her ground. 'I didn't know anything about chillies, either.'

'But I'll have to explain everything. Maybe we could do it in the winter. God, with Stephen wanting me to research things, and you and Daisy wanting to turn me into a writer, I don't know when I'm ever going to get my hoeing done. You hoeing? Or is Carter Stoke doing it all for you?'

Now Tessa loses her cool. 'He's just being neighbourly. I think he likes to be able to escape from those sisters of his. Imagine the responsibility the poor boy has. I'm the vicar's wife. It's my job to...'

'Give him solace in his hour of need?' Tessa freezes, stares. Ellen's face cracks. She bursts out laughing. 'I'm sorry. I'm sorry. I'm not accusing you of anything.' But Tessa can't recover. Ellen's yard wheels around her. She thinks she's going to be sick. She stumbles back, collapses onto the mounting block, blacks out for a second.

'Are you all right?'

Tessa nods, unable to speak.

137

'Shall I get you some water?'

Tessa shakes her head: anything in her mouth might make her sick.

The world comes slowly to a standstill around her. She must remember to eat lunch in future. Cycling around these villages is more exhausting than scooting across flat London with lots of sets of traffic lights to catch her breath at. She changes the subject. 'What's Stephen asking you to research? Surely you do enough for the benefice?'

'I said I thought he'd better ask you. Hasn't he mentioned it?'

Tessa hasn't seen Stephen for long enough to have a conversation with him for over a week.

Stephen knows his fear of chickens is irrational. But ever since he was attacked by Ellen's cockerel he's kept well away from his parishioners' sharp-clawed, vicious-beaked, gimlet-eyed friends. And now he's come home to find a hen-house has appeared from nowhere and a pair of mangy-looking beasts are pottering about under the fruit trees. The remains of the daffodil stalks have been mown. The whole lawn has been mown. Carter...

We should be paying him, thinks Stephen, turning into the house, into his office, sitting down at the safety of his desk. *We can't afford to pay him! I should be mowing and making vegetable gardens*, he says to himself. 'But I don't want to be a gardener. I want to be a good vicar. A better vicar.' he says out loud, looking up at the ceiling. 'Come on, God, help me out here.'

Long recovered from her unexplained fainting fit, Tessa's mood is light as she comes back from dropping a caramelised garlic tart off for Dyllis. 'No! I didn't make it. Ellen did.' She skips up the front path, rootling for her keys. She can see

Stephen lost in something at his computer in his study. 'Bugger it,' she says, not finding the keys and ducking round to the back of the house where hopefully the door will already be open. She kicks off her shoes and runs barefoot up the lawn to check on her chickens. They already seem perfectly at home. They have water, they have food. They're so funny and bossy, even without their grown up feathers yet. They won't lay for at least another six weeks, Ellen says. Never mind. Tessa carefully clips the lead onto the battery to switch on the electric fence. She's determined not to lose them to the fox before she's even had a single egg out of them.

'Tessa!'

She turns to see Stephen standing in the open kitchen doorway. She waves at him from the other side of her vegetable beds. The carrots have sprouted, she notices, between rows of onions already ten inches high. Ellen says she mustn't touch them or the onion fly and the carrot fly will have the lot before she's tasted any of them. She has salads and spinach and glorious rainbow chard, the multi-coloured stalks lit up by the late afternoon sun. The potatoes have pretty, flat leaves. She picks up a hoe and runs it gently between her rows; not that there's a single weed yet, the soil's too new. A hundred and twenty quid, she thinks, was a bargain price for the pleasure she's getting from this lot. She must pick some baby spinach and take it up for Dyllis to have with her tart.

'Tessa,' Stephen's suddenly standing right beside her, shocking her.

'What do you think?' she asks him, taking one step away.

'We've got to talk.'

139

Chapter 11

Tessa's heart stumbles. Her face burns. Dyllis had seemed off when she saw her earlier. Did Dyllis see Tessa and Carter snogging? Has she told Stephen? Tessa told Carter to be careful!

'What do we need to talk about?' She hangs the hoe back on its nail. She tidies what's already carefully arranged. She's no longer flushing when she exits the shed. Stephen's already gone back into the house. Tessa takes one final look over the valley and the woods. The steeple of Stockford Church piercing the haze transforms the view into a Turner.

Of course the idyll couldn't last. She's sabotaged the perfection by allowing herself to take more. Without Carter, she could have made this work. With Carter on the scene, though, she's been too happy, like a child doing something they know they shouldn't because the glee they get for that naughty moment is irresistible.

She heads slowly down towards the open kitchen door. She straightens her shoulders and holds her head high: this might all be her fault, but she won't slope in hang-dog and give him the physical upper hand before he's even started.

There's wine on the kitchen table and he's pouring two glasses. Tessa takes hers and sniffs it. It smells of fish. She takes a sip. Eurgh! Holding the wine, she leans against the Rayburn, its heat warming her back.

We're like strangers, she thinks. She can't remember the last time they had a friendly chat over supper together. 'What do you want to talk about?' She knows she sounds defensive.

Stephen pulls a chair out and sits down. He puts his head in his hands. 'It's all my fault,' he starts.

What's all his fault?

Hold on. Wouldn't he accuse her if he knew about Carter? Would it be a relief? Break the sultry mood between them with a thunderstorm of shouting?

But from his demeanour it's suddenly clear that this little talk is about nothing new. Something must have happened to make him decide today's the day for their annual you-never-put-the-lid-on-the-toothpaste-ing. It always begins like this. He'll take responsibility for what's wrong in their relationship. And in doing so claim the moral high ground before the battle's even begun.

'What's your fault?'

And anger begins to boil inside Tessa. Stephen's going to say they must spend more time together, not be bored by one another, have contrived little picnics at times inconvenient to them both in order to preserve... Time was, she had nothing better to do. And she made all kinds of efforts until, constantly rejected, she found new pastimes. Now it's not just Carter, it's the life: the baking, the research for Rufus, movies with the girls, the chickens, the garden...

'What?' she wants to know.

Stephen takes his head out of his hands, pushes his chair back, stands up, pulls off his dog collar. He shakes his head, as if clearing it of something.

'Come on,' he says, taking her wine and putting it down. 'Please will you show me round your vegetable garden?'

Wind taken out of her sails, Tessa can do nothing but point out to him that she's planted four different kinds of lettuces.

'I've got to say I'm no big fan of chickens.' He's trying to be conversational but his words come out sulky.

'They only look so scrawny because they're getting their grown-up feathers.' Tessa unclips the electric fence and climbs in with them. They skitter behind the apple tree and peer round nervously. Tessa takes a handful of feed from a bin she's put next to their little ark and squats down, holding the feed out, trying to tempt the chickens to come to her. They stay put. 'Ellen says they'll start laying later in the summer. They need to grow a bit first.'

'They're so mean-looking. Look at their eyes.'

Exasperated, Tessa stands up and confronts her husband. 'When I first met you, I made you bring me down here, do you remember?' Stephen remembers. 'And you fetched me from the station in Stockford in the Mini. You'd been clearing the garden behind your mother's house with a chainsaw and you'd had a bonfire. Your hands were covered with oil and you stank of two-stroke. I never thought you'd be the sort to turn out frightened of chickens.'

One of the hens has bravely come forward. Tessa kneels down and strokes the new grown-up feathers on her back.

'If you'd given me the choice, I'd have said don't get them.' Stephen shuffles from foot to foot. Is it so important he be honest? He knows it makes him sound a wimp. He's conscious that the hands in his pockets are soft and pinkly clean. But he's a vicar, not a smallholder. Tessa climbs out of the chickens' pen.

'I thought you wanted to have a row, when you said we needed to talk.'

'I did,' he says. He looks lost. She doesn't put her arms around him. 'I do,' he says, staring straight at her. 'But I don't know what we should row about,' he lies. He wants her to accuse him. If he can barely admit to his fear of chickens, how can he possibly bring up the fact that he's frightened he'll never be able to make love to her again? 'I can feel it, the row. It's like a scratch I can't itch. All the time. But I can't put my finger on it.'

His thick grey hair stands on end. He's so much more healthy-looking than he was in London. Tessa and Stephen are much of a height. They can look directly at one another. He is gorgeous, she thinks. To look at, anyway. If only she didn't find his shuffling about being uncertain and honest about not liking chickens so unbelievably irritating! And why want to talk now, when he's been conscientiously avoiding her for months?

'I think you just don't like it that I've made a life for myself down here.' Guilt drives Tessa to take a few cheap, cowardly shots. 'You want to come home and find me goodly tapping away in my study, waiting for you to tell me all your excitements. And instead I've got bored waiting and gone to the cinema. Or to research Rufus' house.'

'Rufus!'

'It's work, Stephen. I love my work. Like you love yours. It's great. I've got enough to do I can jump between projects.' She's exaggerating where the work's concerned, but she feels this is what her life is becoming, will certainly be. 'I never get bored. And this....' Her arm takes in the modest sweep of her vegetable garden. 'I never thought I'd have this. This is what I do while you worry about other people's children, about the youth club, and the ownership of the Black Barn. And come home too late to eat and too busy to talk. Would you rather I just sat about and waited?'

'It's great,' protests Stephen. He steps back and almost falls onto the onion bed. 'When I get a proper job you're not going to want to leave.'

Tessa's on a roll. 'Of course I don't want to leave. How many times do I have to tell you? Let's make a go of it. Let's stay here. Our food miles are down. Our carbon footprint's down. I feel as though I'm making a contribution.' She's never thought anything of the sort: cornered by his moral superiority she feels forced to justify herself.

'But I feel...' Stephen stands, empty hands held wide to her. 'Redundant.'

'Well, that's hardly my fault. I've barely seen you for months. So I've made myself a life. What good would it do me if I did need you for anything? I'm fine. I'm self-sufficient. I've had to learn to be. It's not great for us but...'

There's half a tray of seedlings labelled 'Pot Marigold' by the shed. Tessa waters them, and then begins to prick them out, using an old kitchen knife to lever the tiny plants gently apart from one another, tucking one into each corner of the raised beds. Carter says the slugs don't like the smell of them. That if she plants them amongst the cabbage seedlings the cabbages will have whole leaves. He's given her enough to keep the slugs off everything.

Stephen rubs his face and sighs. 'I was in the deli in Stockford last week. April knows more about what you're up to than I do.'

'You have to ask, Stephen.'

'I am now. Let's go for a walk. It's the summer. Come on, Tessa. Isn't that what summer evenings are for?'

Tessa takes a bowl of baked eggshells and smashes them into tiny pieces with a shard of terracotta pot. She scatters shell round some newly emerging kale as a physical barrier against the slug. She's not sure she trusts the marigolds.

'Take that, you bastards,' she threatens. Then, 'Do you mind if I don't walk? Truth is, I'm knackered. I'd really like to go straight to bed with no supper.'

'Is there any supper?'

'I don't know. Can't you be in charge?'

Tessa curls up under the duvet, her face to the window. Downstairs she can hear Stephen pottering. He'll be creating something amazing and delicious and unexpected from the meagre ingredients of her larder. Then he'll be self-effacing about how good it is instead of pleased she likes it.

She rolls onto her back and stares at the ceiling.

She's been enjoying herself so hard she's been refusing to acknowledge the fact that the fun can't possibly last: this dream life, like being in a film, of sex with Carter, talk with Rufus, nights out with Daisy, Ellen and April. She's content. No, more than that. She's actively happy. But her happiness depends on everything staying the same: of it always being now, of things never moving on.

She turns onto her other side and looks at Stephen's bedside table. The black plastic alarm clock, the glass with a dribble of dusty water in the bottom, an illustrated edition of Ted Hughes' *Season Songs*... Tessa reaches over. She looks briefly at the spare, rich poetry and hurriedly puts the book away. Dyllis told her once that Stephen used to be a poetry freak as a boy.

It's amazing that they can still share the same bed night after night and yet have become complete strangers.

He can't just appear like this and try to lay claim to her. He's shown no interest in her or their marriage for months. In fact, he's actively avoided both.

How would it be if she and Stephen met for the first time now? If he wooed her again? If she were single now, is Stephen the sort of man she'd want to ask her out?

She draws her knees up to her chest and hugs them tight.

All the sex... it's lovely, but it's not fair on Carter. He needs a younger model, someone who can travel with him. He doesn't need a nearly-forty vicar's wife whose new best friends are her chickens.

Carter needs to be set free.

Breaking eggs into ramekins over fresh garden spinach, cream cheese and grated cheddar, Stephen kicks himself for screwing up his attempted reconciliation.

He'd been going to suggest he apply for the Stockford job combined with the Hindle benefices. The rural dean said he should. He was going to admit his – he winces – 'erectile dysfunction' and ask for Tessa's support in getting help. So that they could try and have that child she used to talk about when they first got married.

Stephen always assumes it's his job to mend things. It would never occur to him that if he just sat with Tessa and waited, she might begin to communicate with him herself.

In the Rayburn the eggs fluff up like mini soufflés and he puts one on a tray for Tessa with a piece of toast and a glass of orange juice.

He takes it upstairs, hurries the supper in to the bedroom, dumps the tray on the bed and, giving her no time to thank, or talk, or apologise, he runs away downstairs, shutting the door to his office behind him.

It is six more weeks before the crisis comes. Tessa is sitting on a stool in April's deli, deliberating between hot chocolate and a bottle of Organic Orange Squash. She's gone off coffee.

'Hello!' April waves her hands in front of Tessa and brings her back to the present.

'Orange,' says Tessa. 'You know what's really annoying? When I first got here I was put on pills for an overactive thyroid and suddenly I had all the energy in the world. Now I feel they're just making me fat and sleepy.'

'Maybe you should go back to the doctor and see whether you need to keep taking them. Have a blood test. Change the dose. Doesn't thyroid need constant balancing?'

Daisy jingles through the door with a tray of bright red, yellow, green and purple sweet peppers for April to sell. 'What's this?' she says, dumping the tray and looking Tessa over. 'Not another fainting fit?'

Tessa sips absentmindedly at her orange. It spills down her white shirt. 'What's the matter with me?'

April comes round from behind the counter and perches on a bar stool next to her new friend. 'You're feeling fat?' Tessa nods. 'Tired?'

'Yup.'

'Fussy about your food lately?' asks Daisy.

'She's gone off caffeine,' says April.

'Sounds to me as though you ought to do a pregnancy test.' Daisy drops her bomb unconsciously. She's only joking. She's laughing, look.

But Tessa's mouth has gone dry. She's fumbling hard in her purse for change.

Tessa sits for an hour on the side of her bed looking at the white plastic stick with two clear blue lines indicating the delicacy of her condition. The bells of St George's peal four o'clock. Tessa, terrified of being confronted by Stephen when she's hardly taken in the situation herself, hurries up the lane to the empty church where she doubts she'll be disturbed.

'And I'll have nothing from you!' she says, jabbing a finger at the ever-hovering dove above the altar. She turns her back on the dove and looks for somewhere to hide. The door to the tower opens. She climbs the steep stone spiral to the top. The view is breathtaking. She sits in the space between a crenellation and for the first time considers her belly. It's not fat. It's hard. Filled out smooth where once it would have been wrinkled skinny. Sort of flat up to her breasts. She realises she's lost her waist.

She's going to have to go to the doctor to get the pregnancy confirmed. Then what? Tell Stephen she's expecting another man's child? Put a call in to the rural dean to warn her there might be talk? Compose a note resigning from the St George's Tower fundraising committee: well, she can hardly behave like an upstanding vicar's wife if she's to go round spawning the local bad family's heirs – can she? Tessa stifles a giggle. Her eyes brim.

She can't go to Dyllis.

She should go to Dyllis.

The idea of going home to her own mother...

Oh shit!

She smoothes her hands over her stomach once more. There's no way she'll contemplate getting rid of the child. She casts her mind back, trying to remember when her last period might have been. Before Easter? That long?

Her mind whirrs. Stephen will want a divorce. He'll hate her. Then, without her to slow him down, he'll disappear to some Godforsaken concrete wilderness where he'll lash himself with poverty and deprivation as a punishment for letting his marriage fail. Tessa's in no doubt that Stephen will insist on laying the blame for this upon himself.

And what about Carter? No, she does not want to set up home with him. And he's much too young to want to be tied down by Tessa and her baby.

It's not supposed to be like this. She's not supposed to be torn. She's supposed to be allowed to wallow in the glorious miracle of it. All these years of trying and now, when she was convinced she couldn't... At last, at nearly forty, she's to be one of those geriatric mothers she's read about.

Four tractors pulling trailers piled high with silage rumble past and...

'Ah!' She leaps up. The stones shifted. She knows they did. She stares hard at the wall. Nothing. It all looks exactly the same. She must be imagining things. Her heart racing, she skids down the stone staircase and escapes onto solid ground.

In his head Stephen's turned over a new leaf. Without forcing anything, he's going to be home at a reasonable hour every night. He's going to visit his mother at least once a week. With subtle wooing, he's going to make Tessa love him again. He's got a copy of the *Advertiser* on the front seat of the car along with a lamb neck fillet for a stew, some new potatoes, and a hunk of Ellen's goat's cheese for afterwards. Or he could bake it with mint and serve it to Tessa with bread as a starter. He hopes Tessa's made some bread.

He's going to look in the back of the *Advertiser* for a lawnmower. It's not fair to use Carter like this and not pay him. Stephen's going to help with the garden. It'll do him good. Bulk him up a bit. Make him sexier – maybe – more like he used to be when Tessa, so London in her gold ballet shoes, thick black tights and grey flannel shorts, first stepped off the train at Stockford station and commented archly that he might have taken the straw out of his hair before coming to fetch her. He feels ridiculous worrying about how sexy he looks. He's not vain.

But he looked this morning and what he saw was not alluring. He's not fat but his belly's sagging. His shoulders are naturally broad but his thin arms hang off them, out of proportion to the breadth of his chest. Without muscle he has a sloppy barrel-shaped torso, stick legs, and these spidery arms: he looks like an out of condition troll, he thinks. And he needs a haircut. Vanity, vanity. This morning he flexed his biceps in the bathroom mirror and nothing happened.

He's going to start with mowing.

And he's going to ask Tessa to help him with the problem over the ownership of the Black Barn. Marriages need joint projects to help them move along. He's given this advice to other couples for nearly twenty years. Relationships don't stay still. People change. To keep a marriage fresh you have to

149

find things in common and invest in them in order to tie yourselves together. That's why so many couples divorce when the children leave home.

And he is going to tell her about his problem. Maybe they can work on it together. At least he'll feel better for being honest with her. And, though Stephen knows he can never refuse an outside request for help, that simply means he must fit the helping round Tessa, not expect Tessa to wait while the Church takes its endless pounds of flesh.

And he'll ask if she'd like it if he applied for the Stockford job. For her he'll try and see if they can stay around here. He won't force her back to a city until she's ready. He'll let her play the country dream until it lets her down too.

'Hello?' he calls into the empty house.

She must be out.

Stephen chops veg for stew, adds lamb to the pot, slips it all into the bottom oven of the Rayburn. It's six o'clock. The calendar hanging on a nail by the phone has nothing written on it for tonight. He sits down and opens the *Advertiser*. Mowers... even second-hand, they're not cheap.

At the chilli farm beyond Bag Enderby, Daisy checks her email: Tessa hasn't sent over the chapter she said she'd have finished.

At the Old Rectory, Rufus tweets: 'Tessa hasn't called for days. The good life's only fun with an audience.' He chucks his BlackBerry onto the kitchen table and goes to the black fridge, fingers a bottle of wine, pulls it out, flips it like a barman and reaches for a corkscrew.

In the churchyard, Carter swings the mower round the rows of lichened headstones as if it weighs nothing. He stops to re-light the stub end of his roll-up and glances down the hill towards the vicarage. It looks closed up. Perhaps she's gone to London. He and Tessa never make a plan to meet: their encounters just happen. He won't wait for her. Nor she him, he thinks, grinning, flicking the end of his fag into the yew beside the lychgate.

Carter imagines what it might be to be free of responsibility, to feel able, like his mother did, to walk out one morning and not come back unless he felt the urge. Tessa says he should be travelling the world. She says at his age he should be sleeping on beaches and climbing mountains and working his passage to South America just for the sake of it.

He hauls on the mower's starter motor again and pushes it hard under the tower, jamming it in between the rough stone buttress and the wall to get that dandelion out.

And in Stockford, April clocks the fact that Tessa's unlocked bicycle's been left leaning against the downpipe outside the surgery for hours now. Even in Stockford somebody will take a bicycle if it's just left there overnight. She steps out and wheels it through the back gate into her yard and texts Tessa to tell her where she's hidden it.

At Clapham Junction, Tessa ignores her bleeping phone, gets off the train and takes the underground to Kentish Town. She's already regretting her decision to come to London. The Tube is stand-up, armpit-stink crowded. In her mind she looks at the still hare drawn on the cover of Stephen's copy of Ted Hughes' poems.

Coming out of the Tube, she crosses the road and cuts right to where her mother still lives in the house where Tessa grew up. Her mother never understood why Tessa married a vicar. She's always had opinions about Stephen which Tessa didn't want to hear. But now Tessa needs a burrow to hide in, and she knows this won't be the first place Stephen will think to look.

She has a key but rings the bell. She hates the idea of disturbing her mother, if not in tantric trance, then potentially in the middle of a séance, or Green Party action group meeting – though Tessa suspects that the Greens might be a bit mainstream for her mother these days. The peeling stucco is out of place now, amongst the bright pastel shades the gentrifying incomers have chosen for their houses. The front steps are still crumbling, though they seem no more broken than they were when schoolgirl Tessa used to sit on them in the late afternoon sunshine, reading Thomas Hardy to escape the city heat.

'Oh my god!' Her mother holds the door wide and, rather than hugging Tessa, she looks at her. 'You got fat!'

'Can I come in, Mum?'

'Where's the God Squad?'

'Stephen's at home.'

'Are you staying?' Tessa has no luggage. 'Only we're a full house at the moment.'

'Can I sleep on the sofa?'

'I wish you'd called before...' Tessa's hurried along a narrow corridor and downstairs to the basement kitchen.

The wobbly table's the same. The cracked Victorian tiled floor's the same. The dresser's still sticky with dusty kitchen grime. A cat stretches lazily and re-positions itself, proprietor of the large, cushioned armchair. Tessa sinks onto a hard chair. She isn't sure she's going to be able to fight the urge to weep.

She takes a deep breath.

'OK, Mum. I need to tell you the whole story and then I'll know what to do. And please... don't interrupt!'

Stephen wanders nonchalantly up the lane, his hands in his pockets, thinking he might find Tessa at his mother's. Or that Dyllis might tell him where Tessa is without his having to ask. He waves at Carter mowing the churchyard.

Dyllis is eating a supper of toast and honey with a cup of whisky-laced tea.

'Would you like some?'

He pours himself a whisky and drowns it at the tap. Outside, skylarks are still singing. He helps Dyllis into the garden and they sit and watch the limpid light of the summer evening drench the view.

'Where's Tessa?'

'I don't know,' admits Stephen.

'You want to be careful, you two. Too much of this ships-in-the-night business and one day you'll find you're poles apart.'

'I tried to talk to her about it the other night.'

'And what did she say?'

'Did you know she's got some chickens?'

'Have you put them to bed for her?'

'What do you mean?'

'Well, if she's off gallivanting somewhere I expect she'd like you to shut them up. Otherwise the fox'll get them.'

Stephen stares at Dyllis, leaps up, 'Shit!'

'Go on,' says his mother. 'Prove you're not entirely useless.'

And Dyllis sits on in the gloaming, a frown criss-crossing the lines on her face. She'd thought at Easter... She must have been wrong then. The other day she'd noticed Tessa outside No.3 looking very hair-brushed-for-a-weekday-morning. Or is it Rufus who's the threat? Suddenly chill, Dyllis rocks herself to standing and shuffles on tired feet back into the house.

Stephen hurries out of the house, visions of marauding

foxes already decapitating Tessa's precious birds...

And things do happen in slow motion. It was the same when the girl slashed his face and broke his nose. It had been as if he watched the event load up, pixel by pixel, on a very slow screen. And now it is the same. The sharp silhouette of the shifted stones on top of the church tower. The slam of the mower into the church wall. The idling of its engine as Carter leans into the buttress to light a cigarette one-handed. The snarling griffon gargoyle's head smashing to the ground, hitting Carter on the shoulder and knocking him back so that he loses his balance and hits his head hard on the edge of the Trester family tomb. The mower shudders to a standstill. The whisky jags at Stephen's chest as he runs to see if Carter's dead.

SUMMER

Chapter 12

Tessa lies in her mother's bed, staring at the cow-shaped crack in the ceiling. She's been lying awake there since she climbed in last night. It smells both warmly familiar and stinking. Her mother always had better things to do than change sheets. Tessa's old room, on the top floor, with its window in the apex of the roof looking out over a Victorian view of brick-backed houses, is let to a lodger described lovingly by her mother as 'lost'. She'll be this month's stray, a person taken on as a project, a person who could be so much more if only she'd let Tessa's mother help her.

Tessa has no patience for these intense, doomed relationships.

She's going to have to move on. Coming all the way to Kentish Town has resolved nothing. Perhaps she can go and stay with Rufus?

She can hear her mother's busy life happening downstairs. The phone rings. The front door slams. An unfamiliar voice shouts a question about whether there's any food in for supper.

Tessa will go in a minute. Head back to Stockford. She's just got to come out with it. Tell Stephen. Tell Carter. They can join in or not. It's up to them. Running away's just made much more of a drama out of what's already a crisis. She hopes Stephen's been looking after the chickens. She won't ring him, though. She's not ready for the questions yet.

The Tube is almost empty. Tessa hugs her handbag over her stomach. She's hungry. At Clapham Junction she buys herself a muffin and a bottle of water. She'll have to be careful what she eats now. Shouldn't she be taking folic acid or something? Or is it too late for that? A sudden shot of fear that she might have harmed this child in some way because she didn't know she was expecting it...

This will be a real conversation with Stephen. Now they're going to have to talk. No prevaricating. No hiding behind habits with the toothpaste.

She's pregnant by another man.

She blinks back tears.

She's been so stupid.

Does she have to choose between the baby and Stephen? He wouldn't want her to. She can't. The baby wins. But...

Tessa comes to when the taxi pulls up. Carefully, she pushes her feet out of the car, pulls herself upright, looks at the plain, friendly walls of the house. It seems half asleep.

She walks round the back. The chickens are happily tearing at the grass under their trees. They've run out of food so she gives them a handful of corn and another of grit so that when they do begin to lay, their yolks will be deep yellow and their egg shells strong.

She fills the can from the rainwater butt and waters the lettuces, though she knows she should leave them until the heat of the sun is gone or the water will make them wilt. She'd pick some leaves for Dyllis if she thought it likely the old lady would eat anything so packed with vitamins.

The back door stands wide. There's no sign of Stephen.

She checks the road at the front of the house: no Mini, either.

The possibility of reprieve is not something she's contemplated. She runs upstairs and turns on the bath. To be able to face Stephen with clean hair and in an ironed shirt somehow improves the situation immeasurably.

Sitting in the Mini with a disgusting coffee from A&E, Stephen stares blindly out of the windscreen. He's got to call Tessa.

He's got to ask her... He switches on his phone, scrolls down to Tessa's number and, at last, presses 'Ring'.

'All right?' A voice he doesn't recognise. Must have dialled wrong. He apologises and switches off. Tries again. The same stranger's voice answers,

'Hello?' There's a pause. Then, 'Hey! You the husband?'

'Is Tessa around?' asks Stephen.

'Nah, gone. Left the phone behind. I could send it on. Hey, shall we send on Tessa's phone?'

Stephen's mother-in-law comes on the line, massively self-righteous. 'Stephen?'

'I...'

'You great fool,' she interrupts.

That's it. He knew it. Tessa has left him. Of course she's left him. Stephen drops the phone. No tears - just hot, agonising lava exploding in his head.

Tessa ties her wet hair into a ponytail. She wears a loose shirt over jeans, the top button of which she leaves undone. She is amazed to find that from one day to the next her clothes no longer fit. In the mirror she examines herself sideways. No bump. More a tree-trunking. She smoothes her hands over her stomach and wishes she could have a picture of what's happening inside. They don't give you a scan till you're months gone, do they? Will there be a little face? Teeny legs?

The house is still silent. No sign that Stephen's even noticed Tessa's absence. The raging need she felt to tell him everything is burnt out now. She stuffs her hands in her pockets and walks out. She doesn't notice the toothy-pegged appearance of the church tower. She's not looking. Instead, she turns right down the lane and up the drive to the Old Rectory. Stephen can come and find her there - if he wants.

Stephen makes it home to find April unloading Tessa's bicycle from the back of her delivery van.

'I thought I'd bring your mother a cake,' she says, cool as a cucumber. 'And I hid this behind the shop last night. Tessa must have forgotten it.'

Stephen marvels at the speed with which a woman's girlfriends can get wind of something happening and be unable to stop themselves coming to sniff about.

'Well, she's not here.' There's an understatement. 'And if you don't mind... A great chunk of church tower fell on Carter Stoke's head last night...'

April's eyes are wide. 'Fell on his head?'

'How else would it get there?'

'Well, at the market today they were saying...'

'Sorry, April, I haven't got time for this kind of gossip. Do you mind?'

Raging, he punches the number for the rural dean into the telephone, leaves a garbled message about the tower, and runs back to the Mini. He doesn't see Tessa's bag hanging on the back of the chair, her jacket back on its hook in the hall.

Who's going to look after Abbie? Stephen hasn't seen hide nor hair of Lauren for weeks now. Did she go off with the new boyfriend? No, his converted lorry's still there, sticking its nose out into the road. Stephen slams the Mini into gear and roars up to the T-junction, past his mother's house. Dyllis is waving him in. He can see April's in there. Women! He has no time for tea and gossip now.

Stephen is of the opinion that God doesn't decree a purpose in anything. Stephen believes that it's up to man to find the purpose. The test should be looked for in every little daily occurrence. Stephen thinks that the man who goes through life taking the easy option is failing to see the point. Man's job is to make the world better, thinks Stephen. God put us here to see whether we'd rise to the challenge of finding a way not to wreck the place. So he failed Tessa and she's left him. Well, he will not collapse into a self-pitying heap. Neither will he let Carter Stoke down.

Somewhere in his boiling brain he recognises that the Carter Stoke crisis has come at a wonderful time. He can rise to the occasion, ignore the fact that Tessa's left him, prioritise Abbie's pastoral care – and then dive into the morass that is the mess Len Fox left the Stockford Parish Office in. Without these jobs to keep him busy he'd be freefalling. He drives away from the void of his personal life as fast as the Mini Clubman will take him.

'I should go home.' The story's told.

'Only to leave again? Stay here,' says Rufus. 'It's summer. The house is comfortable. Let me look after you. Till you decide anything.'

Rufus is a natural in the role of nurse as well as confidant. He disappears upstairs and comes back with a cashmere blanket to tuck round Tessa's knees. He fetches her a glass of lemon barley water. She checks his face for the threat that he might be doing this out of anything other than straight friendship. What happened to the angry young man she had dinner with a few times before she met Stephen?

Tessa hugs her knees. She thought she'd come home and find Stephen looking for her. It seems as though Stephen hasn't even noticed that she's gone. Her head droops.

This is going to be so public. So many people are going to feel they have a perfect right to pronounce on the situation. Mrs Trester...

'What about Carter?' asks Rufus.

'He doesn't want me. I don't want him to feel trapped. I want to set him free.'

Rufus squats down beside her chair and gives her a sympathetic hug.

'Darling, this is so hard for you. You've got to be brave. But there's been an accident. Well... something happened. I heard about it at April's this morning. It seems last night Stephen got drunk and then attacked Carter in the churchyard. Carter's in hospital.'

'What?'

Carter looks bigger than ever, uncontained, despite the tight enveloping of the hospital bed. He's in hospital-issue pyjamas.

'I'm sorry. I didn't think to bring you anything,' says Stephen. 'How are you feeling?'

'I gotta get out of here, Vicar,' says Carter. 'There's nobody home for Abbie.'

'Where's Lauren?'

'I wouldn't trust her to feed my hamster, not while there's that Ryan around.'

'He still living at your place?'

'In and out. Can't stop him, can I? 's not my name on the rental. Tell Abbie there's beans in the cupboard. Unless...' Carter looks at Stephen. 'Would Tessa look after her tonight? She'd be no trouble. Promise. That way I know she'll get a square meal at the end of the day. Leave it to Lauren and she'll end up with half a ten of Lambert and Butler and a can of cider for her tea.'

'Lauren's not up to getting her girls back, is she?' Stephen doesn't know how to tell Carter that Tessa's gone.

''s my Mum's fault Lauren's so off the rails.' Carter stares out at the heat haze boiling above the roof tops around the hospital. 'Lauren was so needy. Mum couldn't handle it. Nan always said Mum went a bit mad when she had Lauren. So they never bonded right.'

'I knew your Mum, once,' says Stephen. 'She was a couple of years older than me. I thought she was the most beautiful...'

'That's what all men think.'

'Not like that!' Stephen blushes. 'She ran away for the first time when I was sixteen. I remember the village all talking about it. Her mum just said she'd come back when she was hungry.'

'That was my nan,' says Carter. 'Me and Lauren lived with her in the old cottages before they were condemned. My granddad taught me gardening. Weeding for him kept me in penny chews from the post office what used to be at the back of the pub. If my nan hadn't of died after the move to No. 3 then Mum wouldn't of had to come back. Mum got landed with two teenagers on top of baby Abbie.'

'You turned out all right.'

'Yeah, well... mums and daughters.'

'Would you like me to come and fetch you home tomorrow?' Stephen asks.

''f you won't have Abbie, will you check on her?'

Stephen can promise nothing. He can't look after Abbie if he's alone in the house. He won't ask Anna Trester: Anna's would be a cold bosom to be cast upon in anybody's hour of need. Perhaps he'll be able to take Abbie home to Dyllis. Abbie could have his old room. Stephen can sleep on the couch.

'I'll do what I can,' he says.

Stockford Primary provides a full stop to the road at the top of the Withy Green Estate. At the end of the day the children spill down into their homes or to the high street where they wait for minibuses to return them to the outlying villages.

Stephen finds ten-year-old Abbie sitting on a wall in a row

with her six-year-old nieces, Lauren's daughters, Trixie and Belle, the little girls waiting to be collected by their Nanna. He parks the Mini and steps out.

'All right, Vicar?' Abbie's face is insolent. Stephen can see the bulge of the pack of ten fags in the pocket of her hoodie. She's chewing gum. Her hair's scraped back as it was the day he saw her in the smoking cinders of the Black Barn. But she got herself to school this morning. To look at her, nobody would know that she hadn't been washed and brushed by a proud mother this morning.

'Come sniffing after little children, have you?' she asks.

Stephen can't help but laugh. She's certainly sharp.

''fraid not,' he answers, leaning against the wall beside the girls and nodding at the teacher supervising the children's collection. 'Carter's had an accident,' he says. If Abbie's going to play hard boiled, he'll treat her as such. 'He didn't come home last night because he's in hospital.' He looks down and sees Abbie wide-mouthed.

'Hotstipal?' she says, shocked into childish pronunciation. Stephen can almost see the cogs moving in her brain. She knows that without Carter she has nobody to look after her. The fear of social services flashes behind her eyes.

'Only for one more night.'

'Oh, fuck that then,' and she jumps off the wall, breathless with relief. Stephen can see the Hindle Green bus idling at the bottom of the hill. Abbie starts running for it, sending her nieces' Nanna spinning as she thunders past.

'Wait!' Stephen cries. He sprints after her, only catching up as she puts her foot on the step into the Hindle Green bus.

'What?'

'You could spend the night with Trixie and Belle, here, in Stockford. How would that be?'

'Fuck off! They Nanna combs them out for nits every

162

single night. She'll make me have a bath with them. That's disgusting.'

'Well, come and stay the night with my mother then. I'll follow you to Hindle Green. Take you home for tea there.'

'I can look out for myself.' And Abbie pulls herself up into the bus and the doors slam in Stephen's face. It's no picnic being a man unrelated to a girl-child in need of help.

'Mum, you've got to help me.'

'About bloody time too!' Dyllis waggles a crooked finger at her son. 'There's no easy way out of this, Stephen. You know that. And no blaming the Church or work or any of that business either. This time you're going to have to really take stock and look at your life and make changes that you'll stick to.'

'No! I need your help with Abbie. She's on her own up at No. 3. I need you to persuade her to come and spend the night here. Carter's in hospital with a great hole in his head until tomorrow at least. She's only ten and has already been left home alone for one night.'

'That was Carter in the ambulance, was it? Nobody came to tell me. You weren't answering and I saw Anna Trester's car but couldn't get there fast enough to ask. What's going on?'

'Mum, please come with me and talk to Abbie.'

'She won't want to come here.' Dyllis hauls herself to her feet and shuffles about collecting newspaper, book, pills. 'Why should she leave her house? I'll have to offer to stay there the night.'

'You can't. It won't be comfortable enough.'

'Needs must, Stephen. Bring my buzzing cushion. Though why a child so patently capable can't be left alone for one evening...'

'She's only ten.'

'Time her mother came home to look after her. That Kat...! Wait... Why can't Tessa look after her?' Stephen clams up. The pain on his face is enough to make his mother reach out and touch his cheek.

'Oh, darling,' says Dyllis. 'Is it that bad? I thought that was why you'd come to see me. I have been watching. There are things I've seen that at the time seemed perfectly ordinary. But now... And there's been no sign since she went out all bright-eyed and bushy-tailed this morning. Stephen, you've got to go and talk to her or you're going to lose her altogether.'

'You know where she is?'

'At the Old Rectory, of course. Where she always is. Carter's been acting as go-between.'

'Rufus?'

'For God's sake, Stephen. You can be astonishingly dense.'

The bush telegraph, having been tripped into action by April, is continued on its way by Daisy, who calls Ellen Wiseman about goat's cheese for her stuffed, preserved chillies and mentions that April says Tessa's disappeared.

And then Anna Trester telephones Ellen on joint benefice church business.

And before the day is out the Bishop knows, via the rural dean, that the shoe-in they'd found for the Hindle parishes is not the answer to all their prayers.

'Don't tell me he's lost the plot again,' says Bishop Arnold. 'His boss in London swore that all he needed was a bit of rest.'

'Anna Trester says his wife's left him. There's talk about something going on with the sexton who's in hospital with a vicious head injury. Of course Anna's not the most

164

compassionate of women and she is a notorious gossip so I've no idea how much of all this is true. But she was implying that Stephen smashed the fallen gargoyle on the poor man's head. It's probably all rubbish, and I'll go and check the situation out myself as soon as I can. But I suppose we should be prepared to think again re: the Stockford job. Be no good putting a single man into that great big old house. Shame, because I told him he should apply when we spoke about it. Practically promised him the job. Because of course *she* told me she thought the country would be the perfect place to have children so I assumed they'd be trying. Not splitting up.'

Dyllis marches into No.3 Pratt Cottages as if she owns the place. In the kitchen she finds Ryan and Lauren passed out. Abbie's curled up in the small space next to Ryan's feet, watching telly, forking sardines into her mouth straight out of the tin.

Stephen shakes Ryan's shoulder.

Ryan squints through one eye. 'What?'

Dyllis won't have any of the pussy footing she can imagine Stephen's composing in his head. 'Are you in loco parentis to this child?' To make herself clear, she's standing straight, pointing at Abbie.

'You social services?' Ryan struggles to sit. He's been lying on the contents of a spilt ashtray and a damp patch where his can of cider fell over. 'Lauren!' he pushes at her, shoving till she opens one eye.

'What?' Lauren comes to and stares about, bleary. Abbie rolls her eyes to the ceiling and goes to throw the empty sardine can into an overflowing cardboard box next to the kitchen sink.

'It's Mrs Wilkinson from across the road,' explains Abbie. 'You know, the crippled lady. The vicar's mother.' Lauren relaxes enough to recognise her neighbour.

'You are clearly not up to looking after anybody,' says Dyllis to Lauren.

'What you doing?'

Focusing, Lauren points at Stephen, who's filled the sink with soapy water and is washing up.

'Just...' he grins. 'A helping hand. You can't have had time...'

'If I wanna leave the washing up to fester for a fucking month it's none of your business.' She lights a cigarette with a shaking hand.

'Lauren, you know Carter's in hospital?' says Stephen, drying his hands on his trousers.

'Yeah! 'cos you bloody attacked him with a bit of stone for no good reason. I heard you was drunk an' all. We should call the police on you. He should sue you. Make a mint, he could. Damages and that.'

'I didn't...' Stephen reels before this accusation. Drunk? 'I wasn't...'

'Carter's every right to sue anyone he sees fit,' says Dyllis, trying to defuse the situation. 'But in the meantime who's going to look after Abbie? She's only ten. She can't be left in the house alone.'

'She'll be all right.' Lauren pulls Abbie to her.

Abbie grimaces and pulls away. 'Get off!'

'I could babysit,' says Dyllis, prim as a Victorian governess.

'If you're going out...' Stephen says. 'I'd offer but if I'm supposed to be Carter's assailant... I'm sure Abbie would prefer my mother for company. Or she could stay at Mum's for the night. Wouldn't that be more practical?

'She's not going anywhere with you stone-throwing weirdo. She's staying here with her family.'

'Well, the door's always open,' says Dyllis, smiling at

Abbie. 'You know my house. You call it the witch's house, I think.' Abbie flushes.

'Just fuck off out of here!' cries Lauren. 'Fucking busybody nosy parkers.' In Lauren Stephen recognises the glittering eyes, the sweating face, the shaking desperation of the junkie already aching for their next fix. How can he persuade Abbie out of here?

The child reaches out and touches Dyllis' gnarled hand. 'You got a piano. Can I have a go of it?'

Dyllis smiles widely at Abbie. 'Of course you can.' She's already edging towards the door. Abbie's following her.

Stephen watches them go. He's got to persuade Carter to try and get in touch with Kat. Lauren needs help. Carter's right: Ryan is a disaster. And why would anyone think he'd want to attack Carter? At least for the moment the crisis here has been averted.

And at last Stephen can go and try... No! Just go and claim Tessa.

Tessa's been given smoked salmon on toast for supper, then hot chocolate, then a spare toothbrush. She's too tired to focus on the fact that she's pregnant, and that the village suspects her husband of putting the father of this baby in hospital. That can't be true. Stephen doesn't know about her and Carter. Stephen doesn't care. Clearly. If the village is talking so hard he'll know she's at the Old Rectory. If he was interested at all, wouldn't he have turned up here? Her situation is entirely unresolved. She pulls on a pair of her host's pyjamas and snuggles into the comfortable reach of the walnut sleigh bed with which he's replaced the old wrought iron number that had come free with the attic. The duvet crunches with new feathers, the linen is cool and crisp. Tessa knows that tomorrow she must face the future. But for now this is so comfortable, and her eyes are so heavy and the bed so warm.

She can hear Rufus on the telephone downstairs.

'Yes. It's all so deliciously Lady Chatterley...'

More French farce, thinks Tessa. She's grateful that Rufus has no friends in the area other than her. What if she had invited everyone to dinner with him? He'd have been swept up to become part of her new girls' gang and he might now be on the phone to April instead of this friend of his in London, easily could have been spreading the news locally that the vicar's wife's got herself up the duff by the sexton.

'I know,' he's laughing. 'Rural life: it's so filmic. Hardy? Oh, I see... her name! Ha! Do you think an up-dated re-make? Bags I be Angel.' Tessa rolls onto her back. She stares up at the beams supporting the roof. How can she find out if Carter's all right? She left her phone in London. She doesn't know his number.

This attic room is barnlike with its bare elm floorboards, vaulted ceiling and low windows open to the warm starlit sky.

There's a tiny flit in the dark and Tessa realises there are bats dancing in and out of the night.

And at the end of the drive, standing beside a crumbling gate post, staring up at the same, starlit sky, stands a lone figure. Stephen's so convinced Tessa won't want to talk to him that, having got this far, he doesn't dare walk up and knock at the door for fear of her rejection.

Chapter 13

Self-discharged, Carter sits on the low wall outside the main door to the hospital, his head patched with a great square of dressing. He's smoking a roll-up, squinting at the sun.

Stephen pulls up, grunts a welcome, and the two men sit in concentrated silence while Stephen drives through a fresh-laid, speckled egg of a June morning. Mist in the valley burns off to reveal a ragged robin bobbing bright pink in the hedgerows. In the meadows red cows wrap long, rough tongues round sheaves of grass between the buttercups. The first of the dog daisies are out. The birds are deafening. And Stephen's mood is black as a funeral.

Today, Stephen hates the country – no, more than that: he hates his job, he hates being angry, and he hates God in the way a child in the playground hates their best friend, in a punching, scratching, crying sort of way. But he's not a child, and there's nobody to comfort him. He's got to take two weddings in tumble-down St George's this afternoon.

All Things Bright and Beautiful followed by spoilt tears because the 'Danger Keep Out' tape will ruin the photographs. Stephen is under no illusion that either couple will be strict church attendants for the rest of their married lives. Besides, they're making their vows to each other, before God, not *to* God.

Why have to take a wedding today? Why have to think about anything other than Tessa today? And now, because he wasn't brave enough to face her sending him away, he's missed the moment for storming in and dragging her back to his cave by the hair - as if that were ever going to be Stephen's style. Is he supposed to show how very much he loves her by standing back and letting her go?

Carter hears Stephen snort and says nothing. Carter's made a few decisions himself during his night in hospital.

'Can we do it again?' demands Abbie. She's sitting on the piano stool. The lid is open and there is music scattered around the floor.

'Please!' insists Dyllis, bringing a tray into the room and edging it carefully onto the table by her chair. She shuts the door behind her and curls her gnarled fingers around a milky cup which she gives her young visitor.

'Please!' says Abbie, putting the tea on top of the piano and waiting.

Dyllis edges herself onto the seat beside Abbie, whose hands hover in anticipation over the keys. 'Ready?'

'Ready!' And together they pick out a mad duet of *Chopsticks*, Dyllis' weak bass hands completely drowned by Abbie's enthusiasm at the top end of the piano. Abbie's laughing fit to burst when the front door opens and in comes Stephen, followed by a hobbling Carter. Abbie's face is wide with pleasure. Her straightened hair has come away from its ponytail. Her sleeves are pushed up to her elbows. She reaches for her tea and sips.

''s great here, Carter. She's not nearly as much of a witch as they say she is.'

'Thank you very much.' Dyllis pulls herself to her feet and finds her balance. She takes Stephen's arm. 'A word, Darling.' And she propels him through the kitchen door and closes it behind him before she turns and smiles at the others. She must get them out of here, sharpish.

'One more round to show Carter. Please, Mrs Wilkinson.'

Dyllis' kitchen hasn't changed since Stephen first brought Tessa to meet his mother here: the yellow formica-topped table, the red and white painted kitchen units, the faded geometric-patterned Seventies curtains framing that lovely view over the water meadows.

Tessa hasn't been sick once in the past three months, but she feels nauseous now. She grips the kitchen surface above Dyllis' half-sized dishwasher. Stephen stares at her: he looks as frightened as she is. She realises he's terrified of what she might say. She wraps her arms across herself. And chin jutting, eyes glaring, she comes straight out with it. 'I've been having an affair.'

'You always had a thing for Rufus.'

'Not Rufus.'

Not Rufus? And the penny drops. Of course. Stephen doesn't wait for the rest of the story. Boiling, he slams into his mother's sitting room and grabs Carter by the collar, half strangling him, and yanks him out onto the garden path, where he punches him hard in the nose and then again, for good measure, in the solar plexus.

Carter folds, winded, groaning, onto the concrete.

To stop himself kicking the fallen Carter, Stephen runs to the vicarage and slams himself inside.

Standing across the road in the lychgate to St George's, Anna Trester stares: for once in her life she's actually witnessing the action. Around her, florists are bustling in and out of the church, a video camera's being set up by the lychgate. A pageboy is skidding up and down the grass Carter mowed before the accident: dark green circles stain his pale blue satin bottom. Spluttering to herself, Anna goes inside to practise her voluntary.

And in Dyllis' kitchen, shame pins Tessa to the worktop. She's made such a mess of things she doesn't know where to start making amends. Poor Carter: none of this is his fault. She strains to hear that he's all right. There's shuffling as he stands and his deep, polite, gentlemanly, forelock-tugging voice insists to Dyllis that Abbie can get him home. Tessa doesn't move.

And then there's Dyllis coming through the kitchen door. She eases herself onto a chair and waits for Tessa to take the other. Tessa simply hugs herself and doesn't move.

'That'll teach me to assume I know what's going on without asking,' says Dyllis. 'There I was thinking it was Rufus. Or that you'd just left Stephen because of his generally insupportable behaviour – which I would have understood.'

Tessa doesn't know where to start explaining.

Dyllis is thinking out loud. 'It must have been around Easter. I remember thinking how happy you looked while we were at Ellen's for lunch. And Stephen snored very, very quietly in the basket chair by the fire and you were irritated by it. So it wasn't him who was making you happy. I thought you might have been pregnant.'

And now Tessa can't stop the tears welling. Dyllis always knows everything. She's the wise witch in Tessa's story. If only she weren't Stephen's mother.

'You are pregnant?!' Dyllis puts two and two together and easily gets the right answer.

Tessa nods, dumbly.

'And it's not Stephen's?'

Tessa can't stop her hands going to her stomach. She bites hard on a tiny moan of despair.

'Oh come on, Tessa, stop standing there as though you're a naughty schoolgirl waiting to be sent home in disgrace.'

Tessa sits. 'Dyllis, I've been so stupid.'

Dyllis reaches a crumpled hand across the table and takes one of Tessa's. 'I know that biological clock was deafening you. I'm not forgiving you for abandoning my son. But I do understand that the urge could not be denied. We're only animals, after all.'

'I'm not!'

'Oh yes you are.'

Inside No. 3, Carter finds Ryan counting tiny zip-lock plastic bags into his pockets. Carter's only been away forty-eight hours and the place is a tip. It smells of spilt beer and cigarettes. Lauren has that pasty, gleaming grey look that says she's using. 'Only smoking,' she lies. She'll lose her teeth. And the rest.

Abbie's face when she sees the squalor gives Carter all the courage he needs.

He takes a tiny slip of paper of his own from where it's hidden behind the telephone on the wall and dials the number written there.

'Mum?' he says. Lauren and Abbie stop what they're doing and stare at him in amazement. 'Mum, if you get this, you gotta come.' Carter glares, defiant, at his grown-up sister. 'I got things to say.'

Stephen forces himself to prepare to take these weddings. Habit has him polishing his good shoes. He knows the appropriate sermons off by heart. Don't go to bed on an argument. Criticise for the first year only and then love your spouse for the foibles they won't change. Practise being nice. Good manners will keep a marriage going for a life time. Make a project of your lives together. Don't blame one another for the daily grind. HUMBUG!!!!

He storms up the lane to St George's where the congregation for the first wedding is already milling about. Stephen smiles at no one, shakes not a single hand as he rattles the door to the vestry and swears because he's forgotten the keys and he's going to have to go through the body of the church and be watched. Can people see the flames burning out of his ears?

Carter Stoke! So bloody obvious. It wasn't that Stephen had been blind. Dear God, no! He'd seen them together every minute they could get. But he'd never thought. And it's not her he hates - much. It's that stupid young man for being so good-looking and muscular. Is Tessa really so swayed by the way a person looks?

He slips the flower-embroidered wedding stole around his neck over the starched, white surplice. How can he take a wedding now? He looks up at the plain wooden cross which stands on top of the cupboard in the vestry and jabs a V sign at it. He has to take the weddings. He can't lose his job as well as his wife. Then he would have nothing. Or maybe that's it: maybe he should just walk away and leave it all. In the mirror he practises a smile. It looks like the rictus grin of a hanged man.

He steps out onto the chancel step.

The bride at the far end of the aisle waits triumphant on her father's arm.

The groom looks as if he might be going to be sick.

Mrs Trester strikes up a turgid rendition of Pachelbel's *Canon in D*.

'Dearly beloved...'

Mrs Trester throws her eyes heavenward. Stephen's forgotten to give the notice about not throwing confetti in the churchyard.

The day's weather started too well. By the time the second wedding comes round there's soggy pink paper mashed all over the church path and Mrs Trester is steaming.

Having joined those two couples in wedded bliss, and in an effort to calm himself down, Stephen works his way round

Tessa's garden. He picks broad beans, a lettuce, and a bunch of virulently orange pot marigold flowers and puts them in Tessa's bicycle basket. He adds the first two eggs: those mangy little birds are laying at last. His mother won't eat any of this healthy fare and Stephen has no appetite.

So he sets off for the Old Rectory. The sun breaks through and the wet road steams. He needs to apologise for attacking Carter this morning. He and Tessa need to communicate. He desperately wants her back. He'll never take her for granted again. He'll resign from the church. Get a job labouring – anything so long as he's not in an office. God can find somebody else to speak for him. From the Old Rectory gate he can see the front door standing open. He pushes the bicycle up the drive and stands for a minute by the front door, wracked with uncertainty. He just wants everything to be like it was the day before yesterday. He leaves the bicycle with its basket of offerings leaning against the rain-spattered stone inside the front door. And then, once again, he turns and walks away.

'He loves you, he loves you not,' says Rufus as Tessa unpacks the bicycle basket. She doesn't deserve Stephen's kindness. What other man would react to the news that his deserting wife was having an affair by bringing her offerings?

'Besides, you're with Carter now.' Rufus is in mischievous mood.

'Don't!'

'What are you going to do, Tessa?'

'Go back to London. Find a flat. Get a job. Pick up the pieces.' So much for the dream. Well, she never felt she deserved it anyway.

'What did Dyllis say?'

'That she doesn't forgive me.'

'Stay here with me.'

175

'I can't.'

'I need the company.'

'I haven't any money! I wouldn't be able to pay you rent or anything.'

'Be my housekeeper in exchange for bed and board.'

Tessa stares at Rufus. Is he serious? 'What about the village?'

'The villagers will love it! Their very own little soap opera happening on their doorstep.'

'Don't!'

But Tessa doesn't have anywhere else to go. Even with village gossip hissing about on the wind, Tessa can't bear to leave. She knows she's still chasing an impossibility but if Rufus says she can stay, she'll struggle on until there are only cinders of her fantasy left to sweep up.

If she's going to stay with Rufus, Tessa needs to fetch her computer from the vicarage. And her nightie, and toothbrush, and some clean pants, and a shirt or two. So, hearing the familiar raspberry blow of the Mini spurting up the hill, and assuming Stephen's gone to the wedding reception at Bag Enderby Hall, Tessa goes home, tiptoeing around the house. Up the garden, the chickens scratch about beneath their fruit trees. The earth round the veg is black where Stephen's watered.

The kitchen door is open. Inside she finds a coffee cup and toast plate in the sink. The last crust of her own bread and a jar of Marmite are on the table with a file labelled 'St George's Tower'. Upstairs, she puts a random collection of what might be essentials in a bag with her laptop and the notes for Daisy's chilli book. It's nearly finished. She'll be paid, but not enough to live on for long. She takes the notes she made for the smallholding book, too. It must be possible to persuade Ellen. Daisy's publisher said she'd be glad to look at an outline. Tessa just has to pitch the idea right to her friend.

Outside again, she says a sad goodbye to the chickens and gives them each a handful of corn.

She lumps the bag onto the back of her bicycle and ties it on with a bungee. It's only then that she notices the gaping hole in the top of the church tower and the red and white striped tape measuring off a 'Keep Out' area.

'Tessa!' She's so surprised she drops the bicycle and her deodorant and toothpaste roll out of the bag onto the path. Stephen scrabbles to collect them for her.

'Stop. Before you say anything, please let me speak.' He looks up at her, his eyes sparkling. This is his big chance to sell himself to her. 'Please. Let me talk to you.' And Stephen picks up the bicycle and leans its unwieldy bulk against the log pile. He takes Tessa's hand and draws her up the garden. He pulls her down to sit on the grass between the vegetable beds and the chickens. 'Please, Tessa.' Tessa pushes her legs out in front of her, hooks one ankle over the other. It's not comfortable but she doesn't move again: she doesn't want to look as if she's fussing.

'It's not just Carter,' she warns him.

'What happened to us?' Stephen scratches his head and the wiry mess of it stands up - unbrushed, unwashed. Tessa sits on her hands so that she won't reach out to soothe his fiddling. He won't want her touching him now.

Tessa takes a shaking breath   'I'm pregnant,' she says. And there's nothing but a beat. And then another. She can't bear to look at him. The self-justifying and the begging for forgiveness tumble about her head, but she bites hard on them. He doesn't want to hear her pathetic excuses for ruining their lives.

Besides, his silence tells her everything she expected. Keeping her eyes on the lush, water-coloured valley beyond the house, she pushes herself to her feet. She brushes down her dirty jeans and stands up straight to get her balance. She has pins and needles in her left ankle where the weight of her right has been sitting across it. She limps down the grass, pulls the bicycle off the log pile and pushes it round the side of the house. And all the way back to the Old Rectory, the puddled tears spill.

Winded, Stephen watches her leave. He can think of nothing to say but, 'Wait! Your post.' It's such an inappropriate response to what she's just told him he holds his tongue. He'll do his howling in private.

And Anna Trester, who saw the weeping Tessa pass by her kitchen window, tells Amy at the farm shop when she rings to change her milk order. And Amy tells the cow man, and the cow man tells the postman, who never gets to Hindle Green before five, and the postman takes the news back to Stockford. It wasn't the sexton after all. He was just a red herring. Anna Trester saw it all and she knows. The vicar's wife's left him for the film star. What is the Church of England coming to? Anna rings the rural dean and tells her and the rural dean looks at her figures and wonders if it wouldn't be better just to close Stephen's little churches. What congregation there is wouldn't mind driving in to Stockford on a Sunday, would they?

Chapter 14

Tessa's caught up in a pregnancy machine. She's passed along from midwife, to scan, to doctor: rebalance the dose of thyroid-controlling Carbimazole, start taking folic acid.

'Isn't it too late for that?'

'Better late than never,' the platitudinous midwife palpates Tessa's rock-hard stomach with an ultrasound dipped in ice-cold gunk.

'Amnio?' asks the doctor at the hospital, ticking the box before she's had a chance to answer.

'No!' protests Tessa. The idea of invading her baby's space with a giant needle is anathema.

'You're nearly forty,' says the man. 'There is a greater likelihood of Down's Syndrome.' He leaves the box ticked.

'Whatever happens, I won't want to get rid of it.' How could she face Daisy's daughter, grown-up, responsible, life-enhancing Jelly, if she even considered what the doctor clearly thinks the sensible response?

'Nooo...' the doctor's unconvinced.

Tessa wishes Stephen were with her to be the righteous one. Stephen never lets the system bully anyone. But she hasn't heard a word from him since she walked away the other night. And why should she? She's been having an affair and the affair has got her pregnant. Tessa will be surprised if she ever hears from Stephen again. She knows he'll be working his fingers to the bone. Without her, there'll be nothing to stop him.

On the bedside table in her attic she props the grainy black and white printout of what the scan saw inside her: a tiny alien-shaped profile, a looming fist. She must talk to Carter.

Tessa sits on Rufus' back doorstep, waiting. The side door in the wall creaks and she drops her head into her hands. She's just as terrified of this confrontation.

Carter squats down beside her. He doesn't touch her. He only knows she's left Stephen and that's enough to stop him touching her. He doesn't need pressure: doesn't want commitment. He'd have gone for someone available if he did. He's right to be nervous. Tender loving care isn't what their friendship's about. She turns her head up to his and is blinded by the sun.

'I'm pregnant,' she announces to the glare.

And time slows down while Carter arranges himself beside her, ever so slightly away so that they don't touch. They lean their backs against the warm stone and close their eyes against that sun. She has nothing more to say. She dreads his assumption that she'll have an abortion. The urge to escape is powerful, but she has nowhere to run to.

She hears the rustle of Rizla paper and smells the tobacco as he makes up a cigarette. He strikes a match against the boot scraper and it fizzes as it flares. He exhales hard and then he says:

'I gotta be honest, right?'

She nods. 'Absolutely.'

'Then I'm not ready to have children.'

'You don't have to have this one.'

'You gonna get rid?' He can't hide the hope in his voice. She knows she shouldn't hate him for it. 'Never!'

'What you gonna tell the vicar?'

'The truth.'

And the fact of her pregnancy throws up all the reasons why she and Carter will no longer spend any time together. She's forty: she's never going to give up on this probably only chance to have a child. She can't explain to Carter that her biological clock has been deafening her to the exclusion of reason. She can't expect him to understand. Why should he? He's twenty-two: young enough to spawn any number of children. He won't want to spend any time with a woman whose focus from now on is the safe nurturing of this little bean within her. When he's with Tessa he wants to escape the responsibilities of his life: not be weighed down by more. She can feel him itching to get away already.

The door from the kitchen grates on the flagstones as it opens.

'What are you two doing here?' Rufus is carrying a basket laden with Ellen's home produce that he's bought at the farmers' market. 'Have you come to invite yourself to lunch, Carter?'

Lithe as a cat, Carter unfolds himself. 'I'll just get on with mowing that front lawn,' he says. And Rufus smiles his thanks and pulls Tessa away, into the kitchen.

'You look terrible,' he says.

Tessa hides from life in Rufus' house. She allows him to ferry her about when she needs to go to hospital appointments. He feeds and waters her while she works on Daisy's chilli book. And, without Ellen's encouragement, she puts together a proposal for the smallholder's manual. Tessa can see herself spending next spring and summer helping Ellen with the bees, with the seedlings, with the farmers' markets, building a book out of the experience, while the baby gurgles in its basket nearby.

She doesn't like to examine too closely the question of what she and this baby are going to live on.

Rufus appears in Tessa's dusty bedroom eyrie. He's carrying L plates, the form for a provisional driving licence, and a textbook for the driving licence theory exam.

'You can't be a single mother in the country and not be able to drive,' he insists. 'Come on, I'll take you for a spin now.'

'You've got to be joking!' Tessa's terrified of bumping into anyone who might want a row with her: Dyllis, Stephen, Carter. She's going to hide at the Old Rectory as long as she possibly can, doing business by email and showing her face to nobody.

'I'd like to live here,' says Abbie, her feet dangling off the piano stool, a cup of milky tea in her hands. 'Everyone's always rowing at our house.'

'What about?' Dyllis leafs through old sheet music for simple tunes she might be able to teach the girl. Dyllis wonders if Abbie would ever apply herself to the dull repetition of scales and arpeggios which would exercise some real strength into the child's hands.

'Carter's gone mad. You know he's rang...'

'He rang...'

'Whatever. He's rang Mum up and told her she gotta come and sort things. He wants to get rid of Lauren and Ryan and he don't want no more responsibility for me. I reckon he reckons it's his turn to split. He's back working, right, even with them...'

'Those.'

'Them great big black eyes where the vicar hit him.'

Dyllis looks at Abbie's brave little face, her determined chin and defiant stare. Does she really think Carter's going to abandon her?

'Has the vicar been round to apologise for punching him?'

Abbie screws her face up. 'What he want to do that for? Carter been sneaking about with the vicar's wife, he deserves to have his nose broke.'

'What if Carter goes and your mother doesn't come?'

'I'll come and live with you.' Abbie grins. Dyllis can't help but smile back.

'Do you miss your mum?' asks Dyllis.

'She's magic,' says Abbie.

Dyllis misses Tessa.

Kat waits in the cold, dark wind tunnel which is Platform 9. She texts the time of her arrival to Carter. He'll have to drop her back to the station, too. She's bringing no luggage.

The train hisses to a halt and Kat climbs into it. She may be sitting facing forwards but she's going backwards. When they quiz her, 'How is it, Mum?' she'll shrug and tell them that she's working, earning, that that's the important bit.

She should have known better than to leave them again. But when he called... it was her chance to get her revenge and escape for a while. Besides, she's never been able to turn that man down. Of course it hasn't worked out how she imagined. But she's not ready to go back. Not yet. The possibility of her man's fulfilling his promises is a drug she's been addicted to since long before he gave her Abbie.

And there might be evidence. That mad rush down to Stockford with Carter's Jerry-cans. She must have been off her head. Nobody's come for her yet. If the police can't make the puzzle fit their assumptions, they move on, don't they? They should have thought wider, thinks Kat. Still, she wouldn't like her face to jolt anyone's memory. Be just her luck if the little girls' Granddad Barry had been poking his nose through his nets that morning, making sure there was an even number of blades of grass on his perfect lawn. He could have seen her...

The train rumbles west. The huddled suburbs fade away, and the patchwork fields and grey stone church towers of picture-postcard England unfold into view: river meadows and cathedrals, lone oaks and a high sky bunched with fat, white clouds.

Kat picks at the contents of a railway chicken sandwich, not eating it, watching the passing verdure with suspicion. The country makes her feel claustrophobic. It's so empty, there's no hiding in it. So big there's no escaping it. In her mind she sees Carter and Lauren's father. Even though he's dead now the thought of him has her ripping her empty cappuccino cup into a mess of tiny pieces.

In spite of his appearance, Kat can't hide a smile when she sees Carter waiting outside Stockford station. Wads of dressing on his broken head, and yellowing purple eyes only enhance for her the strong set of his jaw and the good square of his shoulders. She loves his summer-streaked, reddish, curling hair. He's her boy. They nod at one another but do not touch. Carter leads the way to the pick-up parked on a double yellow outside.

'Wouldn't be able to get away with that in London,' says Kat, as she hauls herself into the truck.

There's no talk as they curl through the lanes up to Hindle Green. The only other vehicle they encounter is a monstrous black four-by-four coming too fast round a corner, which forces them into the hedge, and which Carter looks after, frowning instead of shaking his fist.

'That was Carter!' says a white-faced Tessa.

'Slow down! Keep your eyes on the road.' Rufus clings to the seat for safety.

'I told you this was a bad idea.'

'Just do what you're told.'

'Take me into town and I'll kill you. I won't be able to get down the high street without taking people's wing mirrors off.

184

Why do you have to drive such a tank?'

'Change down. We're going to turn right here and go back the other way. Check your mirror. Indicate!' There's a horrible grinding sound and the Lexus jerks, pants, and stalls. A lorry load of shorn ewes misses them by inches, its horn howling.

'I'll drive the rest of the way.' Shaking, Rufus climbs down from the passenger seat. Tessa, too flustered to find the door handle, has to wait for him to come and let her out.

The Stokes are in their habitual places, Carter leaning against the wall between the sink and the telephone, Lauren at the table, Abbie at the bottom of the stairs, picking at the skin around her nails. Ryan's been banished to his van for the duration of this conference. Kat faces her children. There's no running and hugging and welcoming home. Instead, there's a waiting to see what direction the situation will take.

Kat starts. 'You kept the place nice.' In just these few months since Kat left, Abbie's all growing up. Painted nails and product keeping her hair silk-smooth. Kat wants to be able to squeeze her and feel if Carter's feeding her right. But if she touches any one of them she'll never leave. And that won't work.

'So what's this about, then?'

'You gotta chuck her out.' Carter points at Lauren. 'She's usin' again and she's got a waster of a boyfriend who lies about doing fuck-all all day long, eating my food off of my table when he fancies. He's dealin' out of this house.' Now Carter points at Abbie. 'Tessa saw him use her as bait one night in town. I got her away. But it's not right a ten-year-old girl should be living in a house with packets of brown stashed away all round the place. She's bright. You said yourself. It's not fair to put bad influence in her way.'

'So I chuck 'em out. How you gonna keep them away?'

'Court order. You wanna be able to ring and report them if you see them within a mile of here or Stockford Primary. Which means they gotta leave the area.'

'But what about her girls?' she points at Lauren. 'Don't you want your girls back?'

'It's never gonna happen, Mum.' Lauren sniffs and wipes her nose on the back of her hand. She needs to be defensive to save face, but she's never been so relieved to see her mother in her life. If only Kat would stay. 'They're never gonna give the twins back to live with me when they Nanna give them all that perfect home with nit-combing every night and fish fingers three times a week and swimming on Sundays.'

'They would if they thought you'd do the same,' says Carter. 'Vicar had it all set up...'

'Vicar?' asks Kat. 'What you having to do with the vicar?'

'He's all right.' Carter flushes. 'He woulda helped us...'

'If...' Kat's eyes burn into Carter's head and he knows she can see everything laid out in his mind.

What's the point trying to manipulate the situation to his advantage if she can see through to his plans anyway? 'I wanna get away, Mum,' he says. 'You chuck Lauren out and come back and care for Abbie. That's what I called you here to tell you. It's my turn to bunk off.'

'Where?'

'That's my business.'

'What you got to run away from?' asks Kat.

And united for once, Lauren and Abbie fall about laughing.

'And who's Tessa?'

They shout over each other to tell her: that old Mrs Wilkinson's son Stephen is the new vicar. He was stabbed in

London. Nearly died. Nearly bled to death. In Abbie's mouth the story gets wilder and wilder. And by the time she's got to Carter's secret trysts with the vicar's wife she's dragged Kat to sit with her on the sofa and Kat's taken the elastic out of her daughter's hair and set it free and felt her ribs through her hoodie and decided everyone's too thin.

'I tell you what,' says Kat, eventually. 'I reckon I knew him when I was a girl. He used to follow me round everywhere.' She makes a lovelorn face that has Abbie giggling. 'I reckon I might drop down and see him.' She has to get out of this house: find space to think.

'I'll take you,' Abbie pulls her mum out of the settee and towards the door. 'It's all moved and changed round here. The Church sold the vicarage. It's called the Old Rectory now. Where you working in London, Mum?'

'I'm working in a pub, darlin', like I did here, before the Horseshoes got sold off for private housing.' Kat walks upright, holding Abbie's hand firmly, looking straight ahead for fear of those judgemental village faces twitching behind their nets. There's the 'Keep Out' tape around St George's tower. Carter's kept the verges nice. Them horse chestnuts is lookin' a bit ragged.

'The old pub's up for sale again, Mum. Someone might buy it and open it up again and then you could come and work there and live here with us.'

'Oh, my little Abbie. You're doing so well without me. Might ruin everything if I come back.'

'Stay one night, Mum? You might frighten off that Ryan and then Carter won't chuck Lauren out and we'll be just us, like we was.' Abbie knows she's being little-girly; she dances along, dragging her mother by the hand. This is how her mother likes her. And Abbie will do anything to persuade Kat to stay. Should she tell about Dyllis and the music? Will Kat

187

be pleased or go storming off to the old woman's house accusing her of child molestation?

At the vicarage gate, Kat turns to Abbie and tells her, 'Go on home. I won't be long.' Abbie stares up at her mother, rejected. Kat drags her fingers out of her daughter's hand and walks up Stephen's garden path. Abbie sinks to the ground by the hedge so that she's hidden from the house, but her mother can't escape without her knowledge. The sun's hot on her head. She picks daisies, pulls the petals off one by one. 'She loves me: she loves me not.'

It's a strange business, being confronted by the dream grown older. Especially when the dream, distorted by the kaleidoscope of memory, has been haunting Stephen since the day he and Tessa drove into Hindle Green after the stabbing. The great mane of hair's been chopped short. The happy cheeks have gone. Kat's skinny as a rake. The intoxicating glitter in her eyes has turned to wariness. She hovers near the door.

Stephen wants a blow-by-blow account of her life since he woke up in the hay in the Black Barn and found her gone.

Instead he says, 'You're just the same.'

She smiles at him. 'Yeah, right. You got religion.'

'I can't believe it's been twenty-two years.'

'I was here some of 'em. You'da seen me if you ever come back.'

Stephen pours boiling water into the pot.

Kat stalks about the kitchen, examining the charity shop calendar, the candle sticks on the windowsill, the mugs hanging from hooks under the shelf. 'You like being back, now?'

Stephen puts mugs on the table with the teapot, a bottle of milk, a packet of Digestives. He pours two cups, takes his and leans against the Rayburn. It's a hot summer's day but the kitchen's always cold with its concrete floor under the lino and north-facing window.

'We came because of the job,' he says. 'And Mum's not getting any younger.'

'Proper cripple she turned into, didn't she? Still independent, though. Not the needy type, your mum. Bet she likes having you here.' Kat picks up a notepad on which someone's started a list about a christening, the rural dean rang... She puts it down again.

'Tell us about your wife, then,' says Kat, picking up her tea, looking about for sugar, seeing none, sipping anyway.

'What do you want to know?'

'Turns out she's been running about with my boy. And now he's called me home because he wants to go away. Reckon, less you just married a dolly bird half your age, she's gotta be too old for Carter.'

'He wants to go away?'

Kat leans against the sink. Up the garden she can see the leafy raised beds and the chickens under the trees. There's a yellow courgette-turned-giant marrow half eaten by mice where it hangs down into the grass. 'You into all that?' she asks. Stephen shakes his head. Great, thinks Kat. Women never want to leave their gardens. Kat doesn't mind if Carter goes travelling on his own. Well, she does: then she will still have to come home to look after Lauren. She can't take Abbie to London. Wouldn't be right. But Carter going off with some old woman: that wouldn't be right, neither.

'I hate it here,' she says, surprising Stephen with her honesty. 'I don't fit. How can I? My feet grew out of this land yet I'm as foreign to it as you are. I used to be a carefree girl who knew much too much about what she could do with her booty. Well, I got cocky and look where that got me. In London, everyone's got their story so they leave you be with yours.'

She turns and Stephen's giving her a critical stare. She narrows her eyes at him. 'What?'

'I've got to ask you,' he says. He looks down at his shuffling feet. Stills them. It's now or never, Stephen. His heart thumps in his ears, his hands in his pockets are balled into fists. He doesn't know what he'll do with the information, but he has to know. 'Is there any chance that Carter could be my son?'

And Kat's surprised into laughter. For the first time in as long as she can remember, Kat is overwhelmed by great big belly laughs which bring pink to her cheeks and leave her out of breath. There's the girl he used to have a pash for.

She wipes her eyes. 'Oh my God! How long you been worrying?' she gasps.

Since it seems she's been honest with him, he finds it easier to be candid in return. 'It only occurred to me when we got back here,' he says. He smiles, nervous still. 'I can't remember now exactly what happened,' he says. 'I remember the Black Barn. The cider. I had such a crush on you.' There's a limit to how embarrassed he needs to make himself. He misses out the crucial moment which means surely Carter can't be... and yet... can he remember? Is he right? How many people was seventeen-year-old Kat having sex with that August? 'And I remember waking up and finding you gone,' says Stephen. 'And I came back home to find my father had died in the night and there was never another chance to talk to you. I never saw you again.'

'God, that would be a turn up, wouldn't it? Your son having it away with your wife.'

'She's pregnant.'

Kat raises her eyebrows: her eyes widen. 'Nice.'

'It's not mine.'

'That's a mess.'

And Stephen's face is so bereft, Kat could come round the table to hug him. He's not changed from the little boy lost who followed her around. An only child of intellectual types who went neither to church nor pub and so were always strangers in the village. Now everyone's an incomer. But then... the Wilkinsons were foreign as the Poles when they first arrived during the war.

'Well, Carter's not yours, neither.' Is she putting him out of his misery or doling out disappointment? 'Promise,' she says. 'Not just saying. No way is he your child.' She remembers Stephen's clumsy fumbling, his over-excitement, his disappointment when he climaxed... She's not going to make him cringe with all the details. 'You'll have to believe me.'

Stephen breathes out. His face is wiped of expression when he looks up at her. What difference would it have made?

'You wouldn't have suddenly fancied bossing him around like you was his dad, would you? Carter's not the type to be told what to do ever, I'll tell you that. None of my kids never had no dads and they's the strongest, toughest lot I know. They don't need nobody.'

Stephen thinks of Lauren and holds his tongue.

'So you got no kids and I got three, and two grandkids.' Kat's proud of this. In what Kat's saying, Stephen hears Kat's old mum's favourite refrain: he might have all that education and a nice wife and all that, 'But it don't do nothing, do it?'

He smiles. She may be right. 'Why won't you stay and look after them?' he asks.

'Look at what I did to my Lauren. They're all better off without me. Carter's right. Abbie's sharp as a knife but if I stay round to screw up her chances...'

'Just because Lauren went off the rails...'

'You know why that happened? 'Cos of the dad I made

sure she never knew. That's why. Carter and Lauren got the same dad. First time it was me playing silly buggers and then I got more'n I bargained for.'

'Who was it?' He wonders if she'll tell.

And for a second she pauses. She eyes Stephen. He knows that the less he says, the more she'll tell him. People can't bear an empty silence. He waits. She takes a breath. 'I been working at the Horseshoes, remember?'

'Someone you met there?'

'Old Jack Trester used to come in a lot. He was a horrible old lech. Ogling my tits and all that. But I was seventeen. Half of me knew it was horrible. The other half? Well, it was a laugh, wasn't it?'

So much for playing it cool. Now Stephen knows his mouth's hanging open. Kat always hated Jack Trester. For what he did to foxes, for his snooting about the place, for the way he kept his son hidden away. She'd had a highly developed sense of fair and unfair, which had rubbed off so much on Stephen he'd found himself regurgitating her self-righteous comments in his early days at the seminary.

Stephen goes into the larder and finds a bottle of wine. This has gone way beyond a tea and sympathy session. He opens it. Pours two glasses.

Defiant, Kat tosses no-longer-existent locks. 'I'm not proud of what I did.'

'What did you do?'

She takes a glass, doesn't sip, puts it down.

'I left you sleeping in the hay in the Black Barn. I come back to Hindle Green on your bike and I broke in to the Trester house through that old engine room at the back, like old Jack told me I could. I don't know if I thought I was just gonna have a look about, or take anything, or what. I was excited as when we tried to set the hound puppies free, remember that time? When he threatened to shoot us? I can't believe I'm telling you all this. I never told nobody.'

'People always tell me things. I've got a blank face. Makes me good at my job.' Stephen finishes his glass and pours himself another. Kat hasn't touched hers. 'And I never tell.'

'It's a gift.'

Stephen doesn't usually push it: but this is hardly ordinary parish pastoral care. 'What happened next?'

'Carter happened.' Kat sips at her white wine. 'Carter...'

'And Lauren?'

'I went away after that first time. No shame.' She smiles at the memory of her younger self. 'At that age everything's possible, isn't it? You never think. So off I went to seek my fortune. Bright lights, big city. Thought I might be an actress. Got a job in a pub. Didn't realise I was expecting Carter till I was almost seven months gone. At first, the baby and me, we lived together in this squat. But that was no good. So I brought him home and gave him to my mum to look after. She was still living in them old houses on the Stockford Road where I grew up. Trester hadn't knocked 'em down so he could build one of his executive homes there yet. When Granddad died, old Jack served notice on my mum so he could make some more of his millions.'

Kat runs her hands through her spiky hair, looks up at Stephen, defiant as Abbie lighting a fag outside the primary school. 'That was when I made my big mistake.'

'Which was?'

'Old Jack, before, he said any time I needed anything, I should tell him. He said he could help me. I went to beg him to let my mum stay on in her old house. Maybe it was a bit ramshackle, but it was our home. You'd gone off, then. Travelling. Wherever it was your mum sent you after you got out of school.'

'To learn Spanish and walk to Machu Picchu and get over my religious mania. She never understood that the phase she thought I was going through was the only thing that made sense to me then. You'd gone. Dad was gone. Reverend Jones was sinking deeper and deeper into the drink. I think Mum still fantasises about me being a city banker and making millions. But what's the point of all that? I ended up working with missionaries in the favelas outside Sao Paolo in Brazil.'

'Well, while you were off discovering yourself, old Jack blanked me in the Horseshoes. There was a new girl behind the bar for him to make eyes at. I wanted his attention. And he'd promised me... Under all that bluster I was proper innocent.'

'He wouldn't help you?'

'Because of Carter I reckoned he owed me, right? So when he ignored me in the pub, I saw red. I started shouting all over the bar, meaning to tell about Carter and what old Jack done to me and he grabbed my arm – stronger than he looked, he was, even though he was already sick with that first bout of stomach cancer he had – and he dragged me outside.'

Kat sniffs, pulls herself together.

'Out back, by the bins, he told me what he thought of us Stokes and my son.' She smooths her hands out on the table, the fingertips stretched wide from one another. Her hands are very clean. Scrubbed red. 'And that's how I had Lauren,' she says. 'Poor girl. No wonder she's a screw-up.'

'He raped you?'

Kat sits up and throws her head back, proud. She swirls the wine in her glass but doesn't drink it. 'I'm s'posed to be going back to town tonight. I come down to tell Carter to pull hisself together and get on with things. But it's more complicated...'

Stephen shakes his head. 'Carter needs you now.'

194

'And Lauren's got herself in trouble again. He's a nasty piece of work by all accounts.'

'He's just another lost boy. If you stayed and chucked him out at least Lauren might be saved.'

'In't that against your principles? Chucking people out?'

'I have to be pragmatic. Without him you can get Lauren straight and I can help her get the twins back.'

'You'd still help us, no matter what my Carter did with your wife?'

'It's not Carter's fault,' says Stephen into his empty glass.

If Tessa cycles up to St George's she can be quick enough that she doesn't see people staring – if they are. And at St George's she won't be disturbed by Rufus quizzing her, because he doesn't have enough to do, about what they're going to have for supper, whether they should go to the cinema, what she thinks about his new shoes/coat/Hermes beach towels.

'Abbie!' Tessa's brought up short by the sight of the little girl leaning against the gate to the vicarage. 'What are you doing?'

'Waiting for my mum.' She's on the defensive.

'Your mum home?' Already? That's quick. Tessa smiles despite the fear that grips her: Stephen's at liberty to go off with Kat if he wants. After what she's done, Tessa has no right to intervene, let alone stop him.

'She's been in there for ages.' Abbie nods towards the house. Tessa looks. They're not in the sitting room, or Stephen's office. The famous Kat. Will the village kill a fatted calf? It seems it's Stephen's turn to play fantasy-turned-reality, thinks Tessa, the effort of possessiveness denied staining her neck.

Abbie stands up and brushes herself down. Always immaculate, today she's in blinding white jeans and a tiny, spaghetti-strapped rainbow-coloured top. Her hair, as ever, is

195

smoothed into a ponytail. She tucks a comb into her pocket and sits down again.

'Won't you walk up with me?' asks Tessa, needing to get away from the threat of awkward introductions.

Abbie shakes her head. 'I'm waitin'.'

'How's Carter getting on?'

The stone of the church walls is warm to the touch where the sun's been on it all day.

Tessa pushes the door and steps inside. There's the smell of hot dust and beeswax where the sun's been pouring onto the burnished elm pews all afternoon. There are pink and scarlet shop-bought carnations in stilted little arrangements on the windowsills: it's Mrs Tait's week to do the flowers and she doesn't have much of a garden to pick from. Tessa walks slowly up the nave and stands, dead centre, looking up at the dove, hovering over the altar in its burst of glass sunlight. She misses this. She misses feeling proprietorial about her lack of faith in it. Now... it's none of her business, whether she believes in it or not.

It's ironic that this church should have become her sanctuary when she doesn't believe in what it stands for. But when Rufus bosses her about, telling her what she should be doing with her life, she needs somewhere to escape to. And the walls of St George's have seen so much more than her own small tragedy.

'Tessa?' She whips round, like a child caught stealing.

Stephen's at the end of the aisle, just inside the door. He looks tireder, thinner, sharper-edged. He hasn't shaved.

'You look...' Stephen's smiling at her. His professional smile, she thinks. The one that says, *Talk to me, I'm safe and friendly and full of good advice.*

There's a pause.

He wants to pick her up and carry her home and lock the doors against all intrusion. He wants to spoil her and love her and for her to want to love him back. The carnage of Kat's family life has made him need to nurture the possibility of his own. She didn't move in with Carter. Does that mean he might be in with a chance?

'I've been watering your veg for you,' he says.

'It's yours now.'

'The chickens have started laying.'

'I thought you'd have got rid of them.' They're as polite to one another as strangers at a cocktail party.

'They're my new friends. I take my supper out and we tell each other how our day's been. They look at me as if I'm stupid for working too hard. I tell them they've got each other.' Stephen flushes and bites his lip. He doesn't want to make barbed remarks about being lonely. He has to set Tessa free if that's what she wants. She stands before him, so fragile and determined. He's in awe of her.

Tessa walks slowly back up the aisle. She intends to edge round him. She's frightened he'll be cold if she touches him. Gallant, he steps back. She gives him a little, mannered smile and leaves the church, her mind churning with all the things she could have spoken of. But he's been pushing her away for months. She has to assume that this separation has come as a relief to him.

'Wait!'

She stops under the lychgate.

'I keep forgetting to pass on your post. If you're in a hurry, it's on the kitchen windowsill. If you can wait... I've just got to lock up here.'

'I'll pick it up on my way. I know you've got things to do...'

And, cursing herself for being a coward, she runs for it.

Left alone in the church, Stephen looks up at the dove above the altar. The light's gone and it is dull now. The building feels like nothing more than just a cold, stone barn with benches in it. Numb, Stephen steps out and locks the door behind him.

Chapter 15

As the weeks pass, Dyllis is amazed at how stubbornly both Stephen and Tessa maintain their avoidance of one another. The village is aghast at their separation and panting for a next instalment. Dyllis just wishes that this stalemate might be resolved.

So she posts a card to Rufus, in an envelope marked 'Private', inviting him to tea. At her age she feels she has neither the time nor the inclination for prevarication.

She telephones April and asks her to deliver a box of home-made macaroons.

'What's the occasion?' asks April.

'Mind your own beeswax,' replies Dyllis.

Dyllis has been watching Stephen. He's falling apart. It began with the not shaving. He's become increasingly unwashed. He doesn't bother to open the curtains in the morning. For a vicar, whose office is in his home, he's made the place look unwelcoming. He's not the kind of man who'll go out and find himself another woman. Like a swan, he's mated for life. Tessa might have plans to disappear into the sunset with someone else, though Dyllis doubts that: she's still here, after all – and not living with Carter.

Rufus dresses carefully: beige linen suit, pale blue lawn shirt, brown suede loafers, no socks.

Dyllis loves the outfit.

'The thing about incomers,' she says, coyly letting him carry the tray out to the table and chairs where she and Stephen usually sit for their nightcap in the garden, 'is that they do the country-living look so beautifully. They've invested a lot in coming here and want to blend in. So...' she gestures at Rufus' immaculate turnout. 'Of course, when you've been here for a few years more I expect you won't take so much trouble. Or...' she claps her hand over her mouth. 'Of course, you must always mind very much about your appearance.'

Rufus fears he might blush. He hates it when people guess. Dyllis takes a hold of herself. 'Being an actor,' she says, 'you can't afford to be caught looking like something that's just been dragged through a hedge backwards. Now...' Dyllis gives Rufus time to get rid of his high colour while she settles herself and pulls at the cushion at her back until she's comfortable. She seizes up more and more easily, even on a hot July day, and the buzzing cushion stops her back going into spasm. 'Will you be mother?' she asks.

The delicate scent of the Lapsang Souchong goes so well with the flowering lavender. There's the hum of honey bees, the smell of bruised grass where they trod on it...

'The English countryside is truly heavenly at this time of year, don't you think?' Dyllis smiles at Rufus. She likes this young man. The wildness that was there when she first met him has gone from his eyes, replaced by... 'But dull, don't you think? Ditchwater when you've nothing to get your teeth into. How are your plans going for the house?'

'It's so complicated. All the listed building permissions. I've just cleared out the rubbish and made it like posh camping. The bones of the place are beautiful.'

'They'll make cold bones in the winter.'

'I might get someone to build me a box bed in the kitchen. The problem is that even the doors to the house have preservation orders on them, and the weather screams through them.'

'You need velvet curtains and those sausage dog draught excluder things. People used to stuff the cracks between the boards with newspaper. I remember Stephen pulling out a chunk once and it was a concertinaed page from *The Times* about King Edward VII's coronation.'

'And I'll get plug-in radiators and wash in a hip-bath in front of the fire.'

'You're a romantic.' The boy must have run out of money.

'Is this why you asked me here? Twenty questions on what I intend to do with my house?'

'I want to talk about Tessa.'

That's more like it. Rufus rubs his hands together.

'Where's she going to sleep come the winter? With the baby in another little box bed the other side of the kitchen?'

Rufus doesn't like to think of such hard realities as the winter. On a day like this one, he can't imagine cold. He stands, 'Do you mind if I take my jacket off?' Dyllis smiles and he slings it, flashing the blue and white striped satin lining, onto the back of his chair.

'And will you really want a screaming infant around all the time? Buckets of stinking nappies...'

'Oh, I wouldn't care about that. I like looking after her. Gives me...' Rufus sighs dramatically. 'God! I may as well tell you.' There's something about Dyllis that makes him long to tell. 'I'm here because of a broken love affair. I moved out of someone's house in London and stormed off, telling them I was going to buy the country idyll we'd always talked of, and I found the Old Rectory and bought it on the same day. Mostly out of spite. But I've had no work since, and I should have put my money in the building society like my mother told me instead of spending it all on shoes. So no, there isn't anything to do it up with.'

Dyllis quietly re-fills their teacups, adding a tiny cloud of milk to each. She offers Rufus the macaroons. He takes a raspberry in one hand and a pistachio in the other and puts them in his mouth quickly, one after the other. 'I mustn't,' he groans, through a mouthful. 'I don't keep this figure by chance, you know.' Swallowing, he reaches for a chocolate one. 'If Tessa's going to leave Stephen properly she should go and find a house. But what kind of a house could she afford?'

'Exactly my point,' says Dyllis. 'She can't really want to go. Or she'd have gone back to London and left no forwarding address. We must engineer their falling for one another again. Imagine how unbreakable a love it would be if it were to happen while she was carrying another man's child! Poor Stephen. It must be his sperm count that is the reason they never had children. And now Tessa's pregnant he must feel horribly emasculated. Of course he won't let himself feel anything. He always puts aside his sense of self in favour of the greater good. I blame his father's death. He's been a perfectly good boy ever since, as if that's his way to ward off disaster. But good boys aren't loveable if they aren't really honest-to-goodness good. So Tessa's gone elsewhere. Frankly, I don't blame her. I imagine Stephen doesn't either. He doesn't think he really deserves her, so he's pushed her away just to prove his point.'

Rufus isn't sure he wants Tessa to fall in love with Stephen. He likes having her around. She's a distraction for him. He pretends to be busy on his computer while she strings runner beans, pods a handful of peas and rinses some rainbow chard under the tap in Rufus' kitchen. There are new potatoes bubbling in a pan on the stove, sprigs of mint in their boiling water giving the whole kitchen a clean, sharp smell.

Tessa's thinking hard, too: all her life she's been accustomed to making the best of what she has. Now, presented with an endless array of possibilities around the one certainty that she's going to have this child, she finds she's flailing. It's the guilt. She can't think straight because of the guilt. But she doesn't like the person she'd be if she banished that guilt. Besides, look what she's done to Stephen... Of course, he's free to go after Kat Stoke now if he wants to. Tessa jabs at a potato to see if it's cooked before asking Rufus to 'Come on and lay the table.'

Tessa goes to the surgery for an appointment with the midwife, a vague woman who says things like, 'Have you given me your sample?' 'Have I taken your bloods?' 'Should I be worried about your risk of gestational diabetes?'

Tessa's beginning to feel these appointments are entirely pointless. Having seemed distracted since she walked in, the midwife eventually scribbles nothing of any great interest in Tessa's notes, smiles at her and says, 'Next month then,' before remembering to tell her she must make an appointment if she's to see her again. Tessa's glad of pregnancy chatrooms on the internet: they seem more reliable and informative than anything she gets from this woman.

While she waits for Rufus, she buys herself a sandwich from April's and takes it down Watery Lane. There's a band of grass here, between the main road and the river. Tessa sits on a bench in the shade, munching on her tuna mayo, lost in thought - until a shadow cuts out her light.

Carter looks at Tessa now and she's become a tired, drawn woman, with wrinkles round her eyes. The sexiness is all gone. She doesn't look very pregnant. It's amazing how one day you can't keep your hands off a person and the next you can't begin to see what inspired that lust.

'I just dropped the chainsaw off,' he says. 'Problem with the starter motor. I took it apart twice and still can't get it going.' He squats in front of her, out of reach. Tessa folds the remains of her sandwich into its grease-proof paper and dusts off fhe flour left on her hands by the soft white bread.

Nervous, she says, 'Hi.'

'You been avoiding me.'

Tessa gives him a thin smile. 'I didn't think you'd want to see me any more.'

Carter blushes. 'Well...'

Tessa pulls at a loose thread hanging off the sleeve of her shirt. The thread unravels and suddenly she's lost a button. 'Bugger.'

''s all right.' He puts hands up in surrender. He's even laughing. 'I told you already. I'm too young for babies. I done enough playing grown-ups. Now my mum's back...' He grins. The fact makes him really happy. 'I'm free. Unless...' A sudden fear shadows his face. 'Unless I'm wrong. I mean, if you want me to help... bring it up and that. I won't shirk...'

'Carter, no! I want you to be free too.' Tessa gabbles breathy reassurances. 'I can cope. I mean, it'll always be your child. You'll always know where we are.'

'I been thinking about what you been saying...' he changes the subject with the ease of the young deciding a problem's solved, '...about travel and that.'

Tessa smiles honestly now and for a second he sees the beauty he fell for.

'Where are you going to go?' she asks, loving his callous ability to remove himself from her situation. He is guilt-free, like the woodland spirit she thought him when they first met, the man who charged her forty quid to split a load of logs. She remembers the evening in the Kingsmead Arms when he drank beer from a tankard with a glass bottom before taking her to watch the carnival from April's shop. That was the man she fancied, not this nervous youth frightened of being given a telling-off as well as a child in perpetuity as punishment for not using a condom.

'Dunno,' he answers. 'Just I been thinkin' I should get out

of here before Mum gets bored waiting for me to leave and disappears again herself.'

Stephen's mentor, Reverend Jones, always used to call them fêtes worse than death. He also used to call the archdeacon the arch fiend. He taught Stephen to take the precepts of Christianity to heart, but the organisation of the Church of England with a generous pinch of salt.

This year the benefice fête is to be held in the meadow behind the community hall in Pendle. Mid-July, just after the end of term. Of course the plant stall will be second to none with Ellen Wiseman having been nursing donations well out of chicken's reach on sheltered shelves in her yard. And Daisy never lets the cake stall go under-stocked. There's to be a competition to see who can make the most impressive scarecrow, a scratch 'fathers and sons' cricket match, a fortune-teller (Amy from the farm shop dressed in hoop earrings and a big paisley kerchief as headscarf), a book stall (George Cross and David Tait), piglet racing, guess the weight of the honey pot, a tug of war, a white elephant stall, and as much tea as anyone can drink.

On account of the vicar's estranged wife's living with him, Rufus Stone has not been invited to open the fête. David Tait suggested Bag Enderby's Lady Susie be prevailed upon to declare the festivities open. But Lady Susie's glued to Sir Charles' side at a cripplingly expensive hospital in London and has no idea when she'll be home.

In the end Dyllis, who, thanks to her new friend Abbie has adopted the title Hindle Green's Chief Witch-In-Residence, has agreed to declare the festivities a-go-go from a tiny platform where she plans to spend the rest of the afternoon, shaded by Stephen's father's vast golfing umbrella, holding court and accepting tea and cake from anyone who'll bring it to her.

The point of the fête this year is to raise money for St George's tower.

Stephen joins in the fun to the extent that he cobbles together an old jacket over a stuffed potato sack, a pair of specially-bought charity shop trousers, and a face made from a white balloon drawn with a frown, angry eyes and bared teeth. Stephen stuffs two black, holed socks with newspaper, gives them painted yellow eggbox dips for beaks, red drawing pins for eyes, and ties them to the right arm of his useless scarecrow.

He's embarrassed when he wins overall first prize, beating even the fortune teller's eight-year-old daughter's ghost scarecrow made out of an old sheet and a broomstick, which Stephen thinks very effective. Of course he realises that he must have been given the prize in an attempt to cheer him up.

Behind and around him, the Chinese whispers embroider his story to gory absurdity. Even the rural dean turns up to show the diocese supports Stephen in his hour of need – and see how he's coping. She puts a caring hand on his arm and he can feel her forcing kindness down it and trying to inject her love into him. Her lipstick is a virulent fuschia against her pale, suspiciously hairless upper lip. To shake her off, Stephen mumbles something about checking the plant stall before all the good stuff goes.

'Ignore her,' says Ellen Wiseman of the rural dean as Stephen helps her lift a tray of plants onto her trestle table. 'She's lonely.'

Stephen is impatient with loneliness. If he went to the doctor and described the symptoms following him about like a black dog, he'd be offered anti-depressants. Stephen's disdainful of pills. But his life's in crisis. He could barely concentrate on that trip to Preston. A sprawling, challenging parish, encompassing a group of rotting concrete tower blocks and two schools threatened with special measures. Exactly what he likes to get his teeth into. Except, now... the lassitude's killing him.

Ellen hiccups. She shakes her head. 'George Cross poured cider down my throat at lunchtime. I'm going to have to go to bed in a minute if somebody doesn't find a way to sober me up.'

'I'll get you a coffee,' says Stephen.

'And a really fat slice of butter-iced cake, please.'

On his way to the tea tent Stephen carefully avoids the ring where a Jack Russell's just snapped the head off a guinea pig in the 'Best Pet Competition', the fall-out from which might mean the breaking up of the benefice. He neatly skirts the threat of a mauling by the hunt kennel's puppies, which have been walked all summer by various households in the benefice and are now huge, loping hounds, half feral, farting clouds of stink from the culled deer intestines they're fed on.

There's Carter Stoke, staring at him from the beer tent...

The racing piglets are overtaken by their mother, who objects to being separated from them and used as bait.

'Ough!' The escaped sow takes him right in the solar plexus.

'Ooh!' A collective intake of breath as the fête-goers at last have an allowed reason to stare at him. Winded, Stephen curls into a foetal ball and concentrates on breathing while the piglets chase about all over him as if he's a climbing frame especially arranged for their entertainment. Worried hands, including the rural dean's, fuss as he groans on the ground, shaded by a crowd of concerned faces.

'Poor man. Don't seem right he has to put such a brave face on, with all his trouble.'

'Did his wife really leave him?'

'Mucking about with that Carter Stoke. Vicar threw a

brick at him when he'd had one too many.'

'I heard it was that Rufus Stone.'

'Could have been both at once.' Giggles. Stephen keeps his eyes closed so that he can put off the moment when he must open them and smile and pretend he's fine, right as rain, really...

'Sh!' the rural dean's voice bosses.

'Leave him alone!' It's Carter speaking. Stephen looks up at the hulk of Carter's shoulders silhouetted against the light. He's holding a hand out. Stephen can't not grasp it. He's pulled up.

Carter puts an arm around Stephen's shoulder and steers him away from the rural dean and towards the beer tent. 'Come on, Vicar. Let's really give them something to talk about.'

'Why not?' What else has Stephen got to lose? So, stunned that he's about to buy his cuckolder a drink, Stephen slaps change on to the trestle table serving as a bar and says, 'Two pints please,' smiling ruthlessly at the farmer who grows rapeseed to the delight of Ellen Wiseman's bees, looking him straight in the eye and daring him to comment.

Served, Stephen follows Carter outside and they stand together, watching the sow reunited with her offspring and ignoring the gawping crowd. It is funny. Stephen laughs. Carter joins him. And the people in the crowd say to one another behind their hands that they heard the vicar was emotionally fragile after that stabbing in London, and look at him now.

Stephen wipes his eyes. Blows his nose. Life is nothing more than one minute piled upon another. He should enjoy those minutes. One at a time. Don't waste the present anticipating or regretting. *But what if...* protests his habit before Stephen tells it to shut up. Lying in bed through the dark hours, then he can twist himself up in paroxysms of anxiety. Today he will sip the dark russet, buttery bitter and think not about Tessa, Preston, Len Fox, or a baby who is not his. Instead, for a moment, he'll enjoy the sweet-smelling shade under the breadth of the old horse chestnut, sit down even, lean against its gnarled old trunk while a ladybird busies itself up and down the sleeve of his father's threadbare cream linen cricket jacket.

Carter sits down beside him. For which he's grateful. With Carter nearby, people are too embarrassed to come and quiz him about anything.

Tessa's still living with Rufus because she can't motivate herself to move forward. Everything, from the present to the possible, feels wrong. She smoothes her hands over her bump, tidy as a small half water melon. *Poor thing*, she thinks, *this baby's getting short shrift.*

Outside, Carter rumbles about on the ride-on mower. When's he going? She's shocked at her callousness, but now his youth seems nothing more than pimply to her. Was the affair really animal-driven? Did her biology choose him for some pheromone he gave off, matching the chemical reaction her egg would have with his sperm to make this child she wanted so badly? What a witch she is. Maybe Dyllis was right – or is she just looking for a way to let her conscience off the hook and therefore make her blameless?

The chilli book finished, Daisy invites Tessa and Rufus to a celebratory lunch. Tessa doesn't want to go. Rufus, desperate for a social life, isn't having any of Tessa's claimed illness.

'Stop assuming you'll be the centre of attention all the time,' he chides her. 'This is about Daisy, not you. What kind of a friend are you if you refuse to celebrate with her?'

209

Tessa's welcomed into Daisy's kitchen with a great big hug from Jelly who leads her to the cushioned armchair at the head of the table. Tessa protests, 'I'm not an invalid,' but allows herself to be installed. There's a plate of radishes, sweet butter, and a saucer of sea salt in front of her.

Daisy's brushed her hair and put on lipstick for the occasion.

'Hi,' says Rufus in his special telly voice. He kisses Daisy on both cheeks and Daisy blushes.

'I brought Prosecco,' says April, bursting into the room with Ellen. 'You'll be allowed a tiny bit, won't you, Tessa?'

Daisy decants spun salad leaves into a capacious earthenware bowl and pours a jam jar full of vinaigrette over the lot. She passes the bowl to Tessa with a pair of wooden spoons. 'Toss.'

Tessa turns the salad with fake enthusiasm.

Rufus sits down next to Ellen and holds a hand out to her. 'You must be Ellen Wiseman. Will you tell me about your garden?' Ellen flushes purple and takes her hand away sharpish and then smiles for fear her shyness has made her appear rude.

Daisy puts a steaming bowl of artichokes on the table and a copper saucepan filled with melted butter, lemon and black pepper. 'Anyone not know how to do this?' she asks, taking one. She puts a knife under the side of her plate so that poured butter puddles against the rim. She tears the outside leaves of her artichoke off and dunks them one at a time into the sauce before tearing the flesh off with her teeth and discarding the woody pointed end into another bowl. 'Jelly made the sauce.'

Jelly beams, takes an artichoke herself and shakes her head at April offering Prosecco. 'It'll give me hiccups,' she says.

'Well, if everyone else has a glass,' says April, sitting down and lifting her own so that the sunlight shafts through its bubbles, 'I'd like to propose a toast. To Daisy's book, which would still be nothing more than a good idea if it weren't for clever Tessa.'

'Daisy's book,' everyone choruses. Tessa puts down her Prosecco. The baby flips inside her, bubbling acid reflux. She feels as if she's not really here, that this dreamy mid-summer lunch, with its charming guests and gorgeous food is happening in some way without her. She can't seem to touch it. She's numb to it.

And Rufus is right. Nobody's taking any notice of Tessa. It's Jelly who has the table's attention. She's very serious when she says, 'It shouldn't be Ellen doing a gardening book. Rufus, you're famous. Tessa should help you write about learning to be a vegetable gardener. Everyone will buy it with your name on the front.'

Rufus looks stunned. He has no interest in getting his hands dirty. Rufus likes loafing while other people work around him.

'It would give you something to tweet about,' says Tessa.

'I hadn't thought.' Rufus' under-subscribed tweeting usually features his bleating about his not being able to find work.

April's getting excited about this idea. 'You should be asked to declare the ploughing match open. You could tweet about that. Single-handedly put Hindle Green on the map.'

'The vicar's mother opened the fête,' says Jelly blithely. 'But the vicar didn't look happy. He looked sad, didn't he, Mummy?'

'Only because he was embarrassed his scarecrow won the competition.'

'And he was being hounded by that earnest-looking woman in a dog collar,' says April. 'It was like a farce, him running away from her all the time.'

'Till he got tripped by that pig and went down cold. Took him ages to come round, didn't it, April?' Daisy's not a trouble maker but she's curious to see how Tessa will react to news of Stephen being knocked out. Nobody mentions Stephen's happy afternoon outside the beer tent with Carter Stoke. Nobody's sure what they think about that.

Tessa keeps her face neutral. What scarecrow competition? What woman in a dog collar? Was Kat there? 'I expect he got up and drove home all right, though,' she says. The statement's really a question. Don't let him be injured.

'Of course he did,' says Jelly, blithe and generous. 'He gave Carter Stoke a lift when he got too drunk to drive. In that funny old car of his: you could hear it farting all the way down the road, couldn't you, Mummy?'

Carter and Stephen together? Tessa folds into herself, feeling sick, alone, and stupid: though it's only right she should be punished for behaving like a witch to Stephen and a bitch to Carter.

'They're an odd bunch,' says Rufus, chauffeuring Tessa home later. 'You're sitting there and nobody once mentions the fact you've left your husband – who happens to be their vicar – and are six months pregnant by somebody else. Perhaps they think you're with me?'

Tessa realises Rufus' voice is hopeful when he says this. She looks at him, his determined chin and concentrated driving face. And at last his situation falls into place for her. Nobody's having an easy time. And his isn't self-imposed. It must be tough to be gay and a sexy leading man getting the big heterosexual parts that pay for the roof of somewhere like the Old Rectory to be kept on, or, rather, lifted and re-laid with a great thick layer of sheep-wool insulation. He must spend a lot of time pretending in order to keep up appearances for the female fan base whom he thinks won't fancy him so much if they know he's not interested in them. It's all bollocks, thinks Tessa. Women have never been put off by apparent unavailability: if anything, their interest is only further piqued by it.

'Does it matter that you're gay?' Tessa comes out with it just like that. She's bored with pretending anything. Perhaps if she practises honesty with Rufus then it'll be easier to be clear with Stephen when... when what?

Carter finds a grass snake in the lawn clippings when he lifts the corrugated iron lid to add more. He squats down and watches as it glides out of its old skin. He takes the ghostly sloughed snake shape into the potting shed where he lays it in a shallow cardboard lid of a box that some dahlia seedlings came in months ago.

I'll be like that, he thinks. *Just walk out one summer morning.*

Chapter 16

September. This year the Ploughing Match is held at Green Farm in aid of St George's tower.

April, Ellen and Daisy share a stall selling refreshments. It's not in the spirit of self-flagellation that Tessa is forcing herself to come along and help. The fact is that for the moment she lives in this village and she won't be able to hide in the Old Rectory forever. Quite soon, she's going to have to come out and push a buggy up and down the lanes - otherwise her poor baby will suffer rickets for lack of sunshine. Better give the villagers a chance to get their sneering done before the child's born.

Early copies of Daisy's book are displayed prominently on the borrowed village hall tables and Rufus, after he's officially opened the whole affair, is behind the cashbox on the premise that anything that happens today will be good material for the smallholder's book - which Daisy's publisher has leapt at if it's to be fronted by such an illustrious name from the celebrity circuit. Tessa hopes the match audience will be more interested in Rufus than in her.

'My book's hardly worth doing,' Rufus grumbles as Tessa ties him into a dark green apron featuring the slogan: *April's deli: we're always spring fresh.* 'A twenty-five-grand advance and I have to give half of it to you!'

'Don't be horrible.' Nervous at this public airing of her increasing girth, and irritated that Rufus should feel allowed to act so spoilt, Tessa gives his apron strings a vicious tug.

'Ow!'

'Are you going to be more of a hindrance than a help?' asks April, pushing Rufus out of the way and pouring a bank bag of 50p pieces into the cash box.

But she smiles when the first yummy mummy buys a plate of cupcakes from Rufus, who can't help being charming and uses his special sex-pot voice while pouring the lady a cup of tea.

Villagers buying off Tessa ask pointedly, but not nastily, 'All right?' and Tessa gratefully replies, 'Not bad.'

Amy from the farm shop even goes so far as to indulge in reminiscing about when she was pregnant with her daughter. 'I couldn't stand up like you are. It was awful. I had this pain in my pelvis the whole nine months which stopped me doing anything much. God, it was that much of a relief to get that baby out...'

Only Anna Trester refuses to meet Tessa's eye and waits to be served by April, to whom she remarks, 'Extraordinary, the people we get at these events. Of course *one* turns up from noblesse oblige. But I'm not sure everyone need do that.'

'It's for charity, Mrs Trester,' says April. 'I should have thought most people are here to be charitable.'

'Still, all we need now is for the vicar to turn up and then everyone can forget the ploughing and just sit down and enjoy the show.'

'That'll be six pounds, thank you,' says Daisy, ruthlessly charging Mrs Trester double.

'But...'

'It's for charity!'

As Anna Trester stalks off, Tessa can't help dissolve into giggles. 'Thank you,' she says breathlessly to her new friends.

'She's such a witch,' says Daisy.

'I love her!' protests Rufus. 'She's so up herself she's amazing.'

Tessa sits down to recover from her bout of giggles. All this standing makes her back ache. 'She may be right, though. Maybe I should go home?'

'Of course, you must be knackered.' It's Ellen who says this.

Surprised, Tessa stares at Ellen for a second. Ellen stares straight back. Does Tessa see a hint of viciousness in Ellen's eye? Does Ellen not like her? Why? She used to. Daisy, Ellen and April have included Tessa so enthusiastically in their lives. Perhaps Tessa imagined their friendliness. Tessa doesn't care about Mrs Trester. But she admires Ellen a great deal. Inspired by Ellen, she'd like, one day, to live a life of smallholding and veg-growing and chicken-keeping.

'That was a bit sharp,' says Daisy, conversationally. A few years below Stephen, she and Ellen were at Stockford Primary in the same year as each other: Daisy knows when there's something going on with her friend.

'Ow!' Ellen scalds herself refilling the teapot.

'What's got into you?' asks April, gently taking the teapot from Ellen and putting it out of harm's way.

'That girl doesn't know she's born,' says Ellen.

'Better be honest than spiteful, though,' says Daisy. 'Don't you think?'

'All right, I'll be honest.' And she turns and jabs her finger at Tessa, furious. 'You marry that lovely vicar – OK, so he's a bit all over the place emotionally but anyone can see he's a properly good man – and then he's not enough for you so you run off with Carter Stoke - a child! You get yourself up the duff, dump both Carter and the vicar, and move in with Rufus Stone here – to five star comfort and smoked salmon for supper every night!'

'It's not quite like that,' says Rufus, wishing it were. Tessa's standing now but she can't escape. Ellen and Daisy and April and Rufus make a wall in front of her.

'Most people who move to the area gently introduce themselves: try not to put themselves forward too much.' Ellen jabs a scrubbed-of-mud finger at Tessa - who wouldn't be able to get a word in edgeways even if she could think of anything to say. 'She's barged in, turned the vicar into a laughing stock, turned Carter into a toyboy. She doesn't make a living. She just seems to be expecting everyone else to sort things out for her.'

'She's pregnant,' says Daisy. 'It does funny things to people.'

'It's not fair! Why should she be allowed to get away with behaving like she is just because she's been a bad girl? Wish I had an excuse to move in with you, Rufus, and expect you to feed and water me for the indefinite! Go on,' Ellen says to Tessa. 'Carter's over there waiting for his cup of tea... or more. Or have you no further use for him now you've used him like a prize bull?'

And trying to hide a storm of tears, Ellen pushes away concerned April and Daisy and disappears towards her little delivery van - only to find she's been blocked in by a badly parked Freelander and can't escape. 'Fuck!'

'What was all that about?' April looks stunned.

'She's not in love with me, is she?' asks Rufus.

'She's just tired,' says Daisy. 'It's the end of the summer and she works so hard she doesn't usually have time to think. Perhaps Tessa's situation's just thrown hers into sharper relief and she's feeling as though she's slaving away for nothing.'

'But her place is so wonderful!' protests Tessa.

'Doesn't stop her being lonely.'

'I'd better go.' Embarrassed, shaking, feeling slapped - reminded that she's only an outsider and must do something to repay the welcome she's been given by these people, Tessa forgets to pull off her apron before walking away, back to the Old Rectory and her safe attic hide.

'Shouldn't you be at the ploughing match?' The rural dean's voice is accusing. She dusts Stephen's kitchen chair off before sitting on it. Stephen rinses out a mug. There are no biscuits. He warily sniffs the milk before taking a chance on it. Her eyes scan the vicarage kitchen, taking in the smeared, crumb-scattered worktop and the washing-up in the sink. She makes no remark about Stephen's unshaven appearance. Or the fact that he's still wearing his pyjamas in the middle of the afternoon. 'I wanted to talk to you about the rector. The Crown Prosecution Service say there's no case to stick to him. He's no longer suspected of burning the barn down.'

Stephen leans against the Rayburn. He's always cold these days.

'So they've let him go. His wife went to pick him up this morning. But he's not going back to work. Now he's had time to think, he's the first to admit he's not capable. So we'll be advertising the Stockford Rectorship.'

Stephen knows he ought to feel a jolt of possibility.

'Job for a family man, though,' says the rural dean, giving Stephen a never-mind smile. 'And your contract here is up at the end of the year. So we'll advertise for someone who'll be willing to take on your benefice as well as Stockford. How's your job hunting going? I know you were looking for some urban grit. I quite see that the pace of life here might be a bit on the gentle side for a man like you.'

Stephen wants the rural dean to leave. The job hunting's getting nowhere. Preston said they thought he wouldn't be right for them. And apparently now he's not even suitable to be formally employed to do the job he's been working on for months already. And God is silent.

Carter loves the ploughing match. He'll be competing in the vintage class on Sir Charles' 1951 Fergie T20 with a period plough to match. He's been carefully keeping her fit all summer, taking her out for little drives on warm days, making sure her engine is ticking over perfectly, feeding her the exact mix of petrol and paraffin she likes. Today she has new spark plugs, her oil's been changed, and she's shining with a fresh coat of battleship-grey.

Focused on the matter in hand, Carter saw the altercation at the tea tent and thought it better to keep well away. Now he strokes the old tractor, kisses her bonnet, and looks up to find he's being watched.

'My dad's got one of those back home.' The speaker is a lad about Carter's age with an accent Carter doesn't recognise.

'New Zealand. Outside Napier,' explains the stranger.

Carter nods, not overly interested, and bends to check the fuel filling the optic glass.

The stranger keeps on talking. 'I been sent over here for a year. My dad got me a job with this agency that arranges for blokes to go over for the New Zealand summer and do tractor work.' Carter pulls himself upright. Now he's listening.

'Tractor work in New Zealand?' he says.

Lauren should be allowed to supervise Ryan's final departure. Project number one almost achieved, Kat heads for the vicarage: the assumption that Stephen will drop whatever he's doing on her account is as strong as it was twenty-five years ago. Kat finds the vicar unshaven, in his pyjamas, smelling slightly stale. He protests he should show his face at the Ploughing Match.

'Stuff that load of old horse shit,' says Kat. 'And the prize for best polished bonnet goes to Lady Susie,' she finishes in a strangled posh accent.

'Snooty for someone who won first prize for her corn dolly one year.'

'Reckon I had a crush on that Garry Winters at the time 'cos he'd been given a Raleigh bike for Christmas and I wanted a go of it. And I'd passed my 11+ and fancied myself all la-di-dah for about five minutes.'

'But then your mum wouldn't let you take up your place at the grammar school.'

''cos it don't do nothing, do it?'' Kat and Stephen chorus in unison.

Stephen doesn't have the energy to deny Kat. He goes upstairs and pulls on trousers and a t-shirt and follows her up the vicarage garden where they climb the wall into the meadow beyond.

'Woof!' shouts Kat, waving her arms to the curious cows threatening to come up close.

'Woah!' Stephen joins in pushing off the cows, who turn and lumber slowly up the field. 'Remember that time we were stampeded when we got between those cows and their calves?' he says.

'I heard you forgot that lesson at the fête.'

'I seem to not be able to do anything but make a fool of myself these days. Everyone's staring at me already on account of Tessa and then I get mown down in public by a gigantic prize sow.'

'Carter took you for a beer after, though.'

'Magnanimous cuckolder.'

'What?'

Stephen starts to laugh. Tessa's gone. Tessa's having another man's child. He didn't get the job in Preston. The priggish rural dean doesn't want him here. The sow! He laughs so hard he's forced to stop and hold his sides. He can't breathe. Not caring what he's on about, Kat puts her arms round him and holds him until he stops.

'It's shit being grown-up,' she says, as he catches his

breath. He's shaking. 'Come on, I'll beat you,' and she starts running, a mad childish skitter up towards the woods.

Heat blankets the roof of the Old Rectory. On the cool side of the house, facing north through an ill-fitting leaded dormer window, Tessa's view is of the garden and the orchard and the pointed end of the wood encircling the village.

Outside, mewing buzzards spiral on thick thermals. Rufus' pigs have rings through the ends of their noses to stop them turning the orchard over and killing the trees, but they're happily tucking into the first of the windfalls. And there are acorns ripening in the pollard oaks grown tall in the hedge. The puppy-sized saddleback piglets which arrived three months ago are fat and long now, like small sofas. Beyond them there are two ewes and four lambs working their way methodically across the meadow. Rufus is going to need a gigantic freezer.

And in the distance, beyond the sheep...

Ignoring her painful back, Tessa bends and squints through the window. It's Stephen walking along the footpath leading up to the woods. The path she walked with him the day he first brought her here, when she felt the secret possibility of their children fluttering in her solar plexus. She'd taken his warm, dry hand and assumed he would feel those children too. She should have said something.

He's laughing. Bent double. And by his side, Carter Stoke's mother is laughing too. Tessa can't remember the last time she saw Stephen laugh like that. Now Kat's hugging him! Tessa feels a vicious stab of envy for that easy physical closeness. Perhaps that's what she went looking for with Carter. Tessa's and Stephen's relationship wasn't always so fraught – was it? She could swear she's never seen him so relaxed in her life.

Tessa can't bear to watch, and yet is incapable of looking

away. How does Kat make him laugh like that? Tessa loved Stephen so much she couldn't bear to be honest with him for fear of putting him off. Perhaps Kat doesn't care. Perhaps that's what gives them this joyful freedom. Look at them, running up the path towards the woods. He should be at the Ploughing Match, but for Kat he's prepared to forget the word 'ought'. Tessa moans out loud at her stupidity.

But then she stops, looks down and stares at the rock-hard swell of her stomach: there it is again – a tiny but unmistakeable fluttering, as if there were a goldfish swimming around inside her. The fluttering stops. Desperate for more proof that she didn't smash up her marriage to Stephen in vain she runs downstairs and pours herself a glass of ice-cold water from Rufus' fridge. And now the baby leaps with surprise at the cool of it. Grinning, Tessa takes another gulp. What a way to communicate with the not-yet-born.

There's the muffled sound of cheering from beyond Green Farm as Carter wins his class. The village itself is empty. It's as if Tessa and the baby are alone in the world.

Without examining what she's doing too closely, looking to neither side for fear of seeing that she's being watched, Tessa tiptoes up the lane to the vicarage. The back door's wide open as usual. She steps inside. At Rufus' house the kitchen is like an exquisite, dust-shaken, *World of Interiors* set. She misses the functional ordinariness of this place. Automatically, she picks up the loaf and swings it round to close the bag and stop it staling. There's a cold mug of tea with white bits floating on the surface on the table with half a pint of milk. She can smell the milk from here.

Not touching, she steps through to Stephen's study. There's a slew of files on his desk. His computer's switched off: strange for a man who usually checks his email all day long, like a reflex. Upstairs, his pyjamas are slung in a heap on the floor. She can't resist folding them under his pillow.

In her office, nothing's changed. She loves the apple-green she chose for the walls. If it were a child's room she'd paint trees and animals and leaves and flowers...

If only this child were Stephen's. So pointless to think, but if only...

Lauren sits by and watches Ryan gather his things together. He shoves his stuff into a black plastic bag. He drops his glowing cigarette end into the dregs of the last can of lager in the house. He didn't act so squalid when they lived in his van in the woods. Lauren sits on the sofa, not helping, not offering to go with him.

'You ready to go cold?' he sneers.

'I done it before.' She lights the third last of her pack of ten. She doesn't tell him she plans to give up everything. She's gotta get her mum to stay and she knows the only way is if she plays her mum's game to keep the peace. Lauren knows when Kat disappears that it's Lauren's fault. Lauren had only been home a few weeks when Kat went last time. Abbie's the apple of everyone's eye. Carter's the boy and can do no wrong. Lauren determines to smoke all three fags before her mum gets back. Then she's going to have a bath. She's going put a wash on. Maybe have time for a bit of toast before she starts shivering for a fix.

She's written her mum a note in her wobbly, childish hand. *Ryans gone. Dont let me out nor give me no money neither no matter what. Hide your purse where I cant find it. See you in a week.* She's going to make a bed up for Abbie on cushions in her mum's room. The bit she's dreading most... no, she's dreading all of it. But she done it before in prison. She knows she can do it again.

She watches Ryan dispassionately. She can smell his

greasy hair from here. The unwashedness of him had been what turned her on when he swung her round too fast on the waltzer and she screamed and caught his eye and he dragged her into his van after and had her. Well, she's changed her mind. She don't want to be owned, after all.

It happened so fast this time. So easy. Girls got taken away again. Course he was dealing. How else was he gonna keep himself in lager? And when he gave her her first hit... She was so down without Trixie and Belle. He told her she'd never get them back. He told her they should leg it. That's one good thing. Least she stayed at home, didn't she.

'Where you going?' she asks Ryan.

He slings his bag over his shoulder.

'Fuck you!' he answers and lets the door slam.

Lauren carefully sucks the last tiny bit of nicotine out of her cigarette and grinds it out into the top of his beer can. Then she stands and goes to fetch another bin bag. Anything he's left behind, she's throwing out.

Dyllis and Abbie lick April's carrot cake icing off their sticky fingers. Abbie doesn't have to be asked to pour the tea now. And she's got used to splashing a *nuage* of milk into the Lapsang Souchong after it's poured rather than a good slosh before. Dyllis is punctilious. Abbie likes learning these new words.

'Anyone home?' calls Tessa from the front door. Once she would have walked straight round the back. She's holding out an offering: a bunch of French marigolds and two warm eggs she's taken from Stephen's garden at the vicarage. 'I brought you treats.'

'Out here,' shouts Dyllis, excitedly trying to stand so that she can get to Tessa and grab her before she can get away. 'Abbie, darling, would you get another cup?'

Abbie automatically reaches for a bright blue coffee pot to put the flowers in. She's already got out the cup and saucer. 'Sorry we finished the cake.'

Dyllis' dry, cold claw has reached Tessa's hand and is holding it tight when...

'You fucker!'

They all three turn and stare out of the front window. Lauren's standing at the gate to No. 3, yelling and shaking her fist up the road to Ryan's van which is disappearing in a cloud of diesel fumes towards the T-junction. She's waving a handful of syringes at him and tears are pouring down her cheeks.

'Oh, great,' says Abbie.

'I'll go,' says Tessa.

'No!' But Dyllis does, reluctantly, let go of Tessa's hand.

Lauren's sunk into a puddle of despair by the gate. He's left her a stash for a week...

'He loved me.'

'No, he didn't.' Tessa crouches down to sit by Lauren. This is the bit of Stephen's job she used to love helping with. She picks up the syringes and the little individually wrapped packs of brown and looks at them. 'He was so angry you let him go, he left you enough to top yourself with.' Lauren sniffs wetly into her arm and rubs her eyes with the heels of her hands. 'Do you want me to come inside with you?' asks Tessa. 'I could help you get rid of these?'

Lauren eyes the drugs sideways. The stash will keep her going for a fortnight if she's careful with it. She shakes her head. 'I'll do it,' she says. Tessa knows she won't. Bastard.

'Can I come in?' she asks, not giving up. 'I fancy something stronger than Dyllis' tea.'

Lauren hauls herself to her feet. She's already so busy

working out how she can hide, then use, the heroin that she doesn't waste brain power pushing Tessa away. She's certainly not going to make small talk about the baby, obvious now Tessa's wearing a t-shirt pulled tight over elastic-topped pregnancy jeans.

'If you want.' Lauren's truculent again. All the bullish defiance she felt before Ryan left has drained away. She wants to run after him. She wants to go with him. Where will he stay tonight? Will he be out of Stockford? Lauren groans. Tessa gently ushers her inside and closes the door.

There was another girl, in Stephen's last parish, who had been using since her early teens. Mother of four by the time she was twenty. On the game to pay for her habit. The kids running wild. She was a nice girl, Tessa remembers. There'd be days when she wanted nothing so much as to chuck it. But whatever Tessa did to help, the girl would give in eventually: two or three days, tops, and Tessa would drop in on her way back from work and find her catatonic on the sofa, a needle sometimes sticking out of her arm, or her toe, her eyelid once, where she'd injected herself before passing out, the children playing at her feet. Tessa had tried to get social services to take the children. But whenever they visited, the girl would be clean and the flat tidy and the kids tearaways but not in any obvious danger. She'd be given a warning about the eldest's truancy and left to shoot up in front of her children, to leave them alone while she went out at night. One day she was found dead. Then the kids were taken away. And a new family housed in the flat. And the girl and her children forgotten.

Tessa can see Lauren eyeing the stairs. Tessa sits on the bottom step and says, 'Go on, put the kettle on. I'm parched.'

The drugs and the syringes sit on the kitchen table, on top of the note Lauren wrote her mum. The rubbish bag is abandoned on the floor, so far holding nothing but one sock,

Ryan's greasy hoodie, and the ashtray lager can.

Tessa knows it must be Lauren who destroys these drugs if she's to give up. If Tessa touches them then she can be blamed for whatever happens next. Lauren brings two mugs of tea and they sit together at the bottom of the stairs. Lauren's eyes keep returning to the drugs on the table. 'Till I found all that, I was gonna get myself clean. I wrote my mum a note an' everything. Now...'

'What's changed?'

'A week's supply. More, maybe. For free.'

'I thought you only smoked it.'

'I did. Once. I did.'

'How did you start using?'

'Trying to get at my mum, I think I was. We never got on. Always shouting. When she goes, it's my fault. It's me she can't stand having around.'

'Last time she went you were in prison.'

'Nah. I been out a few weeks.'

'Where does she go?'

Lauren shrugs. 'Don't tell us nothing. Just "It's a chance I can't miss." What chance?'

'You ever ask her?'

'Ask what?' Tessa and Lauren jump. Kat's standing in the doorway. Stephen behind her. Stephen's caught the sun, thinks Tessa. Is he growing a beard? He's so thin. He looks like a wild man of the woods. The horrible thought occurs that they might have been out there having sex. She checks them both for leaves in their hair. Stupid, she thinks, standing, brushing herself down as if she's been resting in a bed of leaf mould herself. Stupid to think she can help Lauren. Stupid to be jealous of Kat if Stephen's looking for happiness with her.

Stephen's face is flushed and his lovely dark eyes are alight with purpose. Tessa edges past him, as if they're strangers in a train, breathing in his strong smell of fresh sweat, leaping back as if she's burned herself when she touches him by mistake.

'Sorry... Sorry...'

Once, Stephen would have given her the thumbs-up at her holding the fort until he arrived. Once, they understood one another without having to explain things. Now he gives her a look as she leaves which she reads as exasperated. She doesn't stop to explain. Instead, breathless, she escapes towards the Old Rectory, hurrying down the road, holding her bump to protect it from jolting, ignoring the mean stare Anna Trester gives her when she drives past, ignoring the woman pushing the buggy up the hill and making remarks out of the side of her mouth to her friend, not waving at the cow man on a quad bike who'd usually shout a greeting but who now passes stony-faced, staring ahead for fear of having to get involved in any way.

Abbie watches Dyllis watch Tessa run away from No. 3 and feels sad for the old woman.

'You wish she weren't having the baby,' says Abbie.

Dyllis shakes her head. 'No. I'm glad. She wanted one so badly. I'm sad it's all so... complicated.' Dyllis can hardly bear it that for a split second she had Tessa by the hand and then she lost her. For a second she feels vicious towards needy little Abbie 'Now, run along home, you. I'm worn out with your pestering.'

Abbie looks slapped. Dyllis immediately regrets this teasing remark, but she's too tired to try and stop her so stands, helpless, as she watches the girl run across the road and slam the door to No. 3. Dyllis sinks slowly on to the piano stool. Needy and little she may be, but Dyllis would hate to lose Abbie's friendship now. The girl's got to learn to stand up to a bit of teasing. She won't get very far in life if she takes offence at the slightest thing.

Dyllis carefully folds away the music they've been working on. Dyllis wishes she could find some *Five Finger Exercises for the Talented but Easily Bored*. There are sheets of manuscript paper too amongst the *Melodies for Little Hands*. They've been composing a tune for Kat. It's the child's birthday in a few weeks and she wants to give her mum a present to mark the occasion. She'll be eleven. And then she'll start at Stockford Comp, the school created by the amalgamation of the grammar, where Dyllis' husband taught French, and the old secondary modern. If she's bright, Abbie will have to take the bus to the county town to do her A-Levels. Abbie's going to need support from home if she's to reach her potential. Dyllis rubs her cold, dry, eyes: does she have the energy for all this?

'I won't have this in my house, Lauren!' Kat's got the syringes in her hands and is breaking them one by one into the bin bag beside the kitchen table. 'Or this!' Instead of flushing them away, she empties the heroin sachets into a saucepan and pours boiling water over the loose balls of brown, and then a squirt of cleaning fluid, and some chilli sauce, which she knows Lauren hates. She starts mashing the mix with a fork. Satisfied it's unusable, she pours the mess onto an old copy of the *Advertiser*, which she folds and shoves into the black bag with Ryan's sock and his hoodie and the ash-filled lager can. She hands the lot to Stephen. 'And don't you go through his bins, you sneaky little bitch. He'll have taken it straight to the dump, won't you, Vicar?' Kat waves Stephen towards the front door, where Stephen bumps into Abbie who has tears pouring down her stricken face.

'You want the stuff, you can go,' Kat continues her rant at

Lauren. 'You can get out of here. Carter made me come back to look out for Abbie, not you.' She puts an arm around a shocked-into-silence Abbie and continues her attack. 'You,' she jabs a vicious finger at her elder daughter who still sits, cowed, at the bottom of the stairs, 'are trouble. You always been trouble. You were born trouble...'

Stephen may be bowed down by his own situation, but he can't walk away from this. Before Kat goes any further, Stephen stops his retreat and steps in. 'What your mother's trying to say,' he says, throwing the black bag onto the doorstep, coming back into the house and giving Kat a shut-up-before-I-shut-you-up look, 'is that she's here for you, if you want to get better. If you want to try and knock it on the head, she'll support you all the way. Won't you, Kathleen?'

Nobody's called Kat 'Kathleen' since her mother died. Certainly not in that tone of voice. Kat stops her tirade long enough for Stephen to usher everyone into the kitchen. He pulls out the four chairs around the table. Sits in one. Waits, while the other three take in what they're supposed to do. As sulky as each other, Kat and Lauren sit down. Abbie retires to the bottom of the stairs, to chew the skin around her thumbs. Stephen leaves her there. This is tough for her. She is only ten.

'What's the story, Lauren?' asks Stephen. Off the hook for the moment, Kat leans back in her chair and raises an accusing eyebrow at her elder daughter. Stephen glares. Kat scowls back at him. For the first time since she's been back, she sees Stephen as the man he's grown into: his hardened face framed by thick grey hair, his wiry hands, his bruised eyes... Kat bites her lip.

As Stephen fully expected, Lauren, under pressure, begins to cry.

Stephen neither reaches out to her nor talks to her. He

waits. They all wait. Eventually, taking a shuddering breath, Lauren gathers herself. 'I wrote you a note, Mum,' she says, between subsiding, hiccupping sobs. 'Then Ryan left. And he ruined everything by leaving a stash. I was gonna chuck it. Before you come back. Tessa and me, was gonna chuck it together. But now you'll never believe me.' And she pushes her chair back and, howling, throws herself upstairs. The bedroom door slams.

Stephen reaches for the folded piece of paper still sitting on the table and flips it open. He sees Lauren's careful, childish writing beginning: *Dear Mum...* He hands the letter to Kat.

Walking home, he's grateful to Tessa for holding Lauren there. Without Tessa, Lauren would have certainly given in to temptation and had time to hide the heroin, probably use some of it. Tessa's always been quietly clever with Stephen's crisis-driven parishioners. She has an instinctive ability to talk people down, to hold them emotionally until the bad moment has passed. He remembers her distress when that addict she'd befriended was found dead. She blamed herself. No wonder she wanted to get away.

Chapter 17

Carter stares at the print-out of the contents of his savings account. It's all gone bar the single quid they made him leave. He's even used up the prize money for winning the vintage ploughing competition. Gone on a flight and deposit to the agency - who say they'll sort out his visa, somewhere for him to stay when he gets there, and work within a week.

Poof! The flashes of the camera booth at the supermarket are blinding. He sits on the bench waiting for the strip of photographs to be delivered. The man at the post office said he could get a passport in a fortnight if he paid a bit extra.

He remembers afternoons in Rufus' potting shed, lying with his head in Tessa's lap while she told him again why he must go. She said a man who spends his life where he was born is a prisoner unless he's travelled first and then decided home is where he chooses above all other places. She'd told him he didn't have to do as his mother wanted. He didn't have to look after his sisters and stay in Hindle Green all his life. He left school at sixteen. He's been working on the land ever since. Tessa cuffed his head when he told her how much he's saved. She laughed at him for still working and told him he'd earned the right to misspend a bit of his twenty-two-year-old youth.

He fingers the envelope containing the written reference Sir Charles has given him. Sir Charles glittered with enthusiasm at the idea of Carter's escape, crumpling the notes he found in his pocket into Carter's hand and telling him with a dirty laugh not to waste it all on beer and women. It's as though people want the adventure through him, thinks Carter, because they can't go themselves. The agency has Sir Charles' phone number in case any prospective employer wants to talk to him in person. Carter's put himself down for tractor, horticultural, any farm labouring work.

He needs a personal reference.

Would Dyllis do?

His flight is at the beginning of October. He's got three weeks to get sorted.

Is he really going to go?

There's a purposeful new-term air to September. Stephen feels like a boy without a school place to go to.

The position for a new rector for Stockford has been advertised, and without irony the rural dean's asked Stephen to help go through the applications. She's said again, 'Of course this job would be no good for you,' even though this time when she dropped in on him Stephen had made the effort to shave and wash up the sinkful of dirty dishes. He'd even gone so far as to square up the files on his desk – though the exertion nearly finished him. And it is exertion: life has become like an assault course through molasses. Mundane tasks like making cups of tea or bathing or choosing what to wear in the morning are enough to send him back to bed to recover from the strain. He has no idea where he'll go when the Stockford job has been given to somebody else. The lease on the Hindle Green vicarage is up at the end of January. He flicks through a three-page rant from a woman who's clearly come to blows with her current parish and has 'a strong desire to move to Stockford' - a place which she considers 'will be more malleable to my progressive ideas'.

He should be fighting for this job. But depression has come upon him with the speed of an unexpected summer storm and he is incapacitated by it. Of course he wouldn't dream of explaining how he feels to anyone else: that might make them feel as if they have the right to try and help him – and what can anybody else possibly know about the depth of these black clouds?

The rural dean clearly thinks him unsuitable on account of his collapsed relationship with Tessa. Stephen knows the diocese can't afford to be so choosy and that he'd have a good chance if he could galvanise himself to bypass the rural dean, and call the Bishop direct. But he was done in by shaving this morning.

He can do crisis management, as in when he forced Kat and Lauren to confront each other the other day. But he drowns in the minutiae of everyday.

He screws up the rant from the woman outside Liverpool and throws it viciously at the fire: it bounces off and rolls under a chair where it comes to rest beside a dustball as big as a fist.

There's the sound of a car pulling up outside. Now what? Len Fox unfolding his angular, praying mantis limbs from inside his dull red Nissan Sunny and hammering on the front door. Stephen scuttles to hide behind the curtains in his office, determined to wait for the rector to go away. But Fox isn't easily put off. He picks his way around to the back of the house. Stephen's forgotten that the kitchen door is wide open. From behind his hiding place he hears the rector barge in and sit down. Stephen stays hidden. After a while there's the hiss and click of the kettle being filled and plugged in.

'Make you a cup, shall I?' the rector shouts. 'Biscuits in the larder, are they?'

Stephen slumps down behind the curtain and covers his face with his hands. Will the rector find the new packet of Hobnobs? Stephen doesn't want to share them; there's nothing else to eat in the house. The man will go eventually, won't he? The curtain's twitched back and Stephen's revealed. The rector eases himself down to Stephen's level, his knees cracking. He's brought a tray laid with tea. He found the Hobnobs.

'I hear you've been having an interesting time while I've been away,' Len begins. He slurps at his tea and grunts appreciatively. He leans against the wall beside the wood burner and eases his legs out in front of him, then blows his nose luxuriously into a worn cotton handkerchief. Still half hidden between the curtain and the radiator, Stephen says nothing.

'You having a row with God as well, then?' asks the rector. Stephen bites his lip now, but his eyes still well like a child's. He wants to howl.

The rector ruminates on a biscuit. 'If you're going to waste your stipend on luxury comestibles, I'd go the extra mile and get the dark-chocolate-covered ones,' he starts. Then, 'You know the story of St Teresa of Avila?'

Stephen doesn't move. No, he doesn't know the story of St Teresa of Avila.

The rector seems pleased to be able to tell it. 'One day she was seen standing on a bridge shaking her fist at the sky, shouting, "No wonder you've got so few friends, the way you treat them."'

'It's not God's fault Tessa left me.'

'Oh, but you blame old Sod, don't you? You blame him for letting you work so hard on His behalf that your wife had nothing better to do than enjoy a dalliance with a gardener half your age and get herself pregnant by him.'

'And then she left me.'

'She didn't go very far, though, did she?' The rector finishes his tea and smacks his lips. 'Now it's decided, I'm looking forward to my retirement. But I can't go till they've found my replacement.'

'They're looking for a family man.'

'Bollocks. You tell that uptight beanpole with a mouth like a cat's bottom that she can stuff her "This job's only

suitable for a family man" line. You should have heard her
when you first came to Hindle Green. She already had you and
Tessa lined up for my job. Practically retired me on the spot,
she did.'

'I don't know if I want to carry on working for the Church
at all.'

'Don't tell me you're having the kind of crisis of faith
which has left you no longer believing?'

'If only.'

The ragged, split nails on the rector's hands are flat and
ridged from age and work. His fingers are swollen, like
bananas, and purplish. They are a reproach to Stephen, who
shakes his head. 'I didn't mean that.'

'Then you'd know how it feels to be lonely.'

Stephen's too angry to be sympathetic. 'I'm fucking
lonely now!' Suddenly he's raging. His head explodes with
snot and tears and the gross unfairness of it all. 'I worked so
fucking hard and this is what I get! Tessa pregnant by
somebody else and gone.'

'She's set you up nicely, though.'

'What do you mean?'

'It's repetitive little things that get you through a bad time.
Believe me. You should expend your energy on the garden in
order to keep your mind.'

'The chickens are eating their eggs.'

'Put a marble egg in with them and they'll stop, for fear of
breaking their beaks. David Tait's wife collects them. The
marble eggs, I mean. He calls them dust-gatherers. He won't
mind stealing one for you.'

Lauren is another reproach to Stephen. Here's a girl to whom
life has dealt a series of difficult hands and every time she
loses, she just picks herself up and goes right on playing. She's

refusing methadone because it would take her all day to get to the hospital, take her prescription and get back. She says she can't waste the time, 'Because I need to get a job and sort my life out, don't I?' Stephen's impressed with her determination but fears that heroin, being much more easily available than methadone in Stockford, she might be caught out at a weak moment. But Lauren's refusing the 'one step at a time' idea. She's taking the bull by the horns and isn't frightened about being gored. She's motivating herself by talking constantly about her twins. Stephen has thought of a potential job for her. He knocks on the door to No. 3 on his way back from his meeting with social services. Carter opens up. Stephen shouldn't be surprised, but still he flushes, steps back.

'I was looking for your sister, Lauren.'

'She's out.'

The vicar looks terrible. Carter never thought Stephen would mind so much about Tessa leaving: he never seemed to care much for her before. Carter would make things right if only he knew how: he didn't mean for Tessa to get pregnant; he knows it was stupid but in the heat of the moment it never occurred to him that she would.

At a loss for what to say next, Carter blurts, 'Vicar, I'm going away.'

'With Tessa?' It's out before Stephen can stop it.

'No.'

No? It seems Carter might have said something right. The vicar looks as though he's coming back from the dead.

Hoping Carter's not going to say he's only off to Newquay with mates for the weekend, Stephen asks, 'Where to?'

'New Zealand,' says Carter. 'For the winter. They need tractor drivers.'

Opportunistic as ever, Carter capitalises on Stephen's stunned silence with, 'But I need a reference. Sir Charles give

237

me one, but I need a personal reference. I was gonna ask your mum. She used to be a magistrate, didn't she?'

'I'll give you a reference.' At last Stephen finds his tongue. Carter's going away – far away – for a long time – without Tessa! Stephen is light-headed with relief. He'd give Carter the coat off his back if he asked for it. 'How long are you going for? Will I have to risk life and limb mowing the churchyard myself?'

Now, when the rector drops round a recipe for tomato sauce and a circled ad torn out of the *Advertiser* for twenty pound's worth of second-hand chest freezer, Stephen rings up and buys it, bringing it home hanging precariously out of the back of the Mini and tied in with bouncing bungees to stop it escaping. Pushing it round the back of the house on the wheelbarrow, he installs it in the shed. Purposeful for the first time in months, it takes Stephen all one Saturday to run the electricity for it out from the kitchen. When he's finished, he feels a deep and unexpected satisfaction. He will fill the freezer with vitamin-bursting veg for Tessa to eat in the winter when the baby comes. She planted it all: the least he can do is harvest it for her.

The rector said he should only decide what he wants to do in the short-term – he can change his mind any time – but any kind of decision will make Stephen feel less as if he's flailing about in sinking sand.

So Stephen calls the Bishop's office, leaves a message, and then books a meeting with the social worker to talk about Lauren.

He's anything but happy. But at last he's learning to compartmentalise his unhappiness, to put it in a Tupperware and freeze it along with the runner beans.

Unable to sleep, he's up and out at six, padding about in

the dew-drench. The garden is a cornucopia, but this early in the morning you can smell the coming autumn in the mist blanketing the valley, a bite in the air as sharp as the juice in the apples ripening over the chicken house.

Because they're there, he picks great heaps of tomatoes, scatters them with cloves of garlic and a little brown sugar, and puts them to roast slowly in the bottom oven of the Rayburn. When they've collapsed on themselves he whizzes them up in the liquidizer he finds abandoned at the back of one of Dyllis' kitchen cupboards and freezes them. Ellen passes on spare spring cabbage seedlings. He pulls the onions, lays them to dry on the cut grass, and plants the seedlings in the vacated bed. For Tessa. Bent double to pinch the little plants into their new home, Stephen snorts at himself: at least the vegetable beds are full of cosy couplings.

Abbie sits on the wall outside Stockford Comp and chews the skin around her thumbs. Stockford Comp is a sports academy. Abbie isn't sporty. There's no music. Abbie jumps off the wall without looking and, still tugging at threads of skin, walks down the hill. She pulls out her mobile to text her mum she'll be home on the next bus. She doesn't notice the tough girls until one's elbowing her in the chest, another twisting the phone out of her hands, a third scattering the contents of her bag onto the road.

They run off laughing. 'What kinda Stoke are you?!'

The phone's judged wanting and is smashed against the wall where Abbie was sitting. She stares after the receding girls, the torn skin around her fingers held tight in her fists, Dyllis' voice echoing in her head: 'You've got a choice.'

Abbie hasn't seen Dyllis since the old woman told her to stop pestering.

Instead, she's been home, watching the people who live at

No.3 Pratt Cottages fail to play happy families. All Abbie ever dreamed of was her mum coming home. And now her mum says someone called Buster's coming to stay. Apparently this Buster is Abbie's supposed dad. With a jealousy-inspiring sparkle in her eyes, Kat says they'll love him. 'Love' is not a word that's bandied about at No. 3 often enough to be ignored.

On the bus, she would have bandaged her bleeding thumbs if her stock of plasters hadn't been strewn in the gutter. She swears she'll let her hands heal for at least a week before picking again. When she gets off the bus at the top of the lane, she doesn't walk down to No. 3. Instead, she rings Dyllis' bell, and stands, waiting, like a stranger, while she listens to Dyllis haul herself out of her chair and come to open the front door.

Dyllis is formal, sitting in her armchair with her cushion buzzing quietly against her back. She should be outside, soaking up the last of the sunshine before the autumn chill sets in. But she's tired. The idea of Abbie coming to stay with her is charming, but impractical.

'I like you visiting,' she says, smiling at the disconsolate little girl sitting on the piano stool. 'Your mother's only just come home. Your dearest wish granted and now you want to come and live with me?'

'You said I have choices,' says Abbie, picking at the plasters on her thumbs.

'Of course you do.'

'What choices?'

'What do you want?'

'Not to be at a school where there's nothing to do but swim, but the pool's closed for mendin', where I can't learn the piano, where I get mugged just to see how tough I am.'

'Did they hurt you?'

'They smashed my phone. My family's got a reputation. I

gotta be a hard girl or they'll carry on beating me up to prove how tough they are.' Abbie looks at her long, not-yet-pianist's, fingers. 'I wanna choose not to be like my sister. I wanna make something of myself. And you said to do that I have to start now. I haven't got time to waste. You were punctilious about that.'

'Nice word.'

'What do I have to do to get a scholarship to that posh school, Queen Anne's?'

Dyllis is against private education on principle. 'Just because something costs more doesn't mean it's any better.'

'I bet they teach piano there.'

'I think I'd better talk to your mother.'

Abbie sighs. 'Do you have to?'

Dyllis likes nothing about private Queen Anne's, but the grammar school in Stockford is long gone and the comprehensive that merged with the old secondary modern to replace it is a crumbling place with no academic pretension. The list of GCSE courses available is designed for the lowest common denominator to leave with a few sparse qualifications. There is no sixth form. And who is she to deny Abbie a chance to go and look at Queen Anne's? Abbie might well hate the look of it, realise she could learn everything she wants to using a good old public library and her own self-will and native intelligence, and then that would be that.

Dyllis telephones Queen Anne's, calling herself Abbie's piano teacher. The registrar she speaks to takes her name and says pointedly, 'We don't have any other of your pupils here, Mrs Wilkinson?'

Dyllis bridles but still makes an appointment for Abbie to go and see the school, though she's warned, 'We don't do full scholarships unless the circumstances are exceptional. And this year's music scholars have taken their places already.'

As far as Dyllis is concerned, it's important that Abbie is honestly presented with the options open to her. And perhaps if Abbie's not going to get any support from home... It's all very well for Dyllis to disapprove of private education when she could have educated Stephen herself all she liked. He grew up in a house full of books and culture and the answers to his questions – or at least the understanding that answers could be found. Dyllis doesn't even know how long Kat is likely to stay around. Will she leave Abbie in Lauren's charge when Carter's gone? Surely not.

Dyllis doesn't want to invite Kat to tea for fear of being thought imperious. Instead, she asks April to deliver one of her carrot cakes, and this she carries over the road, hobbling painfully on her creaking hips, the cake in a bag which bangs against another holding the prospectus for Queen Anne's. Dyllis can go no further without Kat's active cooperation.

It's nine thirty in the morning. Having quizzed Abbie, she knows that Kat will most likely be found polishing the kitchen surfaces, having sent her children off on their various daytime activities. Abbie texted Dyllis this morning, a call which came through via a Stephen Hawking-style electronic voice simulator on Dyllis' landline. 'Good luck Mrs Witch. Remember, my future's at stake. No pressure. Ha Ha.' Dyllis is relieved she's forgiven for snapping at Abbie the other day. She feels the importance of her errand keenly.

'Oh!' The door's opened by a man she doesn't recognise. Abbie hadn't said the Stokes were expecting visitors. This is a wiry fellow wearing a straw Stetson in the house, and cowboy boots to add to his otherwise diminutive height.

He turns and shouts back at the interior, 'Doll!' He ushers Dyllis carefully into the kitchen, his arm resting painfully on her shoulders. Dyllis, a past master at hiding pain, smiles and offers Kat the cake.

Kat glows. The toenails on her bare feet are painted fluorescent pink. She's wearing black leggings under jeans cut into shorts and a white T-shirt emblazoned with the words, 'love me – go on – I dare you' in dayglo green. She's tied it in a knot at her hip. She smiles at Dyllis, content as a cat certain there'll be cream any time she asks for it.

The man in the Stetson throws himself on the kitchen couch and picks up a guitar. He strums.

'Forgive me for intruding,' says Dyllis, arranging the cake centrally on the table. 'Kat, I just wondered... I'd love to talk to you some time about Abbie.' Kat crosses her arms and tucks her hands into her armpits. Stetson man takes a roll-up from behind his ear and lights up. He stares at Dyllis. Interested? Dangerous?

'But perhaps this is a bad time,' continues Dyllis, beginning to turn and make a retreat.

'What you got to say about my little Abbie?' asks the man.

'Do you mind if I sit down?' Dyllis pulls out a kitchen chair. She lowers herself onto it, then holds a hand out to the stranger who just waves back from the sofa. 'I'm Dyllis Wilkinson,' she says.

Beaten, Kat takes a chair beside Dyllis, though she doesn't put the kettle on. She nods at the man in the Stetson. 'He's Buster Mostin,' she says, and adds, with careful nonchalance, 'Abbie's dad.'

Dyllis blinks, zips her mouth, and takes a closer look at the visitor. Kat must be keen: who else would get away with dropping ash on Kat's pristine floor?

'What do you want to say about the girl?' he asks.

Dyllis can't see his charm, though Kat's clearly mesmerised. He's too carefully Sarf London. Will he be sympathetic to what Dyllis is about to say?

'Well, I'm sure you realise, Kat, how bright Abbie is.'

Kat raises an eyebrow and says nothing.

'And she's struggling with bullies at Stockford Comp. Of course the first term at secondary school's often difficult, especially if a child's used to being a big fish at their primary. But if you look into the future then Stockford hasn't got a sixth form and Abbie... Has she told you about our little sessions at the piano?'

'She musical?' Buster strums the guitar. 'Take after her old dad? What you teaching 'er? Bit a rock and roll, I hope.' He plays a few random chords which might conceivably have a bluesy inspiration.

'She's been learning for three months. I've got her onto some simple Chopin. Do you earn a living through your guitar, Mr Mostin?'

'I own my own pub.' The man's half proud, half defensive. 'With a theatre upstairs. When I got time, I play.'

Kat's already shaking her head. 'I won't have it,' she says. 'It won't be right.'

'I haven't even told you what I have in mind.'

'Listen, Mrs Wilkinson,' says Kat, tough, the girl who would have Abbie scar the hard girls at the school and never mind the delicate fingers she might need to make music with. 'I don't want Abbie spoiling. All right? She's a Stoke and she'll behave like a Stoke. None of us did too bad and we had no special treatment. And life will deal her a mean hand, and she's got to be able to cope with that.'

'I've spoken to Queen Anne's,' Dyllis has to say her piece. 'They were a bit snooty. But Abbie's very keen to go and see them. She wants to try and get in.'

'For her to be bullied by the posh girls because she don't have a pony and never learned to ski? Why hasn't Abbie talked about this to me herself?'

'Perhaps she's frightened you'll refuse to even think about the idea. She knows I won't mind if you shout at me.'

Kat huffs, 'Go'orn then, you tell me what you come to say and save me'n Abbie havin' a row, then.'

Dyllis smiles. 'The girls at Queen Anne's are mostly farmers' daughters. No more intelligent than the kids at the comprehensive. Their experience is not so very far removed from Abbie's. And though of course bullying goes on, no matter how expensive the school, at least Queen Anne's offers a wide selection of more academic subjects which Abbie could study on through to A-Level and potentially use to qualify her for university.'

'And what does a trip to university buy you?'

'These days, very little. But she has a good brain. And she wants to learn to use it.'

'What about money?'

'We'd have to discuss that with them...'

Kat pulls at the spikes of her hair. 'I don't see why Queen Anne's would want her.'

'To keep their charitable status, private schools have to function generously within their community.'

'We don't need charity!'

'Yes we do.' At the bottom of the stairs stands Lauren, bleary, pale. She sniffs, tucks her hands into her armpits, looks Buster up and down and then ignores him. 'You don't let Abbie do this, Mum, and I'll think you're the stupidest woman... There'll be no point holding off from the promise of a bit of brown if you're gonna force Abbie to grow up like I did... she could go anywhere, Mum, be anything, see the world.'

'You could of got your exams, Lauren. They do exams at Stockford Comp.'

'At Stockford Comp they was worried about the stupid

245

kids. The rough kids got attention. Anyone who could read and write already got ignored. Nobody took me under their wing like what Mrs Wilkinson done for Abbie. Maybe if they had I wouldn't of gone the way I did. Maybe I'd of made something of myself.'

'Abbie's got enough on. This is Buster, her dad, come to get to know her.'

'What the fuck she want a dad for when she could be getting an education? I mean, no disrespect,' says Lauren to Buster. 'But far as I can tell you just come to bring Mum her stuff. You're not staying. You're not going to be a dad. Are you?' For a second, Lauren looks really worried.

Buster has stopped picking at his guitar. He sucks his teeth, shakes his head. 'Gotta get back for the pub, Doll,' he says to Kat. 'You know that.'

Now Kat gets up to put the kettle on. 'But you brought your guitar.'

'I didn't bring anything else, did I? You know I'm not gonna come and stay here, in the country!'

The man cares not a jot for Kat.

Outside there's the coughing of the old Mini struggling up the hill. Kat stares through all the walls as though she can see Stephen nursing the car up the road. Her face is expressionless. Dyllis pulls the prospectus of Queen Anne's out of the plastic bag, hoping she'll be able to make everybody concentrate a bit more on the matter in hand.

Chapter 18

The school was endowed by Queen Anne in 1709: *For the education of the daughters of gentlemen in the accomplishments suitable for girls of such station.* Waiting in the hall, Dyllis reads a list of the founders.

'Look!' she says to Kat. Ninth on the list of twelve reads: *Carter Stoke, Gent.*

'We was farmers once,' says Kat, her awe of her surroundings bringing out the extreme country girl in her accent.

Abbie sits on a bench to one side, swinging her legs, not chewing at her fingers. Pupils wearing kilts, white shirts and ties sashay past, slipping along the antique oak-block floor on the soles of their regulation black-but-still-New Look ballet shoes. Abbie's chosen to wear a grey, long-sleeved t-shirt and immaculate white jeans with orange baseball boots from the market for her interview.

'I'm not pretending to be anyone I'm not,' she'd said, indignant, when Dyllis commented on the fact that she'd removed the giant hoop earrings for the day. To Dyllis it looks as if the pupils are all pretending to be posh school children in a storybook. Abbie seems enthralled.

'Do you know much about your family history?' Dyllis asks Kat.

'Abigail Stoke?' A tall lady with thick white hair and huge pearl earrings opens a panelled door and smiles.

Lauren's been clean three weeks, four days, nine-and-a-half hours. She brushes her hair, throws away the last, empty cigarette packet, and pulls on one of her mum's sweatshirts and tidy jeans. It's Wednesday morning. She takes the papers she's been gathering, walks down the hill and rings the bell at the vicarage.

Stephen opens up.

'Oh!' says Lauren before she can stop herself. 'You grown a proper beard.'

Amused by the fact that his unshaven appearance has turned into a look that can be given a name, Stephen shows Lauren into the office. 'Sorry about the mess.'

'You need a proper clear out,' says Lauren. Then, 'I wanna get my girls back. And I reckon, to get the authorities to let me have them, I need a job, and you telling them I won't muck them around, and a flat. You could pay me to clear your house out for a start, then you could give me a reference saying I didn't steal the valuables and that.'

Stephen laughs. Lauren's got gall, that's for certain. 'Well, I'll tell the powers-that-be that you're determined; that's easy enough.' He squares off a teetering pile of files so that they won't fall. They leave patterns of dust on the desk, which he swipes away with his sleeve. 'I wish I could ask you to sort all this out but I'm afraid vicars' stipends don't run to help in the house. Couldn't you live at home with your mum? She could be registered as joint guardian. There'll be more support that way. With Carter going off there'll be a room for the twins to sleep in, won't there?'

Lauren looks Stephen straight in the eye. 'Mum ain't got no faith in me. Anyway, I reckon she'll bugger off again pretty soon. She only come back for Carter. If Abbie goes to Queen Anne's like she wants to she won't need so much looking after. Mum won't stick around for me. So I better see if I can get my own flat and then I got to look after the twins and the flat and rely on no one. And if I get a job I could pay for the flat and the girls. But you mustn't tell Mum what I'm planning. She says there've been Stokeses in Hindle Green forever and she won't be the one to let us go. Even though she's always chasing off.'

'The twins' Nanna Deborah won't give them up easily.'

'I'd rather fight her than my mum. Mum's gonna be so mad when Carter goes. I don't wanna be anywhere near when that happens.' Her stream of consciousness ramble takes a hairpin bend. 'Do you think you could get the twins out on a visit to have tea at No. 3?'

Stephen twiddles his pen in his hand. He needs to calm Lauren down without stamping on her enthusiasm. 'You're going to have to make it up with your mum if you're going to persuade the authorities to let you have the twins on a visit. Social services will probably want her to chaperone.'

He stands up and leads the way to the kitchen. 'We're going to need sustenance for all that form-filling,' he says. 'I think there are biscuits left.'

She follows him and, looking up the lawn at the falling-over mess that was Tessa's vegetable patch, says, 'You do need help.'

'I thought I was doing brilliantly.'

'Shame about you and your Tessa.' Lauren knows it's none of her business, but... 'It was terrible her going off with Carter like that when you're a vicar so you must be a good man.' Lauren knows she's digging herself into a hole but she doesn't seem to be able to shut her mouth. 'Still, she ain't left the village, so maybe she wants you back? Course you wouldn't have her now, not now she's gonna have the baby. Sorry. I can't help speaking out of turn.' She doesn't look very apologetic. 'Mum says I've got a mouth like a runaway train when she's not there to control it.'

'Truth is, Lauren, I'd have Tessa back like a shot if she wanted.' And it's out. He's told somebody. His heart beats a tiny bit faster at the thought that Lauren might tell Abbie, Abbie Dyllis, Dyllis Tessa...

249

'Well, you should tell her yourself, then,' says Lauren. 'No point in keeping that a secret. And tell her quick before she goes off somewhere else.'

How could he think it would be that easy?

Spooning sugar into her tea, Lauren helps herself to a custard cream, looks at it, nibbles. It's stale. She puts it down. 'What would you do about the baby?'

'Give it a home.' And it's true. He would. It's not the child's fault Stephen couldn't give Tessa the baby she wanted. She was forced elsewhere by Stephen's careless assumption that Tessa was happy with her lot.

If it hadn't been Carter, she'd have found somebody else. He'd just happened to be the fittest, youngest... Dyllis always says we should remember we're driven by animal instincts much stronger than any logical thinking which makes us feel superior.

'I've made enquiries about a job for you, if you're interested.' Stephen banishes his own problems and returns to Lauren's comparatively resolvable situation.

Dyllis is so exhausted by her morning with Abbie at Queen Anne's that she takes the extraordinary step of actually going to bed on her return. With Abbie, the taxi driver solicitously helped her up the path. She could have carried on, taken to her armchair and the crossword and asked Abbie to bring her a cup of tea with a slug of whisky in it to warm her bones. Instead, she sent the girl home and retreated, like an old she-fox, she thinks, to her lair. In bed, she shivers, though the day is warm.

The Headmistress said that though the school year has already begun, she will consider Abbie's case and let them know in writing.

Dyllis isn't convinced by the school. Will Queen Anne's buy Abbie nothing more than an accent that will alienate her from her family? It was Kat who seemed to like the place, who said in the middle of the interview that Abbie's very likely a direct descendant of one of the founders. The headmistress had smiled in a magnificently patronising way and said if they could prove that fact with a paper trail then Abbie would get a full scholarship, including uniform, school trips, and even the slightest incidental expenses. Daughters of founders are educated at Queen Anne's for free. But, as the headmistress pointed out, there are any number of families called Stoke in the West Country. To which Kat retorted that she reckons there can't be that many who traditionally name the eldest son of each generation 'Carter'.

Abbie sits on the back step of Dyllis' house. The old woman's sleeping and Abbie's finding that she doesn't necessarily need her for feedback: she just relishes the quiet calm of this place to think in. At home, furious with indecision about whether to stay, go, help, run, her mum's on a mission to re-clean everything. Since Kat's return, the kitchen surfaces are almost worn away with the grit in the supermarket-own-brand, lemon-scented cream cleaner.

Abbie considers the concept of a dad. Lauren and Carter never had one. It's not an idea which she can get her head round. The twins' dad did a bunk and joined the navy before they were even born. What's a dad for? She flattens her hands out in front of her and examines the torn skin around her fingers. She crosses her arms and tucks her hands into her armpits. Seems to Abbie a dad is a harbinger of disruption and confusion, someone who turns a mum into a person who disappears unexpectedly, without even saying goodbye.

Abbie scratches her silk-smooth, scraped back hair. She picks up the satchel she took with her to Queen Anne's this morning and walks quietly into the sitting room. She'd been

251

asked to perform her pieces in a big room with windows overlooking playing fields edged with gigantic copper beech trees. She imagines being allowed to spend time in that room, lost in making the perfect three-dimensional abstract patterns which she sees in the air when she plays. She'd forget to chew her fingers if she had that.

Dyllis sleeps sitting up these days, for fear of not being able to right herself when she wakes. Besides, the way she coughs in the morning would break a rib if she was forced to bring up all that phlegm lying down. So, leaning against a nest of hard pillows, sitting on her old candlewick bedspread, Dyllis keeps her eyes closed while she listens to Abbie's careful execution of the studies she's taught her. Dyllis was so proud when the Head of Music asked how long Abbie had been playing and Abbie replied, blithely, 'Since June,' completely unaware how extraordinary her progress has been. Unlike the snobbish headmistress, the piano teacher had been impressed. Dyllis remembers his name. She should write it down. He might give private lessons... She hears a hiccup in Abbie's playing: her finger-work's wrong...

Unable to leave her protégé alone, Dyllis carefully slides her legs sideways and off the bed. She hadn't bothered to take her shoes off: she'd only have to put them on again, so that's one less thing to do. But now those shoes seem to have grown somehow, to be getting in her way, tripping her...

With a thunderous slam, Abbie finishes off her private concert with a wild rendition of the original *Chopsticks* she'd first learnt with Dyllis those few months ago. She doesn't hear the crash in the bedroom.

It's true: Kat does seem to do nothing but clean. But when your house is as immaculate as hers, the slightest smudge

shows like a broken window. Besides, what else does she have
to do? In London, in the pub, there's always the chat as a
distraction while she polishes the glasses. Even out of hours,
when the actors take a break from rehearsing in that minute
studio theatre which is really just an upstairs room with two
rows of benches squashed around three sides, there's somebody
to talk to. And they like Kat. They like her for not giving a
shit about her age, for her air of having been around a bit. To
the actors and the pub regulars, she dispenses advice as if she's
an expert agony aunt.

Here, in Hindle Green, Kat feels herself the object of pity.
A woman with three fatherless children, one about to disappear
to the other side of the world; another a single mother herself
with two children she's judged incapable of caring for; a third
who wants to go to boarding school rather than live at home.
The least Kat can do is keep a clean house: she won't have
them accuse her of filth too.

Kat gives the gleaming sink another, vicious wipe.

If she goes back to London...

But Buster doesn't want her. Not really. That was the first
time Buster could have laid eyes on Abbie since she was a baby
and he bottled it. It was the first time Kat put Buster in a
situation where he had to put his own desires aside for those of
Kat and her daughter and it was all he could do to bring her
bags down before running back to town. If he'd kept her
belongings at the pub, Kat would feel as if he wanted her. But
he drove all the way down here with her clothes shoved any-
how into black plastic bags and was gone already by lunchtime,
having stuffed himself with Dyllis' cake first. He was too
cowardly even to wait till Abbie got back from school. Kat
knows perfectly well the fear of a connection that will tie you
down. She touched Abbie's hair that day she got back and
hasn't managed to escape from the child and the

overwhelming, fear-inspiring, responsibility-weighting love she feels for her - yet.

The list of bad choices Kat has made in her life unrolls before her eyes. And now she has a stint at the farm shop to look forward to. Probably only three customers all afternoon, people rich enough to buy hand-reared pork while her kids will be coming home to...?

It's the repetitive hopelessness she hates. And the sound of her own mother's voice in her ear telling her it has ever been so, will always be so. She resents Carter for leaving and envies him at the same time.

Of course that school won't want Abbie. *We are the bad family,* she thinks, half proud, half resigned.

Across the road, Dyllis' curtains are shut.

Now there's a woman who's never been bored. What does she do that entertains her so?

Wait a minute: her bedroom curtains are shut! In the middle of the afternoon?

Kat never makes it to her shift at the farm shop. Instead, she waits with Abbie for the ambulance to arrive, holding Dyllis' hand and feeling the fluttering pulse butterflying irregularly through the paper-thin skin on her wrist. Through half-frozen lips, Dyllis tells Kat not to be stupid. That it's just a turn. She has them all the time. She'll be right as rain with a cup of tea if she'd be so good as to make her one. With perhaps a tiny slug of whisky to give Dyllis' blood a jolt.

Abbie makes the barely-clouded-with-milk tea (without whisky) while Kat gently helps Dyllis to sit on the edge of the bed. She was found flat on the floor, blood congealing from a wounded temple. How could Abbie not have heard her fall?

'I was getting up to correct her finger-work.' Dyllis' mouth has seized up on one side as if she's had a massive injection of Novocaine. Dyllis rubs at it with her opposite hand: the hand on the same side as the sluggish side of her face seems to have no strength in it.

The wail of the arriving ambulance has the whole village out, staring. Abbie waves frantically to the paramedics and they run up the path through the bungalow's front garden, carrying an astonishing amount of equipment for a tiny woman sitting quietly on the edge of her bed.

'She had a turn,' says Kat, ushering the two men through to Dyllis' bedroom. 'Put the kettle on again,' she hisses at Abbie.

'What do you like to be called, dear?' the first paramedic kneels before Dyllis and feels for her pulse

'Mrs Wilkinson!' insists Dyllis in a weedy voice. For no good reason she seems to be wheezing. It's the talking that's doing it. 'I wish you'd all go away. I'm perfectly all right. My neighbour insisted on calling you.'

The other paramedic is already on the phone.

'Suspected stroke,' he says under his breath. 'She's pretty frail. But sitting up and talking.'

'Now then...' The first paramedic prepares to examine Dyllis. 'Will you let me just do a few routine checks? For our peace of mind...'

'I told you, there's nothing the matter with me bar old age and a certain amount of wear and tear, all self-inflicted,' repeats Dyllis, through gritted teeth.

'Just give you an aspirin,' the man ignores her protests. 'Looks like you might have had a small stroke. The aspirin will help thin...'

'I know what aspirin does, young man.' Dyllis is becoming increasingly imperious.

'And we'll get a dressing on that nasty cut on your head. Did you hit something when you fell?'

'I don't know.' Dyllis feels panicky. She tries to push the man away. 'I don't know,' she wails.

'Patient's a little bit upset,' the other says *sotto voce* into his mobile.

'My feet won't work!' Tears of frustration well in Dyllis' wrinkled old eyes. 'Why won't my feet work?'

Abbie jumps forward. 'Come on, old witch,' she says tenderly. 'Mum and me will get you up.' And Kat and Abbie slip their arms under Dyllis' armpits. Her bones under their hands are frail as a bird's. Abbie's suddenly afraid she might cry.

While the paramedics protest that they should be doing this, Abbie and Kat help Dyllis to stand. Without being asked, Abbie reaches for Dyllis' handbag, checks her reading glasses are in their case. As they shuffle through the sitting room she dives for the book of Sudoku puzzles and the main news section of today's *Telegraph*, which is sitting by the single cigarette stub in the miniature crystal ashtray, and the half-drunk, microwaved breakfast coffee, with the granules still floating in the milk.

Forming a chair with their arms, the paramedics carry Dyllis carefully down the garden path to the ambulance.

Kat notices Abbie's wobbling chin.

'You go and find the vicar,' she says gently. 'I'll stay with her, shall I? You lock up the house. If you can't find the vicar, get Tessa. You know where she'll be?'

Abbie, gulping, nods and without looking back she runs through the house, banging doors and locking as she goes, leaving the key under the pot outside the front door. She runs blindly, past the gawping villagers, fast enough to make her chest hurt, down to the vicarage and round the back to the kitchen door. Too immersed to notice the sound of the ambulance, Lauren and Stephen are still bent tight over their forms.

'Vicar! It's your mother. She's been taken...' And having to tell means Abbie can contain herself no longer. She collapses at the table and drops her head in her arms, her shoulders shuddering with fearful, grieving sobs.

Stephen puts a hand out to the girl's shoulder, takes it back, nods at Lauren to do the comforting.

There's a horrible sinking feeling in Stephen's stomach. 'I'll go and get Tessa,' he says.

He finds Rufus in the kitchen, determinedly working his way through a bottle of wine and raging at a copy of *Hello* magazine. There's no sign of Tessa

Stephen goes looking for her room. Up and up the stairs until he reaches her attic with the rumpled, unmade bed and the notes spread out round her computer, her mobile phone left behind next to a jam jar of michaelmas daisies on her bedside table. He can't exclude her from this. Dyllis will need Tessa. And Tessa will surely never forgive Stephen if he doesn't invite her in now. Stephen puts the note on the bed but decides it'll get lost in the duvet; on the pillow - too intimate. Eventually he leaves it by the computer, weighed down by the stone she's kept as a paper weight ever since he picked it up for her on a pebble beach in Dorset on some holiday a lifetime ago.

Tessa hasn't felt this relaxed in months: an afternoon snapping up half-price special offer multi-packs of babygros, followed by coffee with April who insists on Tessa staying and inviting Daisy and Ellen over to supper.

'I reckon we deserve a night off from our lives.'

'But Ellen...'

'Oh, don't mind her, she's just jealous.'

'She won't want to see me.'

'Look, I'll leave her a message. If she doesn't want to

come then she can stay on her own at home, can't she? Though that would be proper cutting off her nose to spite her face if she did. There's homemade pappardelle for supper.' April shaves parmesan and chops spinach leaves and folds them into the dough.

Daisy calls to say she's got a cornucopia of sweet peppers: should she bring them?

'Should you!' laughs April.

Tessa sits in a basket chair and accepts a tiny glass of Prosecco.

'Time you started taking it a bit easier, my girl,' says April, bossily, giving Tessa a heart-shaped parmesan biscuit straight from the oven. Tessa cradles it with her spare hand so that she won't lose a single one of those lovely buttery crumbs as she tries not to swallow it whole.

And suddenly Daisy and Ellen burst into the room, all noise and baskets and chat and gossip. Tessa stays back, waiting to see if Ellen will still be odd with her. If she is then Tessa will have to withdraw from this group: she's not so stupid that she doesn't realise that new best friends don't always turn into lifelong mates. New friendships are pretty and amusing as sweet peas, but just as fragile.

'I owe you an apology.' Ellen's suddenly at Tessa's elbow. Tessa looks straight at her. Does she mean it? 'I do think you behaved badly. I do think you've had everything you wanted on your plate. And I'm jealous that you're having a baby. But you are having a tough time now. It can't be easy living in luxury with that filmstar.'

There's a beat. And another. Daisy and April shut up and hold their breath. And Tessa prays she's doing the right thing by thwacking Ellen on the arm and saying, 'But the house is freezing, and won't have any heating or hot water in the winter.'

Ellen doesn't snarl. Tessa presses on. 'Don't be jealous of

me. I'm sorry, too. I'm the new girl and you've all been friends forever and I've just barged in on all of you and expected you to like me. I've been the biggest fool and I need you girls to help me live with that. And help me find somewhere to live. I've got to get out of the Old Rectory before this baby comes.'

Ellen laughs. 'Remember the health visitor telling you to get room thermometers and to keep the whole house a temperate 18 degrees when you had Jelly?' she asks Daisy.

Who hoots. 'Imagine trying to get the Old Rectory that hot?'

'What about moving in with Dyllis?' asks April. And then drops the pasta to go and put her arms around Tessa, who for no good reason has begun to cry.

'My fucking hormones!' Tessa wails, trying to get a grip on herself. 'The slightest thing and I just dissolve. I hate it!'

Kat waits outside the ward while low-voiced doctors discuss Dyllis' condition with Stephen. He still looks like a little lost boy, she thinks. He was always like that. When he was a child it was as if he was constantly playing catch-up with life. She remembers his helpless, left-behind cry: 'Wait for me!' as she and her brothers cycled off – she riding Stephen's too-big bike, rushing herself, or her brothers would be gone without her. Well, they're gone good and proper now. And she's still here with Stephen.

She crosses her legs, puts her chin in her hand and her elbow on her knee, and examines him. He's good looking in an educated sort of way: the wire-rimmed glasses, the frown lines caused by too much thinking, and the wiry grey hair sticking up as if his enormous brain's pushing his hair right out of his head.

He bends, and oh-so-tenderly kisses Dyllis' papery cheek. Briefly touching his mother's hand, he turns and comes towards Kat. 'Let's go home,' he says, and he puts an arm around her shoulder. She leans in against him. He's not her type, but she too needs the reassuring pressure, the physical presence of him.

In the car park, he finds she's shivering. He takes his jacket off and pulls it round her shoulders. And she's standing by the old red Mini Clubman and he's so tentative about what happens next that Kat puts up an encouraging hand to touch his cheek.

'It's all right,' she says.

And he kisses her. And she feels the months of loneliness and frustration and fear and unhappiness in the gentleness and uncertainty of that kiss. She holds his face in her hands and her lips are a gift, a balm, a witch's potion to mend a tortured soul. He slips his hands around her back and pulls her to him.

She makes a decision. 'Come on,' she says.

Driving through the lanes, she keeps her purposeful hand on his thigh. He turns left after Bag Enderby, curving along the back road up towards the tower. They park up at the top and get out. And in the cold, black night, he crushes her hard against a tree. Pulling at her clothes, he shoves himself into her with a moan so heartfelt she wonders if they might be falling in love.

Daisy drops Tessa home late that night. Tessa pushes in through the unlocked front door and finds Rufus weeping all over the scrubbed kitchen table.

'What happened to you?'

Rufus sniffs and rubs his red eyes with the heels of his hands. The sour smells of alcohol and bile rise off him. There are two empty bottles of Viognier on the floor beside him. He's halfway through a third, which he grabs now, as if for fear she'll take it away from him. Instead, Tessa cuts two slices of bread, finely chops half an onion, grates cheese, scatters both over the bread, and dribbles olive oil over the top before putting both slices on a baking tray and under the electric grill. This is Stephen's winning supper recipe, her absolutely favourite comfort food. There's a bowl of late cherry tomatoes sitting on the table. She pops three into her mouth while the cheese melts onto the toast.

She puts the food in front of Rufus.

He pushes a mauled copy of *Hello* magazine towards her. The cover features two men gliding under the Bridge of Sighs on a gondola. They're kissing and laughing and camping it up for the camera. Rufus jabs his finger at one of them. 'That – fucking cuntish bastard - is my ex,' he wails. 'And look, he's marrying somebody else.'

'Already?'

'Already! He was supposed to come running after me. Not go about marrying famous film stars who should know better than to expose themselves as homosexuals if they want to keep getting headline work. Fucking shite bastards!'

Rufus shakes his head. Finishes his glass. Pours another. 'You know you can tell how it's wrong?' he says, wagging a finger to emphasise his point. Tessa has no idea. 'Because Joseph looks manic. With me and him it was boring from the start. We were so easy with each other. There was never that adrenaline rush of 'will he, won't he?' I always knew he would. We only split up because he got too square and I got too rowdy. You know, I always thought that if I went cap-in-hand, clean, begging, he'd have me back in a flash.

'We made a great team: beautifully decorated house; clever, cosmopolitan friends, everybody making pots of money. But if it's right, does it have to be boring? That's the big question. If it's wrong – like this...' he jabs the cover photograph again. 'You can tell how over-excited he is. Look inside.' Rufus turns to spread after spread of the two men walking hand-in-hand, dancing at a party, popping champagne corks, sharing a hot tub on a balcony overlooking the lagoon.

He sighs shakily and pushes the cheese on toast away.

'Rufus, you have to eat.'

'You're a good girl, Tessa,' he says. 'You must have made that Stephen a truly wonderful wife. You're understanding. You don't whinge and bother. You just get on with what needs doing. I bet he cries himself to sleep on his pillow every night without you.'

'I expect he's off finding himself a replacement, like your ex did,' says Tessa.

'He's definitely not going to come along and pay for this house now, is he?' Tessa shakes her head. Rufus groans. 'Am I actually going to have to get my hands dirty doing this book?'

'Have you signed the contract yet?'

Almost tipping his chair over with the effort, Rufus reaches onto the dresser behind him and pulls a sheaf of papers onto the table. 'Let's do it now,' he says. 'Pen.'

Tessa doesn't hesitate to let him sign this document while he's drunk. He scribbles his signature in red biro at the bottom of the page where the publisher had put a big arrow on removable sellotape to show where. She's clearly got Rufus' number already, thinks Tessa.

'Hey, talking of marriage...' Rufus slides the contract into the stamped addressed envelope he was sent with it. 'Your erstwhile husband wasn't off looking for nookie – he was looking for you earlier.'

'Why?' Tessa's cheeks burn.

'God knows. Come on.' And Rufus drags Tessa to her feet, out of the house and up the lane to the postbox. 'Before I lose my nerve,' he says.

It's not until the next morning that Tessa finds Stephen's note.

Chapter 19

Dyllis sits up against the yellowing, lace-edged pillows Tessa's brought from home, the thinning fuzz of her hair haloing her lopsided face.

'Don't look at me,' she says to Tessa, who's stroking the skin on her hands, as if the warmth of her own will bring some to Dyllis'. 'And don't make remarks about how cold I feel. I'm an old woman who's had a tiny stroke and isn't even allowed a potter up the ward because they say I'll fall over and cause more trouble. I thought the way to recover from a stroke was to get out and about. Instead, I'm stuck with a view of that hideous old crone over there all day while they evaluate whether I'm fit to go home.' Her long speech leaves her breathless. Tessa smiles across at the opposite neighbour to make up for Dyllis' rudeness. Though she looks rather past caring what Dyllis might think of her.

'She won't go home alive, don't you think?' Dyllis hisses in a stage whisper. 'Nor her, that one in the orange nightie. And *he* wets the bed all the time and harangues the poor nurses to change him. I thought we were supposed to have single-sex wards these days? No wonder everybody's so bad-tempered.'

Tessa wants to ask Dyllis what she thinks about an idea she has for making money, but Dyllis seems to want to talk, not to listen.

'I'm worried about Abbie,' she says. 'I don't want her to go to Queen Anne's.'

Tessa frowns. How can Abbie be going to Queen Anne's?

'But the child wants it so badly. The only way to get her in is to prove she's a descendant of one of the founders: a Carter Stoke of centuries ago, would you believe? You have to research it, Tessa, and make up a paper trail to prove her provenance – perfectly outrageous request but it seems to be the only way to get her in. Then when they have no choice but to offer her a place, I'll persuade her to stamp their offer letter 'Bullshit!' and turn it down. Education's about what happens at home, Tessa. You remember that with this child of yours. You can't expect the system to bring your children up for you. It's your job to set them up to conquer the world. No matter what school a child goes to, it's a child's home which teaches it that it should assume it can do well.'

'Dyllis, you'll tire yourself...'

'No, I won't. You're the one who's going to exercise their brain on Abbie's account. Which will be good for you. It'll give you perspective on your own problems. Now go away and let me sleep. Tire me out and they won't let me go home for a week.'

Dismissed, Tessa stands up.

'I'll do my best for Abbie.'

'You better!' Dyllis' voice is hoarse from talking. She sinks back into her pillows but doesn't sleep. When the nurse brings her a cup of tea she asks if she could have some writing paper and a pen and something to lean on.

'You've had a stroke, dear. You should rest.'

To which Dyllis briskly ripostes, 'In which case you'll save my frozen hand by being kind enough to let me dictate to you. I've no time for dawdling.'

Carter hangs the last of his tools against Sir Charles' shed wall. He's wrapped all the sharp edges in linseed oil-dipped sackcloth. His lawnmower skulks under a tarpaulin in the corner. If the new gardener touches any of this stuff...

If it weren't for Tessa, no way would he be leaving. But he's not ready to be a dad. Ever since he found out she was pregnant he's had this urge to shout, 'It's nothing to do with me!' Which makes him feel guilty, but he can't change the feeling. If that's what she wants, he's glad she's getting the baby. But it really doesn't feel as if it's anything to do with him.

All his life, he's been too settled. It's time he set himself free.

Tessa spent so much time selling him the idea of discovering the world that she's made him curious, given him itchy feet. He feels as if he's already disappearing into the sunset and he hasn't even left yet. Besides, maybe in his absence his mum and Lauren will finally settle their differences. Look where his trying with Lauren got them: a dealer moved in and she started injecting when before she only smoked the stuff.

Instead of selling it, he's insured the pick-up (third party) for Lauren and his mum. Lauren's talking about finding the money to get her licence and go legal. And if his mum learned to drive, maybe she wouldn't feel such a prisoner in Hindle Green. Carter leaves the pick-up parked outside the gate to No. 3 and puts the papers on the kitchen table. Lauren's out somewhere. Abbie's at school – still Stockford Comp. He leaves her a note giving her the email address he's set up at the library. The instructions for accessing it are tucked in the back of his passport.

'TELL ME WHAT HAPPENS,' he writes to her, in careful block capitals.

Checking the time - he has hours, but to the nervous first-time traveller, plane fever fires up easily - he slings his bag onto his shoulder. It's hardly over-weight: some pants, some shirts, a good pair of trousers, and a work pair. He's wearing his steel-toecapped boots. He's looking forward to getting to New Zealand. It's the travelling part he doesn't like. It seems he has to put his life in the hands of a lot of people, all of whom have to get their jobs exactly right, in order for him to arrive safe and sound in Auckland by the afternoon of the day after tomorrow.

Leaving his bag under the hedge, he slopes down to the Old Rectory where he finds Rufus washing hens' eggs, and drying them on kitchen roll, before arranging them in a special china eggbox for display on his kitchen windowsill.

Hovering in the doorway to the kitchen, Carter asks, 'Tessa around?'

And looking at the nervous man, who'd twist a cap in his hands if he had one, Rufus wonders if Tessa's being fair. She'll be all right: lots of people will see to that. But this young man's being forced to travel to the other side of the world on account of her carelessness with her fertility. Does this boy really want to leave his home, his family...? Rufus couldn't wait to get out of Skipton: but Carter's no Rufus, is he?

Rufus wipes his hand on a linen glass cloth. 'She's at the hospital. With Dyllis.'

'Tell her I'm gone, then,' says Carter.

'Wait.' Rufus puts the glass cloth down. 'I'll give you a lift, if you like. It's only an hour to the airport. You can remind me of all the chores you usually do around the place while we drive. We could go via the hospital and see if Tessa's still there? You could say goodbye to Dyllis, too. Wait here. I'll just get my...'

By the time Rufus is back from the loo, Carter's gone.

At last English Heritage, the diocese faculty department, Amanda Davis the architect, and David Tait the churchwarden have come to an agreement on how and when the works on the tower should take place.

Stephen stands at the bottom and watches the scaffolders

fling and clang their way up the tower. He would never, in all his life, he thinks, have been able to skim up scaffolding like that, weighed down with a sack of hooks slung round his waist and two or three long, tubular steel poles balanced on his shoulder. But he's not entirely useless. A tiny smile plays about the corners of his mouth. Not entirely.

He's too buoyed up for the moment by the success of his encounter with Kat to worry about the future. The system works. He can get it up and use it. He can hardly keep the grin off his face.

By four o'clock, the scaffolders are finished and Amanda Davis appears to admire the work. 'Shall we?' she suggests to Stephen, ushering him towards the first ladder. Loath to follow her tight jeans-packaged bottom up the sharp incline of the ladders, Stephen ungallantly goes first.

The top's a mess.

The lead's been pulled away by the falling corner, leaving only half the space there had been to stand on.

'And that's pretty unstable,' says Amanda, kicking at an apparently solid stone which crumbles onto the oak struts holding the roof off the stairs below. 'I told you I thought the water would have got in somewhere. Stone's no more than sponge, really. Soaked with enough water over enough years, it just rots. What's this? Looks as though someone tried to plug a gap with paper at some point.' Amanda squats down in her straining jeans and tugs at a wad stuck between two stones. She continues her history lesson meanwhile. 'These initials in the lead,' she says, 'we can preserve them by cutting them out and re-applying them to the roof after it's been mended and re-leaded and so on.'

'Wouldn't it be better to put them as a plaque on the wall?' asks Stephen. 'Then they won't get trodden on and worn away.'

'Well, it'll be up to English Heritage,' says Amanda. 'You can try and persuade them, though I've never heard of the plaque idea. Here it is!' She pulls the squashed wad of paper free. 'What an odd thing. Who'd think paper would stop water getting into stone?'

The paper is just that, a wad. Stephen takes it and, while waiting for David Tait, whom he can hear puffing up the ladder, he fiddles with it until the leaves, finally, begin to come away from each other.

'Amanda...' Stephen's head shoots up. What's this gravel in David Tait's voice? He's kissing her hand. The churchwarden's smitten.

Stephen clears his throat – in his current mood he doesn't want to cramp anybody's romantic style. 'Well, I'm sure you've got lots of interesting things to show David, Amanda.' He climbs the parapet and onto the first rung of the ladder. 'Here, David, I think you're supposed to wear one of these.' He removes his sunshine-yellow hard hat and hands it over before making his escape.

Outside No. 3, Kat's sitting in the cab of Carter's pick-up, tears rolling down her cheeks.

'What is it?' Forgetting that he needs to get a move on if he's to see his mother before the ward closes, Stephen pulls himself into the cab beside Kat. She pulls a choking, bubbling breath and swallows.

'He's gone,' she says.

Stephen can barely hear her. 'Who's gone?' He moves to put a comforting arm around her, but she pushes him away.

'Carter!' And her grief is a wail. She's inconsolable. 'He didn't even say goodbye.'

'He'll be back.' He might not be.

'What do you know?' Kat's angry with Stephen. 'What

do you know? Fuck buddy for a night and you reckon you can start telling me my business?'

'I'm just...' *Fuck buddy? What?*

'Well, just fuck off and do your holy shit somewhere else. It's my boy what's gone. It's my right to cry over him. I don't need you telling me anything's gonna be good or better or different in any way because he's escaped this shithole and left us all behind.'

Tessa's bumbling home on the bus by the time Stephen makes it to his mother's bedside. He finds Dyllis snoozing gently against pillows Tessa smoothed for her, her breathing deep and regular. She doesn't look as though she's going to die today.

Stephen buys a cup of tea from the machine in the corridor and sits beside his mother. It's astonishing that someone so tiny can breathe so deeply. He remembers her being tall, wearing embroidered flared trousers and shiny platform lace-ups, chasing him around the back garden when he was a child. Her now crippled hands then stretched out to catch and tickle till he couldn't breathe at all. In the memory, his father sits outside the back door, reading the paper and smoking a pipe. Always a slightly distant figure, of the old, children-are-women's-business school, his father was the sort to wear a tie on Saturdays, with a checked Viyella shirt, under a scratchy (to Stephen's cheek) tweed jacket.

How many of his childhood memories are made up, he wonders: pictures of what he assumes did happen; pictures to match the feelings he can conjure of what it was like to be that only child. For Dyllis and his father he was always a good boy. It was only with Kat that he gave in to the opportunity to be bad.

It's astonishing that this tiny bundle of misshapen bones is what remains of that energetic woman. Dyllis snuffles in her sleep. Her eyelids flicker.

She and Stephen have never talked about the past. His father died and it was as if Stephen's childhood finished, was packed up and put away that very day. He's confident Dyllis loves him, though he suspects she loves Tessa more: he doesn't mind, no doubt Tessa's more loveable than he is.

He doubts Dyllis has ever seen the point of his chosen career. There's a secret longing for riches in Dyllis which would have enjoyed Stephen's making millions somewhere. But Stephen... He became a vicar because the job combined all the useful things he felt he could do. And because his faith was so clear and uncomplicated then.

Now? He's angry with his faith. His wife is gone. The bewitching Kat is back but feral as ever. She was right to rail at him this afternoon. She has been alone for years. Did he really think that one desperate clinch in the dark woods would change anything? Nothing about what they did was loving or kind – it was nothing more than scratching an unbearable itch.

He runs his hands through his hair, literally scratching his head. Life isn't about satisfying lust, or longing, but about doing the right thing and feeling content with it. Contentment's a tough state to accept. So much less exciting than agony.

Stephen pulls out the clump of paper Amanda found in the church tower wall and, while he waits for Dyllis to wake up, eases the edges away from one another. It turns out to be one piece of thick, linen paper. There are seeds pressed into a corner. The paper cracks into four separate quarters. The writing on it is in pencil, so faint as to be almost illegible.

If this is found 'tis murder and he must be hanged. Stephen frowns. Turns the paper over. There's more on the back. He squints to read. If the writing had been in ink he wouldn't have been able to decipher a word. He wonders how old the paper is.

First. I married her. She is a lovesome girl who makes a useful as well as a tender wife. None of this is her fault. I made an honest woman of her in the church at Stockford where the rector was understanding enough to oblige. I couldn't bear to marry her here at Hindle Green with her father as witness. He'd have made some kind of trouble. His affliction, I believe, is envy.

Second. The felon in this story is that John Trester who has jealousy of his daughter growing like a canker in his gut. Some might say I should play master of the village on account of my house and property, and put him out. But I cannot deprive my lovely wife of her father. I miss my own more every day and wish he were here now to relieve my boiling soul with good advise.

Three: I am not a religious man. I will not turn to God in this matter, nor shall I pretend in order to make life different.

I pray she be right. That he cannot be such a bad character. She says I am a fool and my fears must be groundless. She says he is as good a Christian as any Churchwarden in the country. Therefore I must doubt this paper will ever come to light, for if it do I should rather have thrown him out with nothing but his blasted cows for company, and whatever hedge he might crawl under for cover, and kept my lovely wife and child for mine while I live on earth and never mind the ever after.

So endeth the testament of a fool for love. Carter Stoke, Gent, August 23rd 1710.

Stephen stares at the paper: *Carter Stoke, Gent?* What was he doing up there on the tower, if Trester had threatened to push him off? Maybe he'd wanted to test his father-in-law, find out he wasn't all bad. The gamble had clearly not paid off.

'Oh good, you're here at last,' a querulous little voice

comes from the nest of pillows. 'Now, this isn't about you, so don't think it's pointed. You and Tessa have made all your mistakes and I've realised there's no knocking your heads together so I shan't bother to try. But you do need to talk to Tessa about Abbie.'

Tessa's old green corduroy coat flaps about her bump as she goes into all the agents in Stockford High Street, asking for lists of flats. She's going to need £1000 from somewhere as guarantee and first month's rent. She has nothing of value except the diamond engagement ring Dyllis gave Stephen to give to her. She'd rather die than hawk that. She should give it back to Stephen. It rattles around in a box with a carved Kiwi god figure and a broken pair of fake pearl earrings. She's never taken her wedding ring off.

Because she's very pregnant, it's no good her going looking for a job. Instead, she steps into the offices of the *Advertiser* and fills in a form: 'Private tutoring. Help with preparation for Common Entrance, GCSE and A-Level. All arts subjects as well as communication and writing skills.' She gives her mobile number and email address for contact and pays £8 for the advertisement to be placed this coming Friday. She knows very little about what's needed for Common Entrance but is sure it won't be impossible to find out. At least she's finally doing something proactive about taking charge of her life.

Public library next for Abbie's family history. The librarian tells her that the place to look would be the vestry of Stockford's parish church.

'Shouldn't those old books be kept somewhere less damp?' asks Tessa.

The friendly librarian nods enthusiastically. 'Much better we have them and give the county less reason to try and close us down. We're such a small library. We need to make ourselves indispensible in the community in order to keep ourselves going.'

Tessa smiles. 'I'll go and see what I can do.'

And in the vestry-cum-parish office of Stockford's church, Tessa finds Stephen sitting behind the desk, staring into space, his beard still unexpected. He looks as though he needs a square meal.

'Oh.' This time she stands her ground.

As Dyllis says: this isn't about Tessa and Stephen. In front of him lies the square of paper from the church tower.

For a second, Stephen stares stupidly at Tessa. This is an opportunity for them to be ordinary with each other, to achieve something together. Of course he's not going to tell her about Kat. Kat doesn't want him. And he wants this smiling, freckled person with the uncontrollable strawberry blonde bird's nest escaping from the pins she's shoved into it any old how. She's beautiful pregnant, her delicacy exaggerated by the weight of the bump she's carrying.

He holds the paper out to her. 'Have a look at this first.'

Tessa walks up the road in the dark. A threat of frost catches in her nostrils and makes her sneeze. The child inside her pulls hard on her back and she can feel her legs swing oddly on her aching, loose pelvis. She pulls her coat tight.

Lights blare at No. 3. Tessa shivers on the doorstep. Abbie opens the door, smiles, and walks back to the kitchen without further invitation. Tessa follows. The house is toasty. This would be the kind of place to live in the winter, she thinks: double-glazed UPVC in all the windows, and nice small spaces to heat. She finds Kat at the cleared kitchen table, poring over the *Advertiser*. Lauren's sitting next to her, not smoking, fiddling instead with pulled threads on the hem of her jeans.

'What's this about, then?' Kat retreats to fill the kettle, and stays leaning against the kitchen worktop.

Tessa takes the kettle being put on as an invitation to sit.

Kat's exhausted, thinks Tessa, and why wary? 'Where's Carter?' she asks.

'Gone,' replies Lauren, and her face, hidden from Kat, says 'Drop the subject'.

'I just...' Tessa's flustered now. Gone? That bridge burned, then. Though she hadn't counted on crossing it: but so long as he was there... She pulls herself together.

'Dyllis has told me about Abbie needing a paper trail to get her into Queen Anne's. Stephen and I got together this afternoon. It seems you might be able to go there after all, Abbie. If that's what you really want?'

'You serious?' asks Abbie, jumping up from her place on the settee, where she'd been curled up, wearing her dressing gown and pink fluffy slippers, not watching the titles as *Coronation Street* begins. 'Turn that off!' She grabs the remote off Lauren and silences the telly.

Relieved the girls are there to prompt her, and too rattled by the news of Carter's departure to analyse Kat's watchfulness more closely, Tessa begins. 'It seems that once upon a time your family were the closest this village had to lords of the manor until one of your tenants...'

'The Tresters...' says Kat.

'You know already?'

Kat shrugs. 'You tell how you found it out.'

'Well, it seems that the Stokes used to live in the house that's now the Old Rectory. And the Tresters at Home Farm were their tenants. Until a Trester daughter ran off and married a Stoke and her father murdered that Stoke by pushing him off the tower of St George's.'

'Get away with you!' Lauren's indignant.

'Trester settled his widowed daughter and her baby son in a cottage out on the Stockford Road with a strip of land to grow veg on and enough room to keep a pig. In the Stockford parish records, she had her child christened Carter Stoke.'

'Does this mean I can go to Queen Anne's?'

'If you really want to.'

'Why didn't the Tresters move into Stoke House?' asks Lauren.

''Cos they was torn up by guilt for they way they treated people,' says Kat.

'Trester gave Stoke House to the parish for the vicar to live in and it became the rectory. He then kept the rest of the land round about,' explains Tessa. 'The Trester family only sold Green Farm off to grandparents of the people who live there now as recently as 1920.'

Abbie's grinning from ear to ear and capering about. 'I'm going to Queen Anne's! I'm going to Queen Anne's!'

'Bad blood,' says Kat quietly, under her breath.

'What?'

'Airs and graces. My mum always said there's no point trying to get above yourself. She used to say, "Don't do nothing, do it?" We was all told that story.'

Her wariness forgotten for the moment, Kat disappears up the stairs, returning a few minutes later with a worn, gold pendant, the size of a penny piece. The back is glass, and in it is plaited a miniature length of dark reddish hair. The front is tooled gold, worn almost away. Inside is a tiny drawing of a baby.

Kat turns the thing over in her hand. 'My mum always said this is a picture of that baby what they called Carter Stoke for his murdered daddy. There's been Stokes working the land in this village ever since.'

'What do you mean by bad blood?' asks Tessa.

'That's Trester blood. Twice more injected. Twice more ruined our lives.'

'Twice more?' asks Lauren.

And Kat, in an unexpected gesture of kindness, reaches out and strokes her elder daughter's hair. She shakes her head. 'It weren't never none of your fault,' she says. 'Just worked out that way. Carter got off scot-free. 'cept now... maybe it's bad, after all. Maybe he'll never come back.'

'Maybe we'll all go and find him when he's made a new life?' suggests Lauren.

'Not so long as I'm going to Queen Anne's,' protests Abbie. 'Which I am now, aren't I?'

The phone rings. Kat leaps for it. 'Carter?' There's a hiatus: nobody dares breathe, until... 'No, I don't want no fucking kitchen units. I don't want windows, bathrooms, bloody plastic glass houses. You just get off the line and don't you dare fucking ever ring me back!'

Dyllis is to be sent home tomorrow. She's been in hospital for five days and is champing to get out.

'I want Tessa to come with me in the ambulance,' she says. 'You have to ring her and tell her and bring her here so that she can come with me.'

Stephen's lost momentum since that afternoon when he and Tessa worked their way patiently through the parish records kept in Stockford Church. He should have capitalised on the situation, taken her out to dinner right afterwards, created a reason for their keeping relaxedly in touch. But his confidence was compromised by the memory of what he did with Kat. And the fact that Tessa was so nice to him: she was ordinary, smiley, friendly but not keen or nervous. She didn't touch his arm a lot or laugh. She took the job seriously, worked with him until their object was achieved, and then offered to go and tell Kat herself, unwittingly letting him off the hook there too. Middle class good manners must be the death of so many relationships, he thinks. At the end of the afternoon she smiled, pecked him on the cheek, and then he let her walk away from him. OK, so this is a massive improvement on the edging-past-not-meeting-his-eye that he's had from her all summer. But all he's had from Tessa since is a terse little text reading: *Great success at the Stokes'. Abbie v excited*. No 'Love'. No 'XX'. So now what?

And what about Kat? He saw her coming out of his mother's house, locking it, putting the key under the mat.

'Kat!' he shouted, running up the road, watched by the cow-man on his quad bike and Mrs Trester zipping by in her car and that new couple who've just bought the executive home old Jack Trester built on the site of the old Stoke family cottages. But Kat marched across the road into No.3 and slammed the door to her own house in his face.

He unlocked Dyllis' door then and inside found the place completely spring-cleaned. Even the top shelves of the kitchen cupboards, untouched for years, had been wiped, and the old crock Dyllis keeps there taken out, washed, polished and put back. There are clean sheets on the bed, and ripening Chinese lanterns from the bush beside the gate sit in a jam jar on the night stand. Stephen wants to go and thank her, but Kat slammed the door in his face. He doesn't want to marry her. He only wants to draw a line under what happened. But clearly she doesn't want him anywhere near her, either.

Well at least his mum's given him an excuse to ring Tessa. So now, adrenalin rushing in anticipation of rejection, he dials her number. And when she answers he garbles in a rush, 'Mum's coming home tomorrow. They're bringing her in an ambulance. Would you come with her?'

277

'Of course I will. You should fill her fridge for her.' Tessa sounds friendly. 'I'll go round and tidy up a bit. Make the bed with clean sheets and things.'

'Kat's already done that.'

'Oh.' So much for the friendly voice.

'She just did it. I didn't ask her,' he blusters. He's sure he sounds as though he's lying.

'What time are they going to bring her back?' asks Tessa's cold voice.

'Around ten o'clock tomorrow. Can I drive you to the General?'

And Tessa doesn't say, 'No. I'll get a lift with Rufus.' To Stephen's surprise she answers, 'Pick me up at nine thirty?'

'It's a date.' And flushing furiously, Stephen slams down the phone. *Date?!*

To take his mind off the carnage of his personal life, Stephen drives into Stockford and parks outside the immaculate cross-cut lawn of Lauren's twins' paternal grandparents. He's rung several times but they've never called back. A drop-in might be a better idea. The more communication he can encourage before the social services start in with their jargon, the more space there might be for a successful resolution to this family's problem.

The doorbell plays a ding-a-ling rendition of the opening bars of *Nights in White Satin*, and a great oaf of a young man answers the door. Gym-honed shoulders strain at the seams of a Naval Marines t-shirt. Stephen racks his brain for the name of the twins' father.

'Kyle?' he asks, holding out his hand. The man shakes it, and nods.

'I'm Stephen Wilkinson, vicar at Hindle Green. I was hoping your mother might be in.'

Stephen follows Kyle into the kitchen where the twins' Nanna is busy preparing what appears to be a celebratory tea. There are plates of sausage rolls and cheesy nibbles and carrot sticks, and mini cartons of apple juice for the girls: and there are stuffed white rolls and mini sausages and, stacked in ice-filled plastic boxes, there are cans and cans of beer.

A tiny, ash-blonde woman Stephen hasn't met before, with boobs as pneumatic as Kyle's pecs, squeezes past him with a tray of carefully arranged crisps and dips, calling over her shoulder, 'I'll put these in the lounge shall I, Deborah?'

'I've come at a bad time,' says Stephen.

'Not at all, not at all.' Deborah's gleaming with excitement. Dressed up to the nines, she's been smoking excitedly out of the kitchen window. She stubs the cigarette out in a Diet Coke can next to the sink and puts the can into the bin. 'Nasty habit,' she apologises. 'This is my boy, Kyle. And he's brought home the lovely Stacey that you saw go through there. The girls are all of a twitter, I can tell you.'

'Goodness,' says Stephen, very confused.

'The girls never met they dad before. Now it's all happening at once. Dad and stepmum-to-be. And she's expecting. Though she's not showing yet, of course. You don't with your first. Not for ages. Do you, darling?' Stacey comes back to fetch another tray of nibbles. 'This is the vicar, dear, where the twins' mum lives.'

'You come to take them back?' asks Stacey. Stephen thinks he sees hope in her eyes.

'Well, I'm here on a diplomatic mission. Sort of. Lauren wondered if she could have them for a sleepover. You know her mum's back. So she'll be there in case...'

'Well they can't go tonight. It's the party tonight. They got new dresses for tonight.' Deborah's loading up with a tray of mixed scotch eggs and Wotsits.

'No, no.' Stephen doesn't want to antagonise her. 'This weekend, perhaps. I could fetch them.'

'I'll take them over,' says Kyle.

Stacey throws him a black look. 'I'll come with you,' she insists.

Stephen never thought it would be so easy. This'll give Kat and Lauren something to do. Kat'll go berserk getting the house ready for the twins. They can have Carter's bedroom. Fill that gaping void, if only for one night.

You only have to ask, he thinks. Sometimes things are so much less complicated than they seem when they're tangled in your mind.

Tessa and Rufus park outside the multiplex and go and find April, Ellen and Daisy, already installed in the pizza place next door.

'It's a date!' insists Rufus. 'Girls. Tessa's got a date!' He plumps himself down next to Ellen and kisses her.

'Get off!' Ellen flushes furiously.

'Date?'

'It's not a date,' protests Tessa. 'Stephen's taking me to fetch his mother from hospital tomorrow, that's all.' She nonchalantly picks up the menu and scans the pizzas for something with anchovy.

'What are you going to wear?' asks April.

'It's not a date!'

'Well, it won't be if you won't let it be,' says April, waggling her eyebrows at Tessa and waving at the waiter to ask for orange juice for the party's teetotallers.

'How do you know it's a date?' Daisy asks Rufus.

'Because he said it was. And when Tessa put the phone down she was stunned as a teenager who's been asked to the prom by the class stud. She turned to me in amazement and

280

said, "Stephen said it was a date!"'

'I just thought it was a bit odd. That's all. Stephen and I are cool. It's fine. It was just an odd word to use. Come on, what's everyone having to eat?'

Tucking into the complimentary olives, April asks Rufus, 'And how are you?'

Rufus squares his shoulders and sits up straighter. 'Just dandy, April.'

'There was someone asking about you in the shop this afternoon,' says April. 'Told me a story that would have me in tears if it were true.'

Now Rufus' smile is a rictus grin. 'What did you tell them?'

She smiles. 'I told them absolutely nothing at all!'

AUTUMN

Chapter 20

For this not-date to fetch Dyllis from the hospital just feels central-casting-pregnant-lady enormous. Her sweater's stretched tight and her pregnancy jeans are bursting at the seams. How big will this baby be?

The Mini pulls up outside the Old Rectory at 9.25 and Stephen gets out, apologising, and apologising again for being early. Without touching her, he carefully ushers Tessa towards the Mini Clubman. The hand he offers to help her balance as she lowers herself into the tiny old car is warm and dry. She takes her own little cold hand back quickly and pulls the seat belt round her tummy. It will only reach round her if she tucks it around the bump.

'Will you be able to see over me?' she asks, nervous giggles catching in her dry throat and making her cough.

'When's it due?'

She's surprised he doesn't know – though how should he? 'They say a bit before Christmas. Not even a couple of months to go.'

He pulls onto the Stockford Road. Only he's turned left instead of right and is driving towards Pendle.

Tessa frowns. 'Are there roadworks?'

'That's where Kat grew up,' says Stephen, pulling up outside a newish executive residence with double garage and carefully laid, herringbone-patterned, red brick drive.

'Really?' It's a bit grander than Tessa had imagined.

Stephen turns to Tessa and looks her straight in the eye. Screwing his courage to the sticking place he blurts out, 'I kissed her.'

'When you were children?' Tessa's heart races. What's she supposed to do with this information?

'Last week.'

Staring straight ahead, Stephen indicates and pulls back into the road. At the next T-junction he turns right towards Stockford. What will Tessa say? She's not reaching for the door handle.

Instead, Tessa's surprised it's taken him this long. She knows it's ridiculous, but she's glad for him. He, on the other hand, just wants to tell her the rest of it, that the point of the whole story is that the system worked!

Stephen slams on the brakes as a Transit pulls out from Watery Lane without looking. He's not impotent, he has his wife in the car: the facts that he proved he's not impotent with somebody else, and that Tessa's pregnant by that somebody else's son seem unimportant now. His fist-shaking at the van's blind back is like a football supporter punching the air.

Tessa begins to giggle first. 'Does that mean we're quits?'

And soon Stephen's laughing so hard he's forced to pull up in the lay-by above Daisy's house. The release of tension has them howling. And they're so happy he daren't risk ruining the moment by telling Tessa the rest.

All the way to the hospital they laugh and chatter and pretend everything's normal and that there isn't the giant bump of Tessa's unborn child, elephantine in that tiny little car. Only when they arrive and find the fragile bag of bones which is Dyllis, hunched over in a wheelchair by the ward doors, her bag on her knee, desperate to get out, is the mood broken.

For fear of revealing that she's grieving for the loss of her already, Tessa finds herself chattering inanely while Dyllis is wheeled into the ambulance. Dyllis demands Tessa's arm to lean on when she finally stands at the door to her own house, Tessa's hand to hold while she takes careful, concentrated steps forward, over the assault course of a tiny ledge, a treacherous doormat, the fringed rug from John Lewis, bought in a January sale in 1973.

Officially, Dyllis is more or less recovered from the stroke, but the skin on the old lady's face is still a deathly grey. At last she's settled, the hum of the buzzing cushion filling the silence while Tessa brings her a cup of Lapsang and a homemade flapjack and puts them on the open desk as directed.

Tessa finds a vase for the bunch of late sunflowers and cosmos which somebody left on the doorstep. Amy from the farm shop comes by with a basket of sausages and pots of soup (after Tessa's suggestion she's discovered there's a good market for freshly whizzed-up old veg in ham stock). The doorbell rings again.

'I brought her fish fingers.' Kat's defiant on the doorstep.

'She'll love those. Thank you for coming in to clean.' It's that *Brief Encounter* voice again. Tessa steps back so that Kat can come in.

She can't imagine Kat and Stephen kissing. Tessa thinks Kat too sharp-edged to be very kissable. Tessa's hand involuntarily goes to cover her bump. Kat will be Tessa's child's grandmother. When they'd caught their breath after their bout of hysteria in the car, she hadn't wanted to ruin the mood by asking Stephen whether he wanted to kiss Kat again.

'Come in.' Kat looks uncertain. Tessa insists. 'I know Dyllis would love to see you.'

But here's Anna Trester who, completely ignoring Kat, barges straight into the house. 'Two fish pies,' she marches through to the kitchen, shouting over her shoulder to Tessa, as if talking to a servant. 'And two chicken and mushroom. I should freeze three of them and work your way through one at a time.'

Tessa turns back to Kat, smiles, 'Please... come in.'

But Kat's already turning away. 'I best get on. Twins are coming this weekend.' In other words: 'I gotta get back to my life.'

And Tessa thinks, *This is my life. I must claim it. Dyllis and Stephen are mine.*

And suddenly Tessa can't look at Kat without laughter bubbling up in her throat. And Kat must never think Tessa's laughing *at* her. She's just hysterical at the whole mess of it all.

When the visitors are all gone, Dyllis doesn't ask about Abbie. Instead she wants to know, 'How was your trip with Stephen this morning?'

Tessa can't possibly say. She's still shocked by their laughter. And his having kissed Kat – the first effect of which is simply to make what she did with Carter less competitively, gold-medal-winningly awful. After all, if he admitted to a kiss, might there not have been more?

And so Tessa doesn't answer Dyllis but goes to make the old lady another cup of Lapsang Souchong, weak, with just a *nuage* of milk, which Tessa pours carefully into the good china teacups which Kat has so recently washed. There is a box of cakes from April as well as Tessa's flapjacks. Nobody's ever going to make Dyllis eat anything savoury again if she doesn't want to. Tessa cuts a Bakewell slice into little fingers and arranges them on the saucer with the tea.

Back in the sitting room she finds Dyllis slumped, her hands held tightly under her chin, fast asleep. Tessa sits on the sofa, watching the old lady's deep, regular breathing, absentmindedly eating the Bakewell slice herself.

Dyllis dreams she's walking across a field. There's Stephen's father, smoking his pipe, wearing a knitted tie with his checked shirt and heavy tweed jacket. He's waiting the other side of a stile, holding a hand out to her. But it's hard walking across the plough. Her feet are heavy with clogged clay.

'Wait for me,' she shouts to him. 'Wait! I'm coming.'

The atmosphere at No. 3 is taut with anticipation. Carter's stuff has been boxed up and put away in the never-used front lounge. Kat's spent some of the rent money on second-hand bunk beds bought off the community notice board at the supermarket. They'll get new mattresses when Kat and Lauren can afford them. The windows are draped in frothing pink curtains. There are teddy bears and dollies and fake *High School Musical* duvet covers. In the bathroom there's a nit-comb in the cupboard and in the freezer there are fish fingers galore. Kat and Lauren spent every penny they could scrape together and got the lot delivered by a mate of Carter's who once tried to take Lauren out.

Now Lauren and Kat stand at the door of the girls' room and admire their handiwork. Without realising it, they've found common ground. Nobody's taken charge. It's been a joint effort – and what an effort – to make No. 3 as welcoming a home as Deborah's on the Withy Green Estate.

The girls are to be dropped off late morning by Kyle. Lauren and Kat sit about, eyeing the clock, not making tea for fear he'll arrive just as it's ready and they'll only have to start again. There's a tray set with matching cups, milk in a jug, and a plate of pink-iced biscuits.

Lauren hasn't seen Kyle for six years.

'All right?'

She jumps out of her skin. He's just pushed the door open without knocking. He's followed by a sour-faced blonde in a midriff-baring t-shirt. The girls lag behind, nervous of the pressure of loving their family. But they run to Lauren and burst into tears when they see her squatting down, arms out, ready to give them hugs they'll never forget.

Lauren can't bear to look at Kyle. What's he got himself into? Any tighter and that t-shirt will burst. And isn't he freezing? She sounds like her mother, Lauren thinks, wiping her own tears, laughing inside.

'Oh, you're gonna have a lovely time with me and your Nanna Kat,' she says. 'They got kittens up at the farm shop, and piglets you can give apples to. And your Aunty Abbie says you can play with her old doll's house. She put it in your room. You wanna come and see?'

'When do you want them fetching?' asks Kyle.

Kat gives him a stolid stare. 'I expect your mum will want them back to be disinfected before school on Monday.'

'Well, we're heading back to Plymouth later,' says the blonde, who still hasn't been introduced. 'You'll have to get them back to Deborah your own way.'

'You tell her she can fetch them after their tea tomorrow. Tell her she'd be very welcome to join us. We eat at six.'

When April said she told the person quizzing her about Rufus yesterday 'nothing', it clearly wasn't little enough. The first photographer arrived just after Tessa left this morning and now paparazzi are arranged around Rufus' front door like a guard of dishonour. But the garden behind the Old Rectory is walled, and therefore private. So Rufus has put on his boots and gone out the back. The pigs trot towards him across the orchard, light-footed in spite of their bulk. Rufus reaches into their bin. It's empty.

Rufus goes to see if Carter got in more pig nuts before he left. And suddenly he stops. He has a house he can't afford to live in. But the potting shed... He opens the door and steps inside. There's running water. And electricity. He frowns. There's a sofa already in here. And Tessa told him how cosy it was at No. 3: the less space there is to warm, the warmer the space can be. This book Tessa's making him write could be called *My Life in a Barn*. He could bring the sheep in at night to keep the place warm. Be better than living with trench foot in the kitchen.

'Hey, you the housekeeper?' Where did all these people come from? What do they want with Rufus? Tessa could go round to the back, but she doesn't want to show anybody that low door in the wall, half hidden by a curtain of ivy. The crowd edges closer, cameras bristling. She's caught.

The questions come thick and fast. 'What's he doing in there?'

'Why did he spend so many years hiding the fact that he's gay?'

Speechless, Tessa's barred from the front door by a tired-looking woman with a microphone. 'You must be the vicar's ex. Looking just about ready to pop. Happening village you've got here. What do you say to the news that your husband's been seen having *al fresco* sex with the mother of the village junkie?' Tessa stares. 'Wouldn't you like to have the opportunity to say your piece?'

Tessa can't move. She thinks she might be going to faint.

And then there's a kerfuffle behind her and pushing and swearing and an arm takes her elbow and a voice says, 'Rufus Stone's sexuality is nobody's business but his own.' Stephen is wearing his dog collar to give him an air of authority. 'How would you like it if people door-stepped you to quiz you about your private life?' he barks. 'Are you squeaky clean? Or you?' he asks another. 'Don't tell me: you're all married with two-point-four kids and live in Godalming and are so fucking bored by the whole experience you waste your life getting vicarious kicks through the excitements of other people's lives.'

289

The journalists flail under this onslaught and Stephen pushes through, propelling Tessa into the sanctuary of the Old Rectory. He slams the door. She leans against the wall, catching her breath, willing her knees not to buckle under her. And before she can thank him, or question him, or tell him just to *wait* a minute, Stephen's turned and barged out into the fray again.

He's been having *al fresco* sex with Kat?

'Nooooooo!' She slumps down to the floor, cursing her hormones.

And this is where Rufus finds her.

'He's been shagging Kat,' she wails at him. 'I've really lost him now.'

'Tell him how you feel,' says Rufus, ignoring the rumpus outside and sitting down beside her. 'I'm here on my own in a house I can't afford because I thought my other half would understand what was going on in my head without my having to tell him. I thought that because we'd been together for years we had some kind of telepathic thing going and he should be able to read my closed face like an open book. When he ignored me, I just went and got drunk and annoyed him. So he ignored me some more. So I decided he was boring. And then he decided to marry somebody else. But the somebody else has already left him because apparently he hasn't got over me - which is why all these people are hanging around outside my front door.'

He takes Tessa's hand and squeezes it.

'You're going to have to be a big brave girl,' he continues. 'Men are simpler creatures than you'd have them. If you don't tell, they don't know. They don't look for hidden meanings in everything you say. They take your words at face value. So write him a letter or something and make yourself clear. Or you might lose him for good when you haven't even once asked him outright if that's what he really wants.'

St George's is always packed for the Harvest Festival. In this agricultural community, people are truly grateful to have got through another season without going bust. So the farmers turn out en masse, the men's faces scrubbed red for church, the women pale under powder.

And the rest of the village is there too. There's been enough going on in the past few weeks and who knows how much of it might be played out in front of them in church today?

Stephen slips his surplice over his head and hangs around his shoulders the stole patterned with sheaves of corn, milk cows, and cider apples embroidered by the old village Women's Institute in the Fifties. To Stephen, St George's is still empty of the God he's always felt here. But the congregation don't need to know that his sanctuary is gone. His stand-off with God is irrelevant today. The people of Hindle Green have come to round off their harvest with a rousing rendition of *Bread of Heaven*. And whatever the state of his private faith, it is Stephen's job to lead them in their song.

'Notices,' he says, before starting the service proper. 'The harvest supper will be at the village hall tomorrow night. Seven thirty onwards.' Mrs Trester nods to show he's right. 'Everybody's welcome.' Mrs Trester raises an eyebrow. She's perched next to her son Jonti at the end of a pew filled, to Stephen's amused amazement, with Stokes: Kat, Lauren, Abbie and the little girls, all shivering in the damp air because they've chosen to leave their coats off their finery. That's the Trester family pew they're sitting in, with the painted crest above it reading '*Contendo, semper contendo*' ('Struggle, always struggle'). From his safe distance Stephen gives them a big, welcoming grin. Kat puts her head on one side, grins at him, and then the people around her see her send him a great big meaningful wink.

'And I'd like to thank you all for the generous time and meals and so on you've given to my mother after her stroke,' he continues. 'She's well enough now that when I suggested I ask somebody to bring her down for the harvest thanksgiving service, she snorted and said she hadn't been to church since she left school and didn't intend to start now.'

A titter runs round the congregation and they stand to sing *We Plough the Fields and Scatter*. In the middle of the third verse some latecomers slip in and the singing around them falters, only to start again, louder, as if to prove the congregation are much more interested in the service than the fact that the vicar's very pregnant estranged wife's just come into church for the first time since Easter, in the company of that film star who bought the Old Rectory.

It's David Tait's turn to read the lesson.

The windowsills are laden with pumpkins, squashes, and heaps of apples. There are jars of jam, and beetroot chutney, boxes of eggs, cabbages, and muddy main crop potatoes, all overshadowed by the last of the colour from people's summer gardens: bright red leaves, fading michaelmas daisies, wilting red and orange-stemmed rainbow chard - which doesn't work well cut in vases - and curling red kale leaves, which does.

'Thank you for coming. Thank you for coming...' Stephen shakes every hand of the biggest congregation he's had since taking the living of Hindle Green. 'Did you enjoy it?' he asks Trixie and Belle as they shuffle past him, keeping their hands lost in the skirts of their party dresses.

'They liked when the children gave an apple to every grown-up. Proper little show-offs,' says Lauren, proudly.

'Thank you for coming,' says Stephen to Kat. She kisses his cheek. There's a slight intake of breath from the queue behind. 'That'll give them something to talk about,' she whispers in Stephen's ear. She ushers her brood out onto the path. He looks after her, desperate to be able to ask if that friendly exchange can be the full stop after their sex in the woods. But she's gone. And he must shake the hands of the rest of the queueing congregation. Until, the crowd dispersed, at the end there are only two people left.

Tessa, to Stephen, is as beautiful as he's ever seen her. Her pale skin's flushed like a doll's cheeks and the sprinkling of freckles matches her hair. Her bump sticks coyly from between the flaps of her green corduroy coat. She's holding Rufus' hand.

'Thank you for coming.' Stephen shakes Rufus' hand first. Rufus is speechless. Not one person has mentioned the spread in the magazine. He's been smiled at and wished 'Good morning', and asked how his sheep are doing and whether his pigs are ready for slaughter. Nobody's sneered or whispered behind their hand or made a pointed remark. Only Mrs Trester pointedly ignored him – but nobody took any notice of her. He's overwhelmed.

So when Stephen asks, 'See you at the Harvest Supper tomorrow night?', Rufus can't help but reply, 'Wouldn't miss it for the world.'

Rufus lets go of Tessa and hurries out of the church. He wishes he had a cigarette. This damp autumn air is just the weather for a romantic pose with a fag in a churchyard. He smiles to himself. Not one person pointed or stared! He's astonished.

'Will you come back and see Mum?' Stephen asks Tessa. There are no breathless giggles this morning. They are as shy of each other as they were the morning after she first slept in his bed, years ago, while Stephen lay sleepless on the sofa, listening to her breathing, staggered that so cool a number as she had agreed to come home with him at all.

Now, in the damply mud-smelling Harvest Festival Church, only thirty foot from where old Reverend Jones married them, she smiles and nods. The letter she wrote him lies in ashes at the back of Rufus' kitchen fire. And it's never the time to ask the difficult questions. She saw Kat kiss him. What did it mean? Are they seeing each other?

His heart races: he wants to ask if she's still comfortable up at the Old Rectory, whether she's found anywhere warmer for when the baby comes, whether she'd consider moving back in with him. The words build up into a jam in his throat. He stands back to let the organist by, 'Thanks, Mr Janson – see you at Pendle for evensong?'

'You had eight o'clock said at Bag Enderby this morning?' says Tessa. It's a first Sunday. She still knows his routine. She and Stephen walk side-by-side down the church path, not touching.

'Nobody there but George Cross, the Major, and Lady Susie. It's not a commercial enterprise taking services at Bag Enderby.'

'I heard Sir Charles was ill.'

'Emphysema. I offered to take him communion when I do the Major's mother on Wednesdays but he wants nothing of it. He said his churchgoing was only ever driven by a sense of duty and example to the village and the estate workers. He's not interested in being shriven in private. He's angry because he's old and frail. Doesn't see the point in God. People often get like that.'

'At least your mother never had a faith to lose.'

Rufus is halfway down the lane now. He looks back to check Tessa's all right and waves. There are still two or three bored journalists waiting outside his gate. Tessa sees him stop and talk to them. They follow him towards the house.

'What is he doing?' she asks.

'Come and see Mum first.'

They find Dyllis in her little upright chair as usual. Her face is a better colour. Her eyes have a jaunty twinkle.

'First time I've seen you two together since Easter,' she says.

Not needled, Tessa puts on the kettle.

Dyllis, the eye of the storm, says, 'Don't bother. Little Abbie's just been in with the twins. She made me something.' It doesn't occur to Dyllis that Tessa might like a drink. Tessa doesn't mind.

'Were the twins sweet?' she asks, coming back with a plate of dunking biscuits and putting them on the table beside Dyllis.

'Oh, bugger those,' says Dyllis. 'April brought meringues.' She rattles the tin.

'I shouldn't eat them,' says Tessa. 'I know April's delicious meringues. They're barely cooked in the middle and she made them with Ellen's eggs, which are certified unpasteurised. Would be a shame to ruin everything now I've made it to this great stage.' There, she's talking about the pregnancy in front of Stephen again. He doesn't flinch.

'Bollocks,' says Dyllis. 'In my day we ate what we were given and nobody worried about pasteurised eggs.' Dyllis offers the tin to Stephen. 'You can have two. Have Tessa's.'

'Mum, I was thinking.' Stephen tries not to spray meringue crumbs everywhere as he talks.

'Don't strain yourself, dear,' says Dyllis. Her face is still a little lopsided but Tessa is so confident in Dyllis' recovery that she allows herself to open a window to counteract the stifling heat from the pre-Health and Safety electric bar fire, which pulses red hot under the mantelpiece.

'Watch the draught!' complains Dyllis.

'You need some fresh air,' insists Tessa.

'I was thinking,' interrupts Stephen in his shut-up-and-listen-to-me voice. Tessa and Dyllis stop squabbling and look at him. 'I was thinking that Tessa could move in with you.'

Tessa closes the window just one notch.

'Don't be silly,' says Dyllis, reaching for another meringue.

'I'm not. She needs to get out of the Old Rectory. When she has the baby...' Now he's talking about it. Tessa hugs her bump, transformed in an instant from elephant to tiny little life, recognised by everybody as something that needs to be taken care of. She smiles.

'Exactly! I'm a frail old woman who's earned the right to decide who peoples her last days. And Rufus might not mind but I'd be useless around a teeny babba. I'd be cross when it cried. I'd fall over all the soaking nappy buckets.'

'I expect Tessa could use disposables,' Stephen wants to sound knowledgeable.

'I don't have a microwave for the milk.'

'I'm going to breastfeed.'

'Not on thyroid medicine, you're not.'

'It's fine. The doctors say it's fine.'

'If Tessa should move in anywhere, Stephen, it should be with you!' And Tessa and Stephen stare at each other, suddenly like rabbits caught in the headlights of Dyllis' clear vision.

Dyllis kicks herself. It was going so well. She thought their turning up together this morning, their easy manner with one another, meant they'd resolved things, talked, been honest. She realises that was just wishful thinking. And now they're separated again by Dyllis' raging through the china shop of their emotions. Stephen sits on the sofa: Tessa stands six feet away by the window; they're no longer looking at each other. Dyllis could knock their heads together.

She wants this situation sorted. There's an urgency in her

which cannot be denied. Exhausted by their blind stupidity, she closes her eyes.

'Well, if you need time to digest the bleeding obvious, bugger off, the pair of you. Take her out to lunch, Stephen. And get down on one knee if you have to.'

'I've got...'

'Some bloody service somewhere. What's more important: your vocation or your marriage?'

'It's my job, Mum,' protests Stephen.

'I know,' says Tessa. She stands and pulls her coat around her. It'll be freezing outside after the tropical heat of Dyllis' house.

Of course she couldn't bring her baby here. Apart from the fact that Dyllis doesn't want her, that old adage: 'A cold baby cries, a hot baby dies' keeps rattling about her head. Poor unborn child. She's at risk of being obsessive about it. She must be careful it feels no pressure.

Tessa's used to having these sorts of arguments in her head these days.

She kisses Dyllis' soft cheek. The old hand, its ancient rings rattling, claws for Tessa's and squeezes hard. 'I did love your flapjacks,' says Dyllis, though her eyes are still closed.

'I'll bring you some more,' promises Tessa.

Trixie and Belle are high as kites on Coke and homemade packet-mix iced cupcakes when Nanna Deborah turns up to fetch them. She and Granddad pick their way up the path of No. 3 as if the old grass and dandelion leaves are poisonous. The twins know Granddad will have spent the afternoon mowing a new pattern around Nanna Deborah's bungalow. Nanna Deborah will have competitively cleaned every corner of the house to fill her time between Kyle leaving and the twins coming home. They protested fiercely when Lauren threatened them with a nit-comb last night.

'No, Nanna does that Sundays.'

'We don't need it more than once a week.'

'We've never had nits.'

'Thought your Carter was a gardener,' says Granddad, wiping his clean feet carefully on the mat before stepping through to the kitchen. 'What's this?'

The girls are rolling around on the floor with a kitten they've named Bubble, free to a good home yesterday from the farm shop.

'Can we take her home with us, Granddad? Can we?' They leap up and hang off Granddad's perma-creased trouser legs.

'She wouldn't like it, Trix,' he says, meaning 'Your Nanna would have a fit'. 'I reckon the kitten's better off here, isn't it?' He gives Kat a meaningful stare.

Kat smiles beatifically. He's taken the bait lovely. 'You can see Bubble next time you come, can't you, girls?'

'But she'll of grown and we won't of seen it and she might of forgotten us and not want to play with us.'

'Not if you come over one night this week for your tea?' suggests Kat. Deborah could kill her. She can deny these girls nothing. And a kitten's a much stronger draw than their, till now, largely absent mother.

'How will they get here?'

'Good point, Deb,' says Granddad.

'School minibus'll drop them off with Abbie. They could stay the night, couldn't you, girls? Go in with Abbie in the morning.'

Abbie says nothing. The envelope from Queen Anne's is tucked between her music books upstairs.

The letter says: *We'd be delighted to offer a place to a descendant of one of our founders.* Also: *We look forward to your confirmation that Abbie will start with us in the January term.* There's a uniform list and a voucher to cover the lot. Abbie's hidden it in the music case Dyllis gave her. So long as the twins are here and the kitten peeing everywhere and Lauren and Kat so nice to each other, and the twins needing chaperoning on the school bus, why would Abbie choose to go away? She doesn't care about the bullies when her home life's this good. *I'm only eleven,* she thinks. Her mum won't stick around forever but for the moment she's going to pretend there's a chance she might.

Lauren runs straight down to the vicarage on Monday morning. She's full of the successes of the weekend. No matter the shakes and the sweating and the sickness and the horrible shits, she's so far off the drugs, she never smoked in front of the girls, and she reckons they all had a pretty good time. Kat wasn't horrible or criticising: she didn't try to make the girls love her more than Lauren. For the first time in her life Lauren felt like a real mum, like someone who could enjoy cooking fish fingers and peas and chips for tea with ice cream and sprinkles for afters. She wants her daughters' lives to be like adverts on the telly. She knows they won't have much money. And she knows that everyday life is more boring than an exciting first weekend, but one weekend is a start. A good start. And she's changed her mind about needing a flat. If Carter comes back then it'll be time for him to move out, won't it? She's had an idea too.

Abbie needs a desk and that to do her homework. She needs not to be woken up every night when Lauren comes to bed. She needs her own room. If Lauren can persuade Abbie to use the front room as her bedroom...

There's no answer at the vicarage door. Lauren, refusing the habitual instinct to feel easily deflated, hurries back up the hill and laboriously writes Stephen a note.

Dear Vicar,

The girls are coming to tea and stay the night again Wednesday. Any chance you could get the social worker? You come too? You can explain all the social services stuff for us. We got a kitten called Bubble. From Lauren xx.

Back down the hill to deliver it.

Back up the hill and a quick cup of tea to accompany the 'situations vacant' section of the *Advertiser*. There must be something. So long as it's close by, she could get a bicycle like the vicar's wife.

Labouring: lots of stuff in schools she'd never get.

Secretary in the council offices. That's a job Lauren'd really like: safe, long-term job with lots of security. And if it's the council they'd have to let her work flexi hours for her girls, wouldn't they?

But she can't type. She doesn't know her way around a computer. She could do a course... But she needs a job, she can't afford to waste time getting qualifications. Her heart sinks: packing at the cheese factory. It'll be shift work, and the girls' Granddad Barry will be her boss. But if she's going to be a grown-up... As she reaches for the receiver, the phone rings.

'Hello?' The voice at the end is so posh it can only belong to Sir Charles' wife at Bag Enderby Hall. The vicar said he'd put a word in but Lauren never thought...

'May I speak to Lauren Stoke?'

'It's me. I mean, you are. I mean, yes...' - what is it posh people say when they're called on the phone? – 'It's me speaking.'

The letter from Preston is under Lauren's note when Stephen gets home. He deals with the note first, calling the social worker on her mobile, passing on the invitation to tea, spending

300

half an hour persuading her that it will be worth her while coming out so late, that Lauren's really on the mend, that an hour spent by her at this stage might speed up the whole process immeasurably later. He rings Lauren and tells her Wednesday night's on.

He wishes he could stay in and have beans on toast tonight. There's a vast swathe of spinach in the veg patch still, but he can't be bothered to go and pick it in the dark, not even for it to be auctioned with all the other contents of the church windowsills after the Harvest Supper. Perhaps, like Ellen, he'll let the chickens roam free over the veg and they can clear it for him. There was a frost last night and the last courgettes droop mouldily now over the edges of the raised beds. Somewhere he read that the thing is not to dig anything up, but to just let everything rot back into the ground ready for spring. Well, if he lets the chickens free over the beds then they'll help, won't they?

He opens the letter from the parish in Preston. It turns out they think him a better bet after all. He allows the contents of the letter to sink in. They're offering him the job. It's the challenging, inner-city based job he wanted: he'll be working with all the problems caused by a whole community struggling below the poverty line, with generations of long-term unemployed, with the disenfranchised, the dispossessed... people whose lives he can change out of all recognition

He drops the offer. It lands on the kitchen table half-unfolded. He sits down and smoothes the paper flat.

He's running out of time. Once she's given birth, she might never be able to see past the fact of the baby to find her way back to him. He understands her need for the child. He wants her to have it. And he wants her. The Reverend Jones said once at a christening that men love women, women love children, and children love pets. This all seems true and reasonable enough to Stephen now.

He can't go to Preston. He has to persuade his current bishop to give him the Stockford job. Then he'll have something to offer Tessa.

He rifles through his telephone book. In order to get what he wants he's going to have to lie, cheat and cast ruthless aspersions in the rural dean's direction. He shoves a V sign up towards old Sod and, grinning, sets to work.

Kat shivers on the doorstep.

'I come to confess, Vicar,' she says. For a second he wonders if her turning up at church the other day had been more than just a supportive move to thank him for keeping an eye out for Lauren. Perhaps she's got religion? And since when does she call him 'Vicar'? She's not pregnant! He feels the colour drain from his face.

'Sit down,' he says. 'Tea? Something stronger?'

'Nothing. Sorry.' She's as nervous as Carter coming to tell him not to bother the social workers because Lauren was using again.

'What is it? Whatever it is, Kat, we can sort it out. Tell me!' She doesn't look as though she's here to pounce on him, though it would be nothing more than his fault if she were.

'You'll know what to do.' She blows her nose, tucks the hanky in her sleeve, lays her hands flat on the table. They are red-raw and thin, and they still shake, no matter if she presses them down so hard that the edges go white.

'I'll help in any way I can.' Stephen sits opposite her. He doesn't reach out to touch her. She must tell him whatever's frightening her without his putting words into her mouth.

'You remember the Black Barn burnt down?' she says. He nods. He remembers seeing Abbie there, lighting up with a wind-proof lighter, chucking her defiant chin at him,

302

disappearing behind the brambles. It seems years ago. 'I went to London that morning,' says Kat. She takes a shaky breath, then another, more confident. 'Had to escape, see?' She looks up at Stephen, straight into his eyes. 'It was me that done it, Vicar. So there's no point getting all friendly with the social workers over Lauren and the twins. They won't let them come and live with their Nanna Kat if she's an arsonist, will they?'

Stephen fetches a bottle of red a parishioner gave him for giving a good sermon at her father's funeral. The Harvest Supper doesn't start for an hour.

'I can't see you burning down ancient buildings.'

'Couldn't bear them Tresters to get more glory. The Jack Trester Memorial Youth Club hall. My fucking arse! Was easy, you know. Carter always kept those big jerry cans full of petrol for the mower. I took them. Walked into town carrying those bloody things all the way in the middle of the night. I shoulda been found out. I was so frightened by the *whoof* of the place going up I dropped my dad's old lighter that I started it with. I hid the jerry cans in the brambles on the railway embankment. They can't of found them 'cos they never went after Carter. I had my bags packed ready and everything. Left them at the station before I done it and then went down there and slept on a bench. Took the five fifteen up to town with George Cross. He bought me a sandwich and a coffee off the trolley: said I looked peaky.'

'I think, if you ask her, you'll find Abbie's got the lighter.'

'They won't let her go to Queen Anne's now, neither.'

'But it seems to me it was yours to burn all the time.'

'Wouldn't do no good if I claimed ownership,' says Kat. 'I'm a Stoke. We been the bad family in this village since that Trester Tessa told us about threw his daughter out and took all the Stoke property to be his own. So Lauren's not gonna get her girls back and it's no good your mum trying to get Abbie into that posh school, neither.'

'But no one's going to find out,' he says. 'Nobody cares enough. With the barn burned down, the diocese can build a new youth club on the site: unless you want to contest ownership of the land, that is.'

Kat shakes her head. 'I like the idea of being rich enough to give things away.'

'But you could build yourselves a house on the site.'

Kat shakes her head. 'I already got a house, thanks.'

'Kat, I won't tell anybody about the barn.' The old Stephen would have felt obliged to call the police. 'I'll say even if the law prosecuted you for arson it wouldn't have a leg to stand on. The Tresters had no deeds. And if you really want Abbie to go to Queen Anne's...'

Kat takes a tentative sip at her wine. She shakes her head. 'That's Abbie's choice.' She takes a gulp.

'Kat, about the other night...'

'You're not gonna ask me for another cosy?'

Stephen flushes. 'No!' If he were standing she can see that he would back away. Kat laughs her head off to hide her embarrassment. She'd half liked the idea. He's really not her type. But she's lonely. Stephen always loved her. She misses being admired.

'Nah,' she says. 'My Carter told me Tessa wanted to grow artichokes. Don't matter how posh we might of been in the olden days, we would never of wasted garden space on horrible-tasting thistles. She's more your line than what I am.'

Stephen follows her out of the door. 'Do you feel reassured about the Black Barn?' he asks. In answer, she waves. 'I won't put the social workers off,' he calls into the evening. People walking down to the Harvest Supper at the village hall turn and stare. He grins at them too. He has nothing to hide.

Chapter 21

After the Harvest Supper Stephen stays up half the night, planning.

Things are simpler when they're not tangled in your head, he thinks. So he takes his situation and lays it flat on the kitchen table: a piece of paper for work, one for his mother, one for Tessa, one for the baby, and one for him. Until now his work has always come first, but he's hopeless without knowing Tessa's there for him to come home to, or that he'll be there for her. For the sake of his sanity, they need to be sharing a house. And if he gets the Stockford job he can't expect Tessa to look after Dyllis as well as the baby. So Dyllis needs a regular person to be in charge of her. Someone who'll do it for free, since Dyllis hasn't got any money, and nor has he much... or perhaps in exchange for eggs and salad – if he can persuade Tessa to be the egg and salad-providing part of the team.

At two in the morning he leans back in his chair and rubs his eyes. It would be easier perhaps if he could be a knight in shining armour, galloping about, blinding everybody with the authority in his sword. The various pieces of paper are scribbled all over, but his mind is clear. He won't talk to Tessa until he can present her with a *fait accompli*. Although he's going to have to be quick about it: once the winter weather sets in, the Old Rectory will be no place for a baby.

He makes a list:
1 Call Daisy...

Daisy's attic isn't quite impenetrable. Jelly finds the cot, laced with cobwebs and grey with abandonment. She and Daisy carefully sponge it down with warm water and washing up liquid, polish it dry with towelling dishcloths. The transfers of children gambolling with little lambs are scratched and battered. 'Jonathan used to bash his nee-nah's against them,' says Daisy.

'Nee-nahs?'

'Fire engines. Anything with a flashing light was a nee-nah. He was never very interested in bouncing lambs. You loved them. You used to sit and coo at them while you goodly waited for me to get you up.'

Jelly traces the oval picture and can't remember.

Having leant the pieces of cot beside the attic door, Daisy returns to a white-painted chest of drawers. She wipes down and polishes the top of it, then pulls the first drawer open gingerly, uncertain what she's going to find.

'I put mothballs in here,' she says, almost to herself. She pulls out tiny sheets and hand-knitted blankets, cardigans and bobble hats, mittens, matinée jackets. They smell strongly of camphor, but don't fall apart in her hands.

Jelly sits on the floor and acts as a basket, Daisy laying each carefully-folded item in her lap. 'Is it true I'm called Jelly because Jonathan couldn't say Jenny?'

Daisy nods.

'I used to have to go to hospital a lot when I was little, didn't I?'

'You used to have a bad heart,' says Daisy, picking up the pile of tiny clothes from Jelly's lap and heading for the stairs. Those were vicious days, when Jelly kept nearly dying on her. George had cradled them both in a way she doubts he'd know how to now. How marriages change. She wishes George would take charge of theirs and pull it together as Stephen's trying to do for him and Tessa. 'But the clever doctors made your heart better. I think we'll wash these by hand, shall we? With some special soap? Come on. Let's go on an outing and get Tessa a new mattress for that cot.'

306

Rufus takes his credit card to the local builders' merchants and impulse-buys with the same abandonment with which he used to indulge the desire to drink. A saw, he thinks. And another, smaller, neater saw. He buys a set of wrenches and another of hammers. Wire and plugs. And two vast rolls of what looks like silver foil-backed bubble wrap. Back at the potting shed, he realises he hasn't nearly enough kit. He returns to the builders' yard and buys a drill, and a shiny new set of drill bits. And a jig saw because it looks so clever. And a sander because it's on special offer. When he's unpacked all this stuff from the back of the Lexus there's no room to stand on the potting shed floor. He collapses onto Carter's sofa, exhausted by his enthusiasm. He doesn't have a clue what to do next.

'Anybody home?'

'Stephen!'

'What are you doing?' Stephen surveys the jumble of over-packaged tools with amusement, and a certain gleam in his eye.

'Boy's toys,' says Rufus, hopefully.

Stephen squats down and lifts the drill out of its box. 'Nice toys,' he says, checking the drill for balance in his hand and already looking about for a plug to charge the battery.

'It's got hammer action,' says Rufus. Rufus has no idea what a hammer action is.

'Where's Tessa?' asks Stephen.

'Midwife appointment.'

'And what are you planning to do with all this?'

Lauren takes the bus to Stockford and walks up the hill to Bag Enderby. She's not used to the exercise, but the woods at this time of year are bright with colour and now there's been a frost they crunch underfoot as she cuts through from the lay-by behind Daisy's house, past the dell where she camped with

Ryan all those months ago and across the sheep-filled meadow to the kitchen door of the big house. She finds Lady Susie there, hugging the Aga and drinking milky, instant coffee sweetened by Hermesetas. The house is bitterly cold. Even the kitchen, too vast to heat, is only warm directly around the Aga: the short side of the scrubbed pine table's kept close to it so that Lady Susie can do all her chores there, from ironing to sorting out her famous collection of pelargoniums before putting them to bed in the bubble-wrap-lined greenhouse for the winter.

'It's the mildew I have to worry about as much as the cold,' she says, without waiting for Lauren to introduce herself, and loading the plants into a little trailer she'll pull by hand. 'Would you?' she gives Lauren, who's yet to take off her coat, the two pots which won't fit in the trailer and Lauren follows her along frost-wilted weed-fringed paths to the walled kitchen garden where the ramshackle greenhouse hugs the red brick east wall. Lady Susie arranges the pelargoniums close together for warmth, but not so close that the air can't circulate. She closes the door, and with a sharp kick breaks the bottom pane of glass. 'There,' she says, dusting her hands off on her apron. 'That'll keep the air moving till spring. We're bereft without your brother, you know,' she adds. 'His was such a helpful pair of hands.' She is entirely uninterested in tidying the broken glass. It crunches underfoot as she and Lauren turn back for the house.

Sir Charles is much iller than Dyllis. Since moving at all has him fighting for breath, he sits, day after day, waiting impatiently for the Channel 4 racing to start.

Lauren's job will be to get him up and take him to his chair in front of the telly. His wife gives him breakfast in bed: All Bran, tea, and the *Telegraph*. When Lauren arrives she's to empty the old milk bottle he's peed into and help him onto the toilet. The first time she does this she leaves him to shiver there in private, in spite of being wrapped in a pashmina given to his wife by their daughter-in-law for Christmas. She waits nervously in the hall outside the bathroom, hoping he'll think to call her when he's finished. Will she have to wipe his arse?

He does call. He's pulled the chain himself and his pyjama bottoms have been hauled up his bony hips and are all caught up with his dressing gown. Lauren can't leave him all skew-whiff like that and she asks if he'll mind her just straightening him up. She wants him to keep his dignity.

Poor man. He smells ever so slightly unwashed. When she's got him settled in front of the telly, she fills a big stainless steel bowl with warm water and soaks his feet in it. She'll start with his claw-like toenails and freshen him up slowly.

'I wouldn't want to be that posh for all the tea in China,' Lauren tells Kat when she gets home after her first day as Sir Charles' 'keeper' as Lady Susie describes the job. She's put Sir Charles to bed, like a child, before seven. He has a sliver of fish with spinach and mashed potato at twelve, and a boiled egg for his tea at five. 'Lady Susie makes him hot milk when she goes to bed. All that stuff and no money. I'm surprised he hasn't frozen to death already,' says Lauren. She runs herself a bath in No. 3's warm bathroom and looks forward to a nice hot tea in front of the telly.

'They offered Abbie a place at that school,' says Kat, perching on the laundry basket while her eldest daughter lowers herself into the peach-scented froth of her bath. 'She hid the letter somewhere. The headmistress rang up to ask why I hadn't bitten her 'and off when she held out the offer.'

Lauren looks up at her mother. Kat's arms are crossed tight across her chest. Her lips set in a thin line. Her eyes are hard.

'They'll give her full boarding scholarship, uniform, piano lessons, hot dinner meals, the lot.'

It occurs to Lauren her mum doesn't know what to do.

'How we gonna get her there every day?' asks Lauren.

'She'll board, I said. But you don't want no stranger for a sister.'

'She won't be a stranger. She'll be posher, know stuff. She'll think we live in a small house with no airs and graces. But so what? She'll be educated. I'll make sure she knows how lucky she is. Hey, if she's boarding you could go to London during term-time. You could...' Lauren stops herself saying anything about 'that Buster Mostin'.

'Won't you need my help with the twins?'

'You gotta make up your mind, Mum. You gonna be their full-time Nanna Kat or you gonna disappear again? If you go off again, Abbie can go and board at that posh school and I'll settle for the twins staying with they Nanna Deborah and tea with me one night a week... till I get a flat.'

'But you want them girls with you? You should have them girls... And if Lauren boards at that school, we'll lose her totally.'

'Plus, also, if you went to London I'd have to give the kitten back...' Lauren smiles inside: she feels she's becoming a mistress of manipulation in her old age.

Tessa stands in the doorway of the potting shed and laughs to see Stephen and Rufus furbishing it as a tiny house. There's a wood burner in the corner of what will be a kitchen/sitting room, a tiny cubicle shower and a sink next to what has always been the gardener's loo. Stephen's knocked the partition wall down. 'You don't want to have to go outside to come in again to pee.' There are two bedrooms at one end of the shed. One is already furnished with the wrought iron bed that used to be in the attic Tessa's sleeping in. The posh new sleigh bed Rufus bought won't fit in here. Tessa likes the fact Stephen's hot enough to be down to his shirt. A bit of sweat suits his scrunched old face. He has a farmer's tan still from the summer.

Fully dressed in black cashmere and Levi's, Rufus, a paler, altogether slinkier number, is an uncertain plumber's mate, constantly passing the wrong wrench.

'Don't laugh,' he says to Tessa. 'I'm new to this. If it weren't for the master here...'

'Would you like to help?' Stephen asks Tessa.

'No!' Rufus is horrified.

'She's not disabled,' protests Stephen. He uncurls from under the sink, stands, and hands Tessa a brush and a pot of paint. 'Rufus is after a Scandinavian look,' he says.

Rufus protests. 'Not *Homes and Gardens*. More *World of Interiors*. The rules remain the same, though. It'll look bigger if it's white.'

'No point in ever trying to make a small space look bigger with paint,' say Tessa and Stephen in unison.

'What are you? Matching talking dolls?' says Rufus.

'Well, if it's white you want...' Tessa squats down and carefully opens the paint can, stirring it gently with a stick until the watery surface has disappeared.

'You should be wearing that expensive leather toolbelt Rufus has slung about his snake hips,' says Stephen.

'If I could ever get it round my waist.' Tessa heaves herself off the floor. Over the space-age insulation, the walls are panelled with old scaffolding boards, sanded to a soft, satin finish. 'It's really amazing,' she says. 'Rufus, the book's going to have the most stunning photographs. All the decorators in the land will be copying your recycled chic.'

'Will I have to credit him?' Rufus points to Stephen.

'Better not,' says the vicar. 'I'm not supposed to spend my weekdays moonlighting as a jobbing builder. Though if they don't offer me the Stockford job...' he says this nonchalantly and doesn't look to hear if Tessa's taken in what he's said, '... I won't be so busy when they find someone else to be rector. Isn't it the done thing to change careers mid-life these days?'

'Sounds complicated to me,' says Rufus.

'Have you really applied for Stockford?' asks Tessa.

Stephen shrugs, and grunts as he pulls the join at the U-bend tight. He doesn't recount the lies he told to persuade the Bishop to consider him: the promise of a wife and child to help fill the rectory. The church has no right to peer into the murky hollows of his private life – but it won't harm proceedings if he promises to represent upstanding 'normality' – whatever that may be.

Tessa half stands. But then staggers. 'Ooh!'

Dropped, the paint oozes outwards between the power tools, patterning the concrete floor like a giant slew of spilt cream, curling round the unexpected wet patch pooling at Tessa's feet.

'Shit. I didn't think they were real contractions.'

Rufus stands too quickly from his position as spanner-passer and cracks his head on the sink so that it bleeds and he has to lie down on the sofa with a paint rag to staunch the wound.

His only useful comment is, 'Take the Lexus!'

The baby might be coming early but Tessa's not frightened. She likes the contractions. It means her body's working. The pain arches through her in repetitive, reassuring waves. The rhythm of muscles contracting down her back and abdomen makes sense to her. Like a ticking clock, the more they come, the sooner the baby will arrive. Just touching the car with the very tips of her fingernails she paces round it while Stephen sprints upstairs to get the bag she's packed with two nighties, a feeding bra, nappies, tiny white towelling babygros and a hand-washed cardigan that Jelly wore when she was born.

Stephen slings Tessa's bag in the boot. 'I saw your notes on your desk and put them in.' She hauls herself up into the front passenger seat. She changes her mind, gets out again, and climbs into the back where she can move around more. It'll be a half-hour drive to the hospital.

'I was going to call it Noel if it was late and came for Christmas,' says Tessa, pulling herself around onto all fours and trying out the breathing April taught her: April's never had any children but she's done a lot of yoga in her time. Tessa tries to think of a golden thread spiralling out of her mouth as the contraction slowly subsides. She curls into what April calls the child's pose as Stephen, adrenalin pulsing, shining armour slipping metaphorically into place, jams the giant car into 'Drive' and roars out of the Old Rectory gates, like a knight on a war horse intent on saving a princess. He thunders the Lexus past the Tresters', the vicarage, his mother's house, Pratt Cottages.

On the back seat, Tessa groans and breathes and groans again. 'They started this morning,' she says. 'I thought they were Braxton Hicks. If it comes now it'll be six weeks early.'

'That puddle of water means we've got to get you to the hospital fast,' says Stephen, all knowledge. 'Unless you were planning on having it anywhere else?' She could have a whole birthing plan involving a hot tub at April's for all Stephen knows.

'Hospital!' Tessa insists. 'It's not supposed to come yet. I don't know if it's the right way round or anything.'

'Just keep breathing.'

Kat's scraping the insides of a pumpkin into a bowl. Abbie's at school. Lauren's up at the Bag Enderby Estate. Carter's never rung to say he's arrived safe or anything. What's it like in New

Zealand? His leaving on this adventure puts Kat in mind again of that oft-repeated phrase of her mother's: 'Don't do nothin', do it?' Not so much a sentence as a blanket of negatives useful for extinguishing hope.

It was her mother who said there was no point Kat going to the grammar school, no point in Kat going to London the first time. She was right. Kat's never escaped Hindle Green. Her mother said Kat never really wanted to leave. That was when Kat dumped Carter and Lauren with her and stormed back to London where she moved into the pub and ran it for Buster, and got pregnant with Abbie. Buster... he was happy to get her up the duff. Happy she had the child. Wouldn't have minded if she'd stayed with Abbie at the pub and brought her up there. But there was no way he was ever going to leave his rich wife. Kat went back for more again and again and again. And it was alright, but not altogether right.

That's it. Hers has been a life of exciting promise turning into endless 'alright'. She's still stunned she suggested she and Stephen had a friendly the other night. Will she never learn? Kat's never thought she deserved more than comfort where she can get it.

Kat takes a kitchen knife and begins to cut jagged teeth into the leathery orange skin of the pumpkin. She gave Abbie such a bollocking for hiding that letter saying she had a place at Queen Anne's. Last thing Kat needed was to be made to look stupid when the school rang her up to find out why they hadn't heard from her. She slices triangle eyes and a triangle nose into the pumpkin's face. She puts three tea lights from the supermarket onto the bumpy bottom of the hollowed gourd and lights them with her dad's flame-proof lighter. He had it from his military service in Egypt. She's glad it's not lost. She's glad of the family history she does have. She imagines the story of the locket is true now.

She takes the pumpkin head with its glowing eyes through to the front room, that empty space they never use for anything. Apart from the boxed-up bits and pieces Carter left behind, the lounge is furnished with a suite that's been there since her mother's day, and a coffee table, and the framed school photographs that are hung above the sofa. She pulls the nets to arrange the pumpkin so the twins will see it when they arrive later. The kitten jumps up onto the windowsill to see what she's doing. It gets caught up in the net curtains and Kat has to pull each claw free one at a time. The kitten draws blood. 'What are you like?' wails Kat, indulgently.

If Abbie goes to board at that school then Lauren's right, Kat could go back to London. Move back in with Buster. Run the bar. Be what? The not-quite-loved-enough girlfriend of a man who will never leave his wife for her.

The wife lives in a mansion in Camberwell with a swimming pool in the basement. She's a lawyer.

But what if Abbie doesn't like Queen Anne's? Where will she go then?

And what if Kat didn't go back to London? If Kat promised to support Abbie, tell her headteacher about the bullies instead of assuming she'll just toughen up on her own...

Don't do nothing, do it?

Kat's mother's voice echoes around the un-used room. Kat should chuck everything out of this place and start again. If she had the gall she'd think of something to train as and run a business from it. Rip down the nets. Let the light in. What kind of business? She's got no education to do anything but polish glasses and ring up beer prices on a till. She's a good cleaner. Lauren's a good cleaner too, isn't she? Neither of them can drive. But they've got Carter's van to learn in...

Don't...

'Oh fuck off, Mum!' says Kat into the gloom.

315

Dyllis has never been so glad to be alone. She lies on her back, her head heated nicely by the nearby bars of her old electric fire. She feels no particular pain. On the ceiling she can see the marks where there used to be a pattern of stars to demonstrate to Stephen the movements in the night sky. She puzzles out Orion, the Big Dipper, Cassiopaeia – what a lovely word.

Will it be now? She's astonished to be so calm. It's like being in an airport departure lounge. There's absolutely nothing you can do but wait. She's glad to be in the warmth of her own home. How she'd hate the rush and man-handling of treatment. She's heard of bigger strokes coming after little ones, like earthquakes. The other day must have been a warning. She's glad she had time to write the letter. She hopes he finds it. Perhaps she should have given it to Tessa. But then Tessa would never have left her. And Dyllis wouldn't be lying here contemplating.

Rufus wiped up the spilled paint by spreading it out all over the floor with an old towel. He likes the look of the pale scaffolding board panelling and the ragged white concrete floor. Maybe he'll just leave it like that. While the floor dries he stokes the fire in the kitchen of the Old Rectory, and makes a pot of coffee. Outside it's raining hard. There's a spreading puddle coming in from the back door. Rufus makes a dyke of towels. He's done this before, but the forecast this time is rain for a week.

Shit! If Tessa's having the baby she'll need all the baby stuff Daisy's sorting out for her.

He calls the chilli farm. No answer.

He tries the deli. 'Tessa's having the baby,' he says without introducing himself.

'What?' When April finally understands what he's saying

through the hubbub at the shop he hears her shout across, 'Daisy! Tessa's in labour.'

Jelly comes onto the phone. 'Don't be frightened, Rufus. She'll be all happy in a minute when it's born safe and sound. You'll see.'

The Chinese lanterns bob damply above the puddles on Dyllis' path. Abbie doesn't knock but pushes open the door. 'It's me,' she calls. And stops. And kneels beside Dyllis, where she lies crooked on the rug before the fire. 'It's me,' she whispers, and gently, gingerly, she feels for Dyllis' hand while watching the tiny promise of lingering life pump through the blackened skin beside the healing scab on her temple.

She knows she must run for an ambulance. But there is an urgency in Dyllis' grip which stops her. Instead, Abbie stays, kneeling. She begins to talk about her day at school. How the swimming pool's not going to be open till after Christmas. How those girls can't hurt her now she doesn't bother to carry a phone. How it was pizza and chips and winter salad from Ellen Wiseman's poly tunnel at dinner time. Her voice falters. She sits still. Dyllis' eyelids flicker and a ghost of a smile touches her lips. Abbie won't go and fetch Kat. Kat will insist on an ambulance. Besides, the twins are coming over tonight after Rainbows: it's Halloween. Kat's been slinging black-faced orange bunting about the kitchen for days.

Abbie slips sideways to sit on the floor. She leans over and pulls the rug off Dyllis' chair. She tucks it gently round the old lady's legs. She takes her school sweatshirt off and folds it into a pillow for Dyllis' head. Dyllis' breathing's not laboured. She seems peaceful. Abbie knows Dyllis was never religious, but in her mind the old lady is something of a saint. It is no surprise to Abbie, therefore, that Dyllis should be so comfortable as she lies there, waiting...

317

'Shall I get the vicar?' she asks out loud, not really expecting an answer. She watches Dyllis' face carefully for a sign. She understands that this is an intensely private moment for Dyllis. That Dyllis might rather Abbie weren't there. 'Shall I get him?' repeats the little girl and Dyllis turns the left corner of her lip into a tiny frown and Abbie reads that as a 'No.'

Tessa can't wait to get to the hospital. She knows she's going to have to push. Stephen stops at Daisy's house. Pulling into the yard and honking the horn, he slams out of the driver's door and pulls open Tessa's apparently in one movement. Her face is entirely turned in on itself, concentrating only on what is happening internally. He leaves her breathing on the back seat and goes to try the kitchen door. It opens. He shouts. There's nobody home.

'Come on.' She takes his arm and pulls herself out of the car. She's panting now, she knows she's going to have to push. There's no time to get to hospital. Stephen shuts the slobbering Labrador into Daisy's utility room. Then he takes Tessa into the sitting room where he shoves a low table covered in dog-eared seed catalogues and gap year activity brochures out of the way. He pulls newspaper from the pile beside the fire and spreads it over the threadbare rug. Tessa leans against the wall and Stephen kneels to pull off her shoes.

'Trousers,' she instructs. And he pulls those off too. And her pants. He helps her down so that she can kneel in front of the sofa, leaning her elbows on it, her head dropped into her hands until the next urge to push comes. He kisses her forehead, because he can't not, and runs to look for towels, which he finds in a laundry basket on the first floor landing. He runs back downstairs with five of them.

Tessa's clinging to the sofa, growling into the cushions.

Stephen finds the phone and dials 999: 'My wife's having a baby.'

And while the person at the end of the phone checks the address against the telephone number, Stephen drops the handset and goes to catch the greyish-purple, slime-covered croquet ball that's crowning already at Tessa's rump. Tiny shoulders slide out and Stephen slides his hand underneath to protect the baby so it won't land on its head.

'Once more,' he says to Tessa. 'I think it'll only take one more.'

And she pushes so hard that the child slips out into Stephen's hands in one final *whoosh* of water and blood and mess which Stephen doesn't see. He's busy carefully wrapping this brand new life in the soft folds of Jelly's pink bath towel.

'Can you turn over?' he asks Tessa. And, panting like a one-minute-miler, Tessa turns round, sits, and leans her back against the sofa.

Cradling the tiny bundle with one arm, he undoes Tessa's shirt buttons with his free hand. Then he offers the baby to its mother, who opens the towel so that she can see her child and coo at those miniature tight-shut eyes and upturned nose and count the precious fingers and toes while the frowning baby lies, skin to skin, on the soft cushion of Tessa's chest.

'It's a girl,' says Tessa.

The umbilical cord is still attached, pumping slowly. The baby arches her neck under Tessa's hand and makes a first, tentative mew, and then a cry and then a rude, indignant howl at being propelled into the world at such unseemly speed. Tessa guides the child's mouth to her breast and that impossibly tiny bud snuffles to latch on.

Stephen brushes the backs of his smeared hands against his eyes.

Laughing, 'Have a towel,' says Tessa. And he takes one

and blows his nose on it before wiping his hands and coming to sit beside his wife, shoulder to shoulder, to admire the little beast.

'She's beautiful,' he says.

'Her name's Dyllis,' replies Tessa, laying her exhausted head on Stephen's shoulder and leaving it there. He pulls his arm out from between them and hugs her close. They are a good physical fit. The baby clenches her fists and fights the air as she sucks.

'I shagged Kat,' says Stephen.

'I would have done too, if I were you.'

As the wail of the ambulance comes into earshot, Tessa turns and kisses Stephen through her tears.

Chapter 22

'Stephen was incredible.' Tessa's tucked into a ward with five other new mothers: she's the eldest of them by at least ten years.

Jelly sits on the chair beside her, cradling the baby, her feet placed firmly on the floor to keep herself steady. So long as she has the baby to look at, she's confident she'll be able to stop herself from blurting out the secret plan everyone has been working on while Tessa's away in hospital.

'I told him to get a clothes peg from the utility room to stop the umbilical cord and then cut it with your sewing scissors but he said he'd read he should leave it all till it stopped pumping.'

Daisy wonders if she looked this happy after she had her own children. 'Lucky for you he didn't pick a nice blunt pair of secateurs and hack at it! George would have done. Dunked in gin to sterilise them.'

'When the afterbirth came he knew what it was. I panicked and thought I was haemorrhaging. He's been looking up on the internet what to do when people give birth. He thought I might have wanted to have it at Rufus' and there could have been an emergency. He thinks Rufus is totally useless.'

'What are you calling her?' Daisy opens a Tupperware of pink and yellow iced French Fancies sent by April and offers one to Tessa, who takes two and eats them greedily.

'Dyllis Jennifer Wilkinson,' says Tessa, through a mouthful, reaching for the baby who is mewing for food. She undoes her nightie and frowns with concentration as she tries to get the baby to latch on. 'The medics are just keeping an eye on my hyperthyroidism and say to breastfeed away. I wasn't

321

sure I'd be able to do both. But they reckon it's OK. April says I should dump the drugs and go for acupuncture.'

'April always distrusts medics,' finishes Daisy.

The baby falls off the breast and cries and Tessa patiently begins the process of helping her latch on again.

'Did you know my real name's Jennifer?' asks Jelly, watching the nuzzling baby, fascinated.

'I called her after you.'

Kat lays Dyllis out in her best nightie. She puts bed socks on to keep her feet warm and wraps her in the worn candlewick bedspread Dyllis has had since she was married. The old woman's face is peaceful. The undertakers suggested taking her to their chapel of rest but Stephen is insisting she stay here, laid out on her own bed, Radio 3 burbling softly to keep her company.

'I feel so bad,' says Kat, moving quietly about. 'The twins came for the night and I was that excited I didn't notice Abbie weren't home till well after tea. And then I thought she'd be here. She normally comes home when the twins are there because she wants to see them. But I reckoned her and Mrs Wilkinson might be playing the piano or something so I left them. Till it was late, you know. Really late.

'And then I came and found Abbie curled up, sleeping next to your poor Ma. Mrs... Dyllis had her arm round her. Abbie... sometimes she looks like such a little girl, you know; when children sleep you see their innocence, don't you? And she's been so grown-up lately. But there she was, like a child again, snuggled up with your old mum.' Kat sniffs and blows her nose. 'And Dyllis already gone. I don't know how long she been like that. Abbie won't talk about it.'

Stephen sort of listens to Kat. The sound of her voice is as comforting as Radio 4. Dyllis' unread newspapers are piled

322

beside the door. He has a mad feeling he ought to do all the Sudoku puzzles for her.

In his hands he holds the loose leaves of his mother's letter, her copperplate pulled ragged by the first stroke. Pages. Pages and pages of love and understanding.

'She knew where I was the night Dad died,' he tells Kat. Kat flushes and bustles about so as not to have to look at Stephen. That conversation about a friendly fuck the other night... it's turning into something hideous in her mind.

This is grossly unfair, Stephen tells God. Could he not have spared Dyllis for another week? Couldn't she have seen the baby? Known she'd arrived safely? Her namesake. Daisy and the girls are at the vicarage now, filling Tessa's office with nursery furniture, packing the drawers with nappies and babygros and tiny dresses April found at the charity shop. Stephen's supposed to be helping. But when he walked out of the hospital he got this message and came straight here. He's still driving the Lexus. He should call Rufus and tell him where the Mini is and that the key's in the vicarage kitchen on the hook.

He scratches his head.

'So I'll leave you for the minute, then,' says Kat. She stops by the door. 'You give my love to Tessa? She allowed visitors?'

'Come and see her when she's out,' says Stephen, knowing it'll be hard for Kat to get to the hospital. 'Don't they always say that the baby blues kick in after a few days? That's when she'll need visitors to cheer her up.'

'You staying here the night?'

Stephen nods. He reaches for the first *Telegraph* and turns to the puzzle pages.

Kat says, 'You know the other night... when I...'

Stephen looks up at her blankly. Tessa's allowed her

323

mobile in the ward; he wants to ring it.

Kat shakes her head. She and Stephen are old history. She hopes he's forgotten her embarrassing suggestion. 'See you then,' she tells him, before closing the door gently behind her.

Stephen is grateful Kat didn't push it. Now isn't the time for protestations and denials. He dials Tessa's number.

'She's sleeping,' says Tessa. He can hear the breathless amazement at the fact of the baby still whispering in her voice. 'I'm allowed home tomorrow.'

'I'll fetch you, then. If you like?'

'I do like. I like so much. You were such a hero, you know, Stephen? Second time in my life I've needed rescuing and it was you there again. I've been telling Daisy and Jelly all about it. Knight in shining armour and all that.'

'I'll get big headed.' He can't tell her about Dyllis yet. He knows nothing will ruin her joy about the baby. But he doesn't want her to feel she has to be sad on his account.

'What's the matter?' asks Tessa. His voice isn't right.

'Dyllis is dead.' It's out before he can plug the sentence.

'Oh, darling,' and her voice is so full of sorrow for him his eyes well with tears. 'Where is she?'

'Here, at home. I'm staying with her. I don't want her to be taken away.'

'When's the funeral?'

'Next week sometime. You know,' he pulls himself together, 'you could move in here when it's all over. You and the baby will be much warmer than down at Rufus'.'

Stephen manages to plug his mouth now. Before the baby came and made the situation more urgent, he was going to ply her with chat about the Trester/Stoke history, charm her into wanting him back, bring up the subject of their getting back together gently. His new plan is too drastic an idea to discuss down the phone. His mother's body lies quiet in the next room.

If she were alive she'd be poking him and hissing, 'No! Not now. Not like this. Surprise her.'

Stephen can hear the baby mewing. 'Is she hungry? I'd better let you go.'

'No, she's all right. She's a good eater. She had a bath earlier. And did an enormous, disgusting, oily black poo in it.'

'Nice!'

'Are you all right there on your own?'

'Yes. Yes. It's very peaceful. I'll fetch you home tomorrow afternoon, then.'

Putting the phone down, Stephen goes to the door of his mother's room. He looks down at her cosily wrapped corpse. 'How was that?' he asks her.

Across the world, Carter reads the news-packed email from Abbie. In reply he writes, *Got work at a winery. Tell Sir Charles I'll have some tips for him when I get back. Am sharing a house with some other lads. Tell Mum not to worry about the washing and we're living on takeout – not really. Say hi to everyone. Glad she's a cute girl. Tell the vicar to look out for her or he'll have me to answer to, eh? And don't miss that rare old bird too much, Abbie – she set you up, didn't she? Now you're gonna have to teach yourself to fly.*

Stephen brings the midwives boxes of cakes from April's shop as a thank you. The boot of the Lexus is brimming with bags from Mothercare and Boots, stuffed with a strange selection of things he was told the baby would probably die without, including an all-singing-all-dancing buggy, part of which is this baby car seat, and from the price of which he's still reeling. Stephen feels strongly that he's been had by the cheery sales girls. He's been to the supermarket, too, and bought a quantity of treats for Tessa, malt loaf and bourbon biscuits, iron tonic and clementines. Everything's arranged. If Tessa will allow him...

He finds her sitting on her bed, washed, dressed, ready to go. She's alight with happiness. She allows him to take the tiny bundle she's called Dyllis and tuck her into the seat and carry her down to the car.

He feels... what? Protective? Loving? Certainly of Tessa. When the baby smiles at him and blows a bubble he knows the baby's smile can only be caused by wind, but still he takes it as a compliment. It is a good sign. She has Tessa's eyes. He gently folds back the woolly bobble hat the hospital have given her so that it doesn't cover her eyes.

Tessa sits in the back and holds the baby's tiny head straight all the way back to Hindle Green.

'She was only five and a half pounds,' she says. 'She's going to need her head holding for a while. But they think she's fine. They wouldn't let us go home if they didn't. She's got the lungs of a full-term baby on her,' Tessa chatters, so focused on the baby she doesn't notice which way they're going until they arrive.

The girls wanted to be there to welcome her home but Stephen put them off. This is his time. He pushes at the gate and thinks he'll have to oil it or it'll wake the child every time it opens. Tessa follows. He pulls the key and opens the front door. And he puts the baby, still snoozing in her car seat, down in the hall at the bottom of the stairs, turning back quickly before Tessa can follow him in. Then he scoops up his wife and carries her, as if they were newly-wed, into the hall of the vicarage.

'You would have us here?' Tessa's dumbfounded.

She unhooks the baby from her car seat and, cradling her tiny bundle in one arm, allows Stephen to pull her upstairs. First he shows her the apple-green office, transformed now into a child's room, with a cot and a painted chest of drawers and a Peter Rabbit mobile hanging from the ceiling. Then he shows her the bathroom where there's a baby bath waiting and a pile of tiny towels and a special nappy bag attached to a hanger suspended from the hook on the back of the door. And finally he shows her into their bedroom where the sheets are fresh, there are Chinese Lanterns from Dyllis' garden in a jug beside the bed, and Rufus' gift, a rocking, ash wood cradle, is made up and ready for the child.

'You're my wife.' He turns and looks into Tessa's eyes, willing her to see that these truths come from deep within his soul. 'I want us to be together. Without you I am not half a man.'

'But what about..?' and she strokes the baby's back, protecting her against the possibility of rejection.

'Without her, you won't function; without you, I am lost. We'd better live here all together and when she screams and stamps her foot, we'll have to get her a puppy to complete the family.'

Tessa slips her spare hand under the tweed of Stephen's jacket and hugs the familiar crunch of his waist. And they stand there, breathing one another in, home at last, neither Stephen nor Tessa wanting to break the spell. Until...

'Cooee!' They stare, wide-eyed, at one another and clasp hands over their mouths so that she shan't hear them laugh.

'It's not...'

'Mrs Trester..?'

St George's is packed to the rafters for the funeral. There's even a little marquee put up outside to keep the rain off the overflow. April, Daisy and Ellen stand with their heels on the canvas to stop the tent flapping away. There's no sexton yet, but Dyllis' letter said clearly she wanted to be cremated without any formalities, and then her ashes scattered in the river after a proper church service taken by Stephen.

As requested, or perhaps, given the tone of her letter, instructed, Anna Trester's playing Bach's *Wachet Auf* on the organ as a voluntary. Her effort, as Dyllis expected, is valiant rather than brilliant. Abbie is mouthing to herself the much-rehearsed poem Dyllis wanted her to read. She would have worn her Queen Anne's uniform for this. But since her mum's promised to stay, she's not going to that school any more. Stephen says she must have Dyllis' piano. Tessa's promised to help with her homework. Turns out the library in town will get books in if Stockford Comprehensive doesn't have them. If she changes her mind, because she's a direct descendant of one of the school's founders, she can take up her free place there any time. But so long as Kat's staying, she chooses not to. She'll see what she can do on her own.

'They shut the road through the woods,' reads Abbie for the umpteenth time,

'Seventy years ago...'

Tessa and the baby sit next to her in the front row, with Kat and Lauren. The baby on Tessa's lap is wrapped tight in a patchwork made of crochet squares Stephen found in the bottom of his mother's chest of drawers. It must once have been his.

The congregation rustle to their feet for the first hymn.

Dyllis' letter, found on her desk, had been very specific about what this should be.

I want them singing loudly to send me off. I want an emotional rollercoaster of a funeral. Tessa's to read the 'Nunc Dimittis' because the words are so lovely. I want Abbie to read 'The Way Through the Woods' – remember creeping through the forest with Daddy when you were little in case you saw the

328

ghostly horses, Stephen? – I want 'O God Our Help In Ages Past', and 'Thine be the Glory', and 'God Be In My Head'.

The faith of the Church of England is not something I've ever embraced, but the point of it I've always seen. These are the parts that would have had me on a weak day – including the slushy, pappy, rather hackneyed number I want you to start the proceedings with. I have always been awestruck by your ability to suspend your disbelief and declare yourself a man of faith. I am too much the child of intellectual Fabians, as is Tessa. But we love you, and are kept flitting back to the draw of your light because you have this faith which we admire, while not having the ability to allow ourselves to believe.

Stephen folds his mother's letter into the pocket of his surplice and goes out to stand in front of the congregation. He will read Dyllis' letter, most of it, rather than make a homily.

The service starts with the slow wheeze of a country congregation with a good turnout of bass voices dragged off their fields and out of their offices warming to a roaring rendition...

'Dear Lord and Father of mankind,
Forgive our foolish ways...'

THE END

Lightning Source UK Ltd.
Milton Keynes UK
UKOW02f2034210416

272687UK00001B/11/P